Tar Heel Politics

2000

Paul Luebke

 The University of North Carolina Press

Chapel Hill and London

Tar Heel Politics

2000

Designed by April Leidig-Higgins
Set in Monotype Garamond by Keystone Typesetting, Inc.
Manufactured in the United States of America

The paper in this book meets the guidelines for
permanence and durability of the Committee on
Production Guidelines for Book Longevity of the
Council on Library Resources.

Library of Congress Cataloging-in-Publication Data
Luebke, Paul. Tar heel politics 2000 / Paul Luebke.
p. cm.   Includes bibliographical references and index.
ISBN 0-8078-2452-6 (cloth: alk. paper)
ISBN 0-8078-4756-9 (pbk.: alk. paper)
1. Elections—North Carolina. 2. Political parties
—North Carolina. 3. North Carolina—Politics and
government—1951–   . I. Title.
JK4190.L84   1999   98-16381
324.9756'043—dc21   CIP

02 01 00 99 98   5 4 3 2 1

Contents

Preface

North Carolina, for most of the twentieth century, has enjoyed a reputation as a progressive state. This is in part true. To the extent that the state from a national, especially northeastern, perspective is ridiculed as the home of U.S. Senator Jesse Helms, such ridicule misses the point. Helms is in fact not typical of North Carolinians and stands on the right wing of even the North Carolina Republican Party.

In fact, long before the ascendancy in Washington, D.C., of Jesse Helms, North Carolina's national reputation rested on the political vision of the state's corporate and governmental elites. In marked contrast to virtually all other southern states, North Carolina by the late 1930s had established a centralized state government that provided the basic infrastructure for economic development (highway construction and a statewide investment in public schools and university education, especially at the Chapel Hill campus). North Carolina at that time had also in place tax structures (a corporate income tax, an individual income tax, a general sales tax, and a sales tax on motor fuels, among others) that could have been a model for any of the forty-eight states. By contrast, even today both Tennessee and Florida raise state revenue without the individual income tax and thus lack what most students of public finance consider a fundamental mechanism to avoid unduly high taxation of middle-income and poor citizens.

Despite North Carolina's long-standing reputation for progressivism, the term "progressive" should be applied cautiously. The reality is that the state's political debate remains firmly controlled by two well-institutionalized economic elites with somewhat conflicting interests. One group, the modernizers, consists of bankers, developers, retail merchants, the news media, and other representatives of the business community who expect to benefit from change and growth. The second group, the traditionalists, includes traditional industrialists (in textiles, furniture, and apparel), tobacco farmers, and others associated with the state's agricultural economy who feel threatened by change and growth. Each group is linked with politicians who represent its interests.

Any progress felt by middle- and low-income North Carolinians has tended to trickle down from actions that modernizers have taken in pursuing their own interests. The political scene has changed substantially since World War II, primarily with respect to the major roles that Republicans and blacks play now compared with a half-century ago. Nevertheless, North Carolina remains what V. O. Key called it in his classic book, *Southern Politics* (1949), a "progressive plutocracy." This is the reality of Tar Heel politics.

Two myths stand out about North Carolina politics. The first affords to modernizers a status of "would-be liberalism." That is to say, a Terry Sanford or a Jim Hunt would have taken more liberal stands, especially on tax reform, education, and public transportation, if only the Tar Heel electorate had allowed it. According to this myth, a more egalitarian public policy to assist the less-affluent majority was stymied by conservative voters. The reality is that both Sanford and Hunt in their own times made conscious political choices that were strong responses to the unwillingness of North Carolina's big businesses to pay more taxes and, in Hunt's case, to the cultural traditionalism of many of the state's voters, especially rural and small-town white males. The willingness of North Carolina's two leading Democrats of the late twentieth century, Sanford and Hunt, to fund investments in public education in large measure from a general sales tax that included a tax on groceries made them centrally responsible for the increasing regressivity of North Carolina's tax structure.

Their terms as governor, Sanford's from 1961 to 1965 and Hunt's first eight years from 1977 to 1985, occurred during periods of total Democratic control. Therefore, the persistence of regressive taxation in those years must be placed firmly on the shoulders of the state's Democratic governors and General Assembly Democrats. Further, Hunt, in his third term from 1993 to 1997, made reduction of the tax burden on the wealthy and on big business a priority. During the same period, via a lengthy special session on crime during 1994, he pressured fellow Democrats to vote for an "anti-crime agenda" that heavily emphasized punishment rather than prevention as a solution.

The reality of North Carolina politics is that leading Democrats since 1960 have taken the state down a path of trickle-down economics that virtually any moderate-to-conservative Republican from the northeastern United States could also have endorsed. The notion that North Carolina's poor and middle-income majority will do well if the wealthy prosper first continued to be at the heart of the North Carolina Democratic Party in the late 1990s.

The second myth of North Carolina politics, with two variations, concerns Jesse Helms. The Tar Heel Republican version of this myth has characterized "Uncle Jesse" as the defender of a down-home traditionalism that represents the views of most North Carolinians. This traditionalism would have men at the head of the household, mandatory Christian prayer in the public schools, and abortion and homosexuality outlawed. According to Helms's defenders, the systematic bias of North Carolina's news media, especially the major dailies, forced Helms and his associates to spend millions of dollars at election time in order to set the record straight. Tar Heel Democrats hold to a second, conflicting variation on the Helms myth. To Democratic leaders, the state's electorate was manipulated into voting Helms into office because of the incessant television spots that Helms's campaigns ran for months right up until Election Day.

In fact, Helms's strong traditionalist ideology has not been shared by most Tar Heels. But Democrats have been wrong to perpetuate the myth that Helms had to hoodwink the people to win. He has, after all, been elected five times to the U.S. Senate. The reality is that a clear majority of white voters agreed with at least some of his antichange, traditionalist thinking. Many fundamentalist Protestants voted for Helms because they agreed with him about the "moral decay" of American society, while most corporate executives supported him because he opposed increased government regulation of their businesses. Just as Terry Sanford and Jim Hunt consciously decided to be modernizers, Jesse Helms became a traditionalist by choice.

Tar Heel Politics 2000 has been revised substantially from the edition (*Tar*

Heel Politics: Myths and Realities) that was published in January 1990. The reasons for the considerable changes between editions are threefold. First, the 1994 Republican sweep of the November elections led to a comfortable GOP majority under Speaker Harold Brubaker in the state house of representatives and fundamentally changed North Carolina politics. Tar Heel voters previously had elected Republican governors, as well as U.S. senators and representatives, but never before in the twentieth century was legislative policy made outside the intraparty negotiations and conflicts of the Democratic "family." Until November 1994 the usually more populist house Democrats and the more big-business-oriented senate would negotiate fiercely because of policy and personality differences, but they would adjourn in July or August assuming their respective Democratic majorities would return after the next election to face another intrafamily fight. But beginning in January 1995, interparty negotiations between the Republican house and the Democratic senate became the norm.

Second, this revised edition demonstrates more explicitly the many ways in which the ideological conflict in other southern states and, to a lesser extent, the post-1994 battles between the Republican Congress and the Clinton White House are mirrored in North Carolina politics. In particular, I make clear in this edition that the terminology of Tar Heel politics, dividing the two political camps in the late 1990s into traditionalists (such as Speaker Brubaker) and modernizers (such as senate Democratic leader Marc Basnight and, on some issues, Governor Hunt) has an uncanny parallel to the Washington, D.C.-based battles between Speaker Newt Gingrich and President Bill Clinton that began in 1995. Similarly, the unprecedented November 1997 triumph of Virginia Republicans over the Democrats, when Republicans won the offices of governor, lieutenant governor, and attorney general and gained new levels of power in the Virginia legislature, was a victory of GOP traditionalists over Democratic modernizers.

Finally, this revised edition is informed by my eight-year membership in the North Carolina state house. By coincidence, I filed for a house seat from Durham in the same month in 1990 that the first edition of *Tar Heel Politics* became available. Over the years, house colleagues have asked me how being on the inside has changed the analysis that I first wrote as an outsider to the legislative chambers.

The answer lies primarily at the level of microsociology. As an academic outsider I had misunderstood the importance of personal relationships in helping or hindering legislation. As insiders my colleagues and I know that we sometimes vote for a bill about which we have some reservations because of a friendship with the bill's sponsor or because we are "trading" support (you back my bill and I'll back yours). In the course of my four terms in the state house, it became obvious that ideological and party differences were to be ignored during the evening hours. For example, at least annually I hosted an evening at the Durham Bulls for my state house friends who share my interest in baseball. Similarly, as a member of the Monday night dinner group first organized by Representative Bob Hunter of Marion, I learned that the emphasis was on camaraderie when we met after session at one or another medium-priced Raleigh restaurant. The food was usually so-so, but the laughs were wonderful.

I moved to North Carolina in 1975 from Mississippi. Before that, I lived in the Middle East (Ankara and Istanbul, Turkey), West Germany (Cologne and Frankfurt), and New York City. I spent my childhood in Chicago, Detroit, and St. Louis. For me, southern politics, and especially Tar Heel politics, is more engaging than political life in any of the other cities and countries I have known. In North Carolina I enjoy the interplay of small-town cultural conservatism and the more urbane culture of midsize cities, the beauty of the mountains and the coast, and the friendliness of the people. The struggle of Tar Heel Republicans and North Carolina blacks to gain powerful positions in a state once controlled by white Democrats is both important and fascinating.

I began studying North Carolina politics in 1976 and over the years have published numerous articles on the subject in sociology journals, newspapers, and magazines. Specialists in political sociology, the branch of sociology where I concentrate my energies, are more often than the average sociologist in tune with the stuff of everyday politics. But while most political sociologists are not themselves active in politics, I thrive on it. The mix of scholarly analysis and practical political involvement has been the driving force behind this book. Throughout my years in North Carolina, I have been active in organized efforts to gain increased political power for the state's less-affluent majority. While I doubt that this vision of citizen empowerment will ever be fully realized, I believe it is a worthy goal.

I began this revision during the early months of the new Republican speakership in 1995. Most of the actual writing occurred on early mornings and weekends during the memorable, seemingly endless 1997 legislative session that finally adjourned four days before Labor Day. Although the political battles of 1997 kept my energy level high enough so that I would be able to write with little sleep, I want to thank three friends and fellow social scientists whom I knew I could have counted on had the going gotten rough: Mark Hellman in Durham (with whom I attended Valparaiso University in Indiana in the mid-1960s); Bill Woodward in Chapel Hill; and Bill Markham, my colleague in the Department of Sociology at the University of North Carolina, Greensboro. I also thank Kem Ekechi, a conscientious and computer-literate sociologist, who completed his M.A. at the University of North Carolina, Greensboro, in December 1997. For a very token honorarium Kem, during the summer of 1997, updated all the North Carolina demographic data and election results in this book. In addition, I thank Thad L. Beyle of the political science department, University of North Carolina, Chapel Hill, for his many astute comments on the manuscript of the revised edition.

This revised edition is dedicated to my wife, Carol Gallione. All my friends know of my penchant to collect "archives" in the basement of my home, on the front and back seats of my aging Geo Prizm, and in piles around the computer on which I wrote this book. But only Carol has had to live with my archives, my reading of five North Carolina newspapers most days of the week and every Sunday, and other quirks of this "professor-politician." Without Carol's support this book could not have been written.

Durham, North Carolina
January 18, 1998

Tar Heel Politics 2000

1 The Heritage of the Democratic Party Elite

North Carolina has long been considered a progressive southern state. Although the term is often ambiguous, the general notion of "progressivism" conveys an image of North Carolina as more committed than other southern states to economic and racial change. In fact, beginning in the 1970s, the closer researchers examined North Carolina, the more they came to question the label (Beyle and Black 1975; Bass and DeVries 1976; Ferguson 1981; Wood 1986; Applebome 1996).

In the first half of the twentieth century, however, North Carolina Democrats led the South in their commitment to public school and university education, a state highway network, and industrialization. The dominant interpretation of actions taken by Democratic governors and legislators to achieve such ends is positive (cf. Lefler and Newsome [1973] for a conventional view). Two aspects of this positive interpretation are significant. The first, which few dispute, is that North Carolina's development of an activist state government was unusual for the South. Thus, its reputation among the southern states as relatively more committed to political and economic change seems secure.

The second aspect of North Carolina's favorable image is more controversial. It hinges on the content of the Democrats' programs. In the dominant view, these state investments were positive because they made industrialization possible. Expressed vaguely in history books and in the speeches of successful Tar Heel politicians, progressivism created an environment in the early decades of the twentieth century that enabled North Carolina's manufacturing economy to become the largest in the South.

An alternate view is more critical of progressivism in the early twentieth century. It does not assume that government activism is in itself positive. Rather, it asks who benefited from the state investments. It focuses on the close ties between industrialists and the Democratic Party leadership. It notes the relative powerlessness of workers and the absolute exclusion of blacks from political life. The alternate view, then, suggests that "progressivism" can be a misleading term; it masks the fact that the state's power holders, even as they invested in educational and transportation improvements, were serving the interests of a narrow economic elite (Finger 1981, 12–13).

Political scientist V. O. Key (1949) subscribed to the alternate view of North Carolina's political economy. Although he praised the state's moderate race relations, he emphasized that North Carolina's economic progressivism was in fact conservatism, not liberalism. He characterized the state as a "progressive plutocracy" whose power was subtle but complete:

> Industrialization has created a financial and business elite whose influence prevails in the state's political and economic life. An aggressive aristocracy of manufacturing and banking, centered around Greensboro, Winston-Salem, Charlotte and Durham, has had a tremendous stake in state policy and has not been remiss in protecting and advancing what it visualizes as its interests. Consequently a sympathetic respect for the problems of corporate capital and of large employers permeates the state's politics and government. For half a century an economic oligarchy has held sway. (p. 211)

This book adopts Key's definition of progressivism. According to Key, a North Carolina progressive is committed to economic change and believes that corporate leaders should control this change in order to benefit the state's business community. The public prospers when business does (Key 1949, 214–15). As background to this book's analysis of contemporary Tar Heel politics, this chapter examines briefly some major political events in

North Carolina from the late nineteenth century to the mid-twentieth century. Two points are central. First, North Carolina's moderate reputation in race relations during the early twentieth century ignores the white leadership's harsh repression of black political participation just before 1900. Second, the Tar Heel interest in industrialization says nothing about the economic and political conditions faced by the growing numbers of factory workers. The reality is that business control of laborers went hand in hand with political control of black protest.

Industrialization as Progress and the Crisis in Agriculture

North Carolina's industrialization in the late 1800s was mostly in cotton textiles. It took place primarily in the state's central region, from Durham in the east to Shelby, west of Charlotte, in the western Piedmont. The raw material was nearby in the cotton-growing counties, mainly in the east (Lefler and Newsome 1973). In these early years, North Carolina's affluent citizenry underwrote the cost of mill start-up (Sitterson 1957). Indeed, sociologist Dwight Billings (1979) has concluded that direct continuity existed between the large landowners of the pre–Civil War period and the textile capitalists of the later nineteenth century. Workers, virtually all of whom were white, abandoned farming to search for higher income in the factory (Hall et al. 1987). The mill relied more on the labor of children and women than of men. In part because such a labor structure was cheap, mills in the years before 1900 were highly profitable (Lefler and Newsome 1973, 508–9, 514–15; Durden 1984, 313–14). A major feature of mill life for workers was the mill village, a closed community where housing, food, and religion were available but political conflict was taboo (Pope 1942).

The mill village, which survived in many North Carolina towns until after World War II, was the cornerstone of textile paternalism. Uncle Ben on the hill took care of "his" workers in the mill (Roy 1975). Such a closed social system had clear significance for labor relations in the mill. Workers who came to view their life in the village as family life were far less likely to protest about working conditions at the factory (Pope 1942). Those who did protest found it difficult to win majority support from fellow employees. Preachers at mill churches often castigated union organizers as heathen. The religious message, primarily fundamentalist Protestantism, stressed the importance of otherworldly salvation rather than collective action in this world. In short, emphasis was placed on individual responsibility and obedience (Earle, Knudsen, and Shriver 1976; Pope 1942; Durden 1984, 314).

The development of labor control through the mill village structure patently benefited textile employers at the workplace. Workers taught early to obey their mill supervisors seldom engaged in political protests. At the mass level, then, the industrialization of North Carolina resulted in a disciplined labor force not initially inclined toward unionization. Yet desperate economic times later changed this pattern.

North Carolina's tobacco industry boomed in the years after the Civil War. R. J. Reynolds started his company in Winston, while Washington Duke became the most successful tobacco entrepreneur in Durham. Both cities were built on tobacco prosperity. Increasingly, farmers in the western and eastern Piedmont as well as on the Coastal Plain began growing bright-leaf tobacco to meet the demands of the tobacco manufacturers. But cigarette manufacturing never employed as many Tar Heels as did the textile industry (Durden 1984, 311–13).

Despite the great publicity that accompanied industrialization, most North Carolinians in the closing decades of the nineteenth century remained on the land. For them, economic conditions were dismal. Forty percent of white farmers and a majority of black farmers did not own their own land. Under the crop-lien system, they were continually in debt to the merchants who provided credit. In the late 1880s an economic populist group, the Farmers' Alliance, began organizing in North Carolina and spread "like wildfire across a parched and windswept forest" (Durden 1984, 316). By 1890 the alliance had more than 2,100 local chapters and 90,000 members statewide. Although alliance members focused their anger primarily on the national economic program of the Republicans, they also criticized the policies of the state Democratic Party.

The Democrats, in close alignment with the growing business class, saw no need to respond to the farmers' protests. The Farmers' Alliance opposed the Democrats' disproportionate reliance on the taxation of farmland, their neglect of public education, and their use of ballot fraud and violence to maintain political power. Most of all, Democrats relied on white racism to keep Republicans from winning elections. The unwillingness of Democrats to undertake political reform in the 1890s provided the potential for a political alternative (Durden 1984, 316). This alternative joined the Populist and Republican Parties in a coalition against the Democrats.

The Populist-Republican alliance, which became known as "fusion," depended on the participation of blacks in politics. Although white Populists and Republicans recognized that this gave the Democrats a continuing issue of "negro rule" (Crow 1984, 340), only the combined totals of blacks and whites interested in political and economic reform could oust the Democratic Party. In 1894 the fusion forces won two-thirds of the seats in the General Assembly. They passed a wide-ranging election law that limited Democratic fraud and allowed illiterates to participate by having colored ballots for each political party; returned home rule, which had been restricted by Democrats, to the counties; increased funds for public education; and limited interest rates (Crow 1984, 338). In 1896 fusionists won a similar majority in the General Assembly and elected a reform-minded Republican governor. Blacks held eleven seats in the General Assembly, their largest total in more than a decade.

The fusion forces foundered, however, on an issue that would permeate North Carolina politics a century later. How much should the General Assembly control business? Was the public interest better served by regulating and taxing business or by giving business a relatively free hand? The new Republican governor, Daniel Russell, proposed an economic program to help farmers and small-business people who were hurt by the high freight rates of the railroads. This was in response to a ninety-nine-year lease that the Democratic governor in 1895 had granted to J. P. Morgan's Southern Railway.

Although farmers and small-business people favored Governor Russell's antirailroad stance, most Republicans objected to the antibusiness tone of their governor, and the 1897 session resulted in a standoff between Populists and some Republicans versus the probusiness Democrats and most Republicans. As a result, Russell joined Populist leader and U.S. Senator Marion Butler in proposing a strong program of economic reform in the 1898 election: nullification of the ninety-nine-year lease, increased taxation on railroad property, and stricter state regulation of rail rates (Crow 1984, 340).

The Democrats countered the Populist economic program with a violent white supremacy campaign. This campaign was led by Furnifold Simmons, who subsequently dominated the North Carolina Democratic Party for three decades while serving in the U.S. Senate. Simmons and other Democrats organized white government unions and established paramilitary units known as Red Shirts and Rough Riders. The Red Shirts and Rough Riders harassed Populists, Republicans, and especially blacks. Historian Jeffrey Crow summarized the Democrats' 1898 campaign this way:

"Armed men broke up fusionist political rallies, disrupted black church meetings, whipped outspoken blacks, and drove black voters from the polls. Simmons enlisted the financial support of business people and manufacturers in the state by promising not to raise taxes. But the cry of 'negro rule' led by Josephus Daniels's (Raleigh) *News and Observer* overwhelmed any public discussion of the economic issues involved in the campaign" (Crow 1984, 340).

The worst violence of 1898 took place in Wilmington, where black and white Republicans controlled local government and a black-owned newspaper, the *Wilmington Record*, was published. Democratic leaders in Wilmington secretly trained Red Shirts in the months before the November election. The antiblack sentiment was so strong that Governor Russell was persuaded to withdraw the local fusion ticket for the General Assembly. Nevertheless, the violence continued. Two days after the election, the Democrats began the so-called Wilmington Race Riot. The *Record*'s offices were burned, black and white Republicans were dragged to the train station and sent out of town, and the local Republican government was forced to resign. Democratic replacements were sworn in on the spot (Crow 1984, 341). Only days after the election, the *News and Observer* commented that "Negro rule is at end in North Carolina forever. The events . . . at Wilmington and elsewhere place that fact beyond all question" (Lefler and Newsome 1973, 559).

Halting Economic Populism and Institutionalizing White Racism

The Democrats successfully used the race issue to regain a majority in the General Assembly in 1898 (Lefler and Newsome 1973, 559). Beginning in the 1899 session of the General Assembly, they repealed the election laws of the fusionists. This ensured the demise of the Populists' economic reform program because, under the new restrictions, the poor biracial majority could not win many elections. Virtually all blacks and many whites were disfranchised by a new election law together with a restrictive suffrage amendment that instituted a poll tax and a literacy test for all voters. The amendment included a grandfather clause allowing illiterates to vote only if their grandfathers had voted before 1867. Since blacks did not have the vote in 1867, the grandfather clause permitted illiterate whites but not blacks to register. With passage of the suffrage amendment, the Democrats institutionalized for decades by law what the Red Shirts had achieved by violence in 1898: the denial of political rights to black Tar Heels (Parramore 1983, 86–92; Crow 1984, 341).

Business interests were also pleased. Their goal of industrialization could now proceed with little danger that economic reformers would attempt to restrict their activities. The Populist movement, which had begun as the nonelectoral Farmers' Alliance in the 1880s and achieved some goals through electoral fusion in the 1890s, was politically dead by the turn of the century. The coalition of business people and Democrats, shaken by the Populist challenge, used white supremacy to regain power. Black political participation would be an undebated issue in North Carolina politics until after World War II.

Charles B. Aycock: The Education Governor

The Democrats realized the Populist Party had selected issues that mattered to the state's farmer majority—for example, public education and health. On his election in 1900, which coincided with the election of another Democratic majority in the General Assembly and ratification of the suffrage amendment, Charles Aycock sought greater education spending in North Carolina. Although he openly acknowledged that more resources should go to white schools, he nonetheless supported spending for black schools as well. Popular history in North Carolina remembers Aycock as the "Education Governor."

Ironically, he could also be labeled the "Segregation Governor." Aycock was a prominent advocate of white supremacy in both the 1898 and 1900 elections. Social harmony necessitated that blacks be disfranchised, he argued. His education programs were supposed to eliminate illiteracy among whites so they could more easily register to vote (Lefler and Newsome 1973, 561). Thus the education program, as presented by Aycock before the 1900 election, was intended to win white support for the suffrage amendment. He did not propose that it help blacks regain the vote. Indeed, historian Helen Edmonds argued that Democrats advocated education in the 1900 campaign only because illiterate whites threatened to vote against the disfranchisement amendment. In short, were it not for their white supremacy goals, the Democrats might not have even promised educational improvements (Edmonds 1951).

The electoral changes achieved by the Democrats had a major effect on political participation by both races after 1900. Overwhelmingly, blacks were disfranchised. But poor whites who could not pay the poll tax also lost the vote. The number of eligible voters dropped after 1900, and within this smaller group, only 50 percent voted in the 1904 gubernatorial election. This compared with 87 percent participation by eligible voters in 1896, when the biracial fusionist coalition elected Daniel Russell governor.

Historian Paul Escott has pointed out that the growing domination of the Democratic Party after 1900 by corporate interests, coupled with the poll tax, drove poor and working-class whites from the voting booths. These representatives of the economic elite, who had funded the white supremacy campaigns at the turn of the century, restricted the state's political agenda to issues of benefit to them. Economic populism to empower the broader-based white majority was simply unthinkable. Accordingly, many of these non-elite whites lost interest in North Carolina politics (Escott 1985, 261). In Escott's view, the success of Democratic white supremacy shaped both class and racial politics in North Carolina for many years:

> Elite Democrats did more than beat back the challenge of the Populists, disfranchise black people, and stigmatize cooperation between Tar Heels of both races. They imposed an undemocratic electoral system so complete and effective that all future political discourse had a restricted character. The new system excluded a large segment of the population from participation and thereby eliminated a broad spectrum of opinion. Subsequent generations learned their politics within a highly constricted, conservative frame of reference. In this way the events of the 1890s froze political thought and kept it from evolving for decades. (p. 265)

Governor Aycock's education reforms are best viewed in this context. Corporate leaders joined Aycock in a "crusade" for public education. The crusade was successful. Never before in North Carolina had more monies been allocated for school construction. The school year was extended to a minimum of four months, and 800 high schools—650 for whites and 150 for blacks—were planned. But the reason behind this school expansion is significant. Once the Democrats had destroyed the Populists, their new education crusade represented a pragmatic effort to claim the mantle of political reform. In fact, Aycock's education programs differed from the Populists' in that Aycock viewed business as the appropriate direct beneficiary of government policy. Literacy could trickle down to the masses, but they were not to share political power with the elite. The activist government under Aycock and future Democratic governors pledged progress for North Carolina. Nevertheless, this progress "tended to enhance the interests of the business community primarily and to reinforce the existing social, political and economic order" (Crow 1984, 342).

More Progressive Policy:
The Good Roads State

The second major area in which Democrats involved state government prominently was highway construction and maintenance. It is another example of how government investment provided the infrastructure that enabled North Carolina to lead the South in industrialization during most of the twentieth century.

Although the General Assembly did not make a major investment in roads until 1921, business began laying the groundwork for state support almost as soon as the automobile was available. In 1902, textile manufacturer Phillip Hanes became the first president of the North Carolina Good Roads Association. The association called for the establishment of a state highway commission and state maintenance of highways. Before state involvement, wealthier urban counties built roads by assessing a county road tax. But in 1910 more than 90 percent of North Carolina's "roads" were little more than mud tracks when it rained. In 1915 the General Assembly established the State Highway Commission to cooperate with counties in road construction (Lefler and Newsome 1973, 587–88).

As the number of automobiles rapidly increased, from 2,000 in 1910 to 150,000 in 1921, so did the political pressure of the Good Roads Association. Heavily lobbied, especially by association secretary Harriet Morehead Berry but also by Governor Cameron Morrison, the General Assembly gave the State Highway Commission responsibility for both highway construction and maintenance. North Carolina soon gained a national reputation as the "Good Roads State." The road building took place because of the state's willingness to finance a bond issue, to be paid for primarily with revenues from the new gasoline tax (Lefler and Newsome 1973, 587, 600).

Also in the early 1920s the General Assembly continued its commitment to public education. Most importantly, it increased the minimum school year from four months to six and established standards for school certification and teacher salaries. The legislature also made large commitments to higher education, primarily to the state's major white campuses at Chapel Hill, Greensboro, and Raleigh (Lefler and Newsome 1973, 600–601).

Funding Infrastructure:
Taxation in the 1920s and 1930s

By the second decade of the twentieth century many North Carolinians realized that the length of the public school term could not be increased without an expanded source of state revenue. Like most other states at the time, North Carolina relied on a state property tax that required fair tax valuations at the local level. But counties had a self-interest in keeping valuations low in order to pay less to the state treasury (Liner 1979, 46).

In 1913 the General Assembly had proposed constitutional amendments to abolish the state property tax, assigning that tax to local government, and to limit state taxation to income, franchise, and inheritance taxes. Voters rejected these amendments in 1914, but faced with the prospect of higher property taxes after a statewide revaluation in 1919–20, they strongly endorsed the amendments in 1920. Accordingly, the 1921 General Assembly established two new state-administered taxes, an individual and a corporate income tax. North Carolina became one of the first states to end its reliance on the property tax and establish an income tax instead (Liner 1979, 46). As part of the Good Roads program, it also imposed a one-penny-per-gallon gasoline tax.

The Democrats' decision to establish new state taxes, including a corporate income tax, underscored the leadership's commitment to economic change. Business could not prosper if state government was unable to provide services, so new tax revenues had to be found. It is a hallmark of future-oriented business people that they are willing to pay taxes as a last resort in order to fund government programs, although they would prefer that legislators keep business taxes at a minimum.

By the early 1920s, then, state government services included support for both public education and highways. In the interest of efficiency the Good Roads program of 1921 assumed total responsibility for intertown road building. Schools, however, still depended on local as well as state taxation. To avoid raising property taxes, many local governments issued bonds to pay for services. This led to high bond indebtedness on the part of many Tar Heel counties and cities. In 1928 the state ranked second in the nation, after New York, in total bond debt, four and one-half times the national average. When the impact of the Great Depression hit in the early 1930s, North Carolina faced a major fiscal crisis (Liner 1979, 48).

Once again an energetic governor seized the initiative. O. Max Gardner, a textile industrialist, had been elected in 1928. Independent of the financial problems caused by the depression, Gardner believed in efficiency based on centralization (Stoesen 1984, 383). Perhaps because of Gardner's strong beliefs, no other state during the depression "transformed its system of governmental finances as radically as North Carolina" (Liner 1979, 47).

Following recommendations of a report that Governor Gardner had commissioned in 1930 from the Brookings Institution, both state and local governments became more centralized. The 1931 General Assembly assumed control of county roads, prisons, and the public schools. At this time no state except Delaware was totally responsible for public schools, and no state took responsibility for all road construction and maintenance (Liner 1979, 47). The legislature also established the Local Government Commission to supervise local finances and especially to restrict bond indebtedness (Stoesen 1984, 383).

The consolidation of state government took the pressure off the local property tax, which had become especially burdensome for farmers during the depression (Key 1949, 211). But the 1931 General Assembly deadlocked over how to raise additional state revenues. Gardner sided with the farmers, who opposed the sales tax and favored a luxury tax (Lefler and Newsome 1973, 608). The General Assembly enacted neither tax in 1931 and instead passed temporary taxes as well as budget reductions.

The legislature faced another fiscal crisis in 1933. The newly elected governor, J. C. B. Ehringhaus, was handpicked by Gardner (Key 1949, 213). In 1932 he had campaigned against both the sales and luxury taxes. But once in office, Ehringhaus concluded that, given the state's financial problems, the sales tax was the only option. He argued that otherwise North Carolina would be required to continue borrowing over the short term to meet its long-term obligations (Ehringhaus 1934). Further, the new revenues would allow the General Assembly to finance extension of the mandatory school term to eight months instead of six.

Ehringhaus justified the sales tax as if taxes on business or the wealthy were not possible: "If it is a choice between a sales tax on one hand and a decent school on the other, I stand for the school" (quoted in Lefler and Newsome 1973, 613). But in fact Ehringhaus and a majority of the General Assembly were ignoring the recommendations of the state Tax Commission, which had been established by the legislature in 1927 to "digest all available data on taxation" and submit policy proposals (Lefler and Newsome 1973, 604). The Tax Commission opposed the sales tax as "unsound, unfair, and unwise." Instead, it recommended budget cutbacks and a 20 percent increase in income, franchise, and license taxes. These tax increases would have burdened business and primarily the wealthy (few Tar Heels earned more than the $4,000 in taxable income, which triggered the income tax; the governor's salary, for example, was $6,390 in 1933) (Lefler and Newsome 1973, 612; Liner 1981, 34). The increases also would have permitted the repeal of a temporary statewide property tax that had been passed to keep public schools open.

The insurance and tobacco industries led the campaign against the Tax Commission plan. Insurance companies insisted that North Carolina's insurance taxes were already the nation's highest, and tobacco lobbyists, speaking for all industry, noted that corporations already paid 57 percent of all Tar Heel income taxes. Merchants as well as the *News and Observer* spoke out against the sales tax. The Merchants' Association called it "the last resort of despotism" and brought anti–sales tax petitions to the General Assembly, while editor Josephus Daniels campaigned for a luxury tax. In the end the insurance-tobacco-Ehringhaus position prevailed. The General Assembly accepted the Tax Commission's recommendation to end the statewide property tax but rejected the idea of replacing the revenue with taxes on business or the wealthy. Instead it passed a 3 percent sales tax (Lefler and Newsome 1973, 612–13; Liner 1981, 33).

In retrospect, the outcome of the 1933 tax debate is remarkable because it set a pattern that Democratic politicians would often follow until the 1990s. In effect, business persuades the Democratic majority that it cannot afford to pay any more taxes. The sales tax is a lucrative alternative. The lower-income majority, which pays a higher percentage of its income in sales taxes because it spends a higher proportion of its income on necessities, lacks the political organization and clout of corporate lobbies. Democrats who have wanted to modernize North Carolina are known for their willingness to tax in order to provide necessary services such as schools and highways. Significantly, as in Ehringhaus's contention, Tar Heel Democrats will usually argue that the end, adequate schools, justifies the means, a regressive tax. This happened when Terry Sanford, as governor in 1961, advocated reimposing the 3 percent sales tax on groceries (groceries had been exempted in 1941) to improve public education, especially community colleges. It also occurred in the 1980s when Democrats raised the local-option sales tax from one cent to two cents, tying both half-cent increases to specific local government investments to aid school and sewer construction.

The tax structure established in 1931 and 1933 still serves as the basis for state finance. Indeed, the 6 percent flat rate of the corporate income tax did not change until 1987, when it was raised to 7 percent. During the 1990s the corporate income tax rate fluctuated but was scheduled to drop to 6.9 percent in 2000. The 7 percent top rate in the individual income tax, established in 1937 for net income above $10,000, did not rise (to 7.75 percent) until the recession of 1991, even though inflation fundamentally changed the meaning of $10,000. The 3 percent state sales tax was also raised in 1991, and all 100 counties also collect a local 2 percent sales tax. Over time, however, businesses' share of state taxes dropped dramatically. Between 1935 and 1990, for example, the total taxes business paid into the North Carolina General Fund dropped from 60 percent to 20 percent, primarily because the individual income tax had grown much faster than the corporate income tax (Liner 1991; Liner 1982, 40–41; see also Chapter 3). In effect, a once-progressive individual income tax had become much less so by the 1990s.

Democrats and Unions:
From 1900 to the Great Depression

Another component of the Democratic heritage is its antagonism toward organized labor. In fact, the state already enjoyed a reputation as antiunion in the early twentieth century. Not surprisingly, most Democrats, closely aligned with big business, openly opposed unions. The key contribution of Democratic governors was to mobilize the National Guard in order to break workers' strikes.

Beginning around 1900 the American Federation of Labor tried but failed to organize textile workers in Gibsonville, Durham, Raleigh, and Fayetteville. Labor's losses had a sobering effect. Although skilled workers succeeded in establishing unions in a few dozen places around the state, both the American Federation of Labor and its textile affiliate, the United Textile Workers (UTW), largely gave up on North Carolina until the national labor unrest immediately following World War I. The reason was not lack of interest by workers but, rather, the virulent opposition of mill owners. When the UTW conducted an organizing campaign throughout the South from 1913 to 1918, it specifically exempted North Carolina because of "strong anti-union sentiment" (Lefler and Newsome 1973, 584).

The actions of three governors (Morrison, Gardner, and Ehringhaus) between 1921 and 1934 illustrate the pattern of elite antiunionism. These governors, directly or indirectly tied to industrialists in the cities and small towns of the western Piedmont, believed unions interfered with progress.

The ideology of progressive North Carolina excluded labor organization just as it opposed black political participation.

The position of a fourth governor, Thomas Bickett, who was elected in 1916 from agrarian eastern North Carolina, constituted an exception that proved the rule of antiunionism. In 1919 Bickett refused to take sides during bitter confrontations between workers and mill owners in and around Charlotte and pressured the dismayed mill owners to reach a settlement (Hall et al. 1987, 188–89).

When Cameron Morrison, the "Good Roads Governor," was elected in 1920, industrialists had a friend in Raleigh. Morrison was linked professionally and through family ties to the Piedmont business elite. Further, he had begun his political career as a Red Shirt, harassing blacks in the eastern Piedmont counties near Rockingham just before 1900 (Hall et al. 1987, 194; Abrams 1978, 426). In 1921 striking union members in Charlotte and Concord asked Governor Morrison to mediate their dispute with management, but he refused to meet with them. Shortly afterward, at the request of Cannon Mills owner Charles Cannon, he called out the National Guard. When the guard allowed strikebreakers to enter the mills, the strikes ended (Hall et al. 1987, 194).

Max Gardner's term as governor from 1929 to 1933 was punctuated by strikes both before and after the depression began. Gardner was generally considered to be more progressive than Morrison, who had defeated Gardner in the 1920 gubernatorial primary. But Gardner, an industrialist, consistently sided with the mill owners. In 1929 he sent the National Guard to Gastonia, where a Communist-influenced union was organizing a strike, as well as to Marion, where the anti-Communist UTW was involved. Both strikes were broken (Hall et al. 1987, 215).

During the depression, mill owners' plans to cut wages often met with resistance from workers. The strikes were usually spontaneous and received little assistance from national unions such as the UTW. Cone Mill workers in Greensboro in 1931 appealed to Gardner to intervene in their dispute, but he refused. In 1932, strikes in textile and furniture factories in the High Point area were so serious that a local newspaper editor and state legislator asked the governor to mediate. Under those circumstances Gardner did oversee a labor-management settlement. In the same year, again recognizing serious conflict during a textile strike in Rockingham, Gardner was willing to intervene, but he backed off when local mill owners refused to negotiate (Bell 1982, 31–39).

Governor Ehringhaus responded to the 1934 general strike that took place across North Carolina, primarily in textile mills, by mobilizing 14,000 national guardsmen. Some mill owners, grateful for the troops, drew a parallel between worker rebellion in 1934 and black political participation before 1900 (Hall et al. 1987, 332–34). In the eyes of business, blacks and unionized workers were equally illegitimate political actors.

North Carolina workers in the first third of the twentieth century could win labor-management battles only if a neutral governor were willing to pressure recalcitrant industrialists into negotiating with unions. This rarely happened. More commonly, when the governors sided with the owners, the owners could wait out the strike, since the strikers ultimately faced starvation. While the strike went on, the National Guard's presence allowed management to try to resume production with strikebreakers.

In the half-century following the 1934 general strike, the National Guard intervened in a major labor dispute just one more time. In 1958 Governor Luther Hodges, a former executive of Fieldcrest Mills, sent guardsmen to Henderson during a strike at Harriet-Henderson Yarns, the effect of which was to help strikebreakers cross the picket line. As in the case of Governors Morrison and Ehringhaus before him, Hodges's loyalties to industrialists spelled doom for the local union (Clark 1997).

W. Kerr Scott: A Populist Interlude in the Post–World War II Era

Max Gardner became a dominant force in the Democratic Party after his election as governor in 1928. His political organization, dubbed the "Shelby Dynasty" after his hometown west of Charlotte, controlled the governor's office for two decades. But in 1948 Kerr Scott defeated the dynasty's candidate by advocating greater concern for the state's rural majority. Governor Scott's "Go Forward" program included a $200 million bond issue for secondary road construction, a huge amount for that time. Scott also promoted measures to improve schools, public health, and rural electrification (Lefler and Newsome 1973, 627). His administration stretched the Democratic Party's progressive ideology to include neglected areas of society. Identifying social needs, the General Assembly appropriated the funds, through bond issues and direct expenditures, to allow state government to assume additional responsibilities.

Two other events marked the Scott administration. First, a young Fayetteville lawyer named Terry Sanford got his start in politics working for Scott. Second, in 1949 the governor appointed North Carolina's foremost advocate for racial and economic justice, University of North Carolina president Frank Graham, to a vacancy in the U.S. Senate.

Frank Graham's Defeat:
The Limits of Democrats' Ideology

At the time of his Senate appointment, Frank Graham had been president of the University of North Carolina for nineteen years. Scott and other political observers were convinced that Graham, as the "best-known and best-loved man in North Carolina" (Ashby 1980, 257), would win the special election scheduled for 1950. But they failed to consider the political realities: Graham was a genuine economic and racial New Dealer in a state whose elite generally tolerated neither.

In the 1920s Graham had supported collective bargaining for workers, and in the 1930s he had advocated both the Social Security system and federal aid to education (Ashby 1980, chap. 11). Further, Graham played a prominent role in the few interracial conferences that took place in the South. Although he opposed mandatory federal civil rights legislation, he did not hide his distaste for racial segregation (Ashby 1980, chap. 12). Conservatives at both the national and the state levels continually accused Graham of being "soft on Communism." Even some of his allies, such as U.S. Senator Clyde Hoey, a former governor of North Carolina, conceded on the Senate floor that Graham had been "careless in association with certain organizations" (Ashby 1980, 245).

Graham was thus vulnerable to the charge that his commitment to economic and racial reform was out of step with the beliefs of most North Carolinians. Willis Smith, a Raleigh lawyer serving at that time as president of the American Bar Association, became Graham's major opponent. Graham led in the first primary with 48 percent of the vote; Smith received 42 percent, while two minor candidates shared the remaining 10 percent.

Smith almost declined to call for a runoff but changed his mind after supporters converged on his front lawn just before the deadline. One of the rally organizers was a young radio announcer from Raleigh named Jesse Helms. Smith's supporters had used plenty of dirty tricks in the first primary. Among them was a fraudulent postcard mailed to whites in every part of the state. Allegedly from the "National Society [*sic*] for the Advancement of Colored People," it thanked "Dr. Frank" for all he had done "to advance the place of the Negro in North Carolina." Smith supporters produced leaflets and ads that declared Graham a Communist sympathizer because of some of his associations over the years (Ashby 1980, 262, 268).

Smith's runoff campaign benefited from a U.S. Supreme Court decision that was handed down between the May and June primaries. In *Sweatt v. Painter*, the Court ruled that the state of Texas had to admit a black student to the previously all-white University of Texas law school. For segregationist Smith backers the Court's decision symbolized the danger of Graham's racial views (Ashby 1980, 262, 268).

Although Smith took the high road in criticizing Graham, leaving the dirty work to campaign staff, his comments paralleled the campaign slurs. On the stump he asserted that Graham's election would mean desegregation. Between the first and second primaries the Smith campaign attacks on Graham became virulent. Reminiscent of the Democratic rhetoric of 1898, one newspaper ad listed the first primary results in selected black precincts around the state and asked, "Are we going to throw away the work and accomplishment of all those patriotic men who freed our state from Negro domination?" Another declared, "White People WAKE UP Before It is Too Late. . . . Do you want Negroes working beside you, your wife, and your daughters in your mills and factories? . . . Frank Graham favors mingling of the races" (Ashby 1980, 265).

The racial theme succeeded in reversing the results of the first primary. Especially in eastern North Carolina, where few blacks voted but where they comprised more than one-third of the population, Graham lost counties that he had won in the first election. But Graham also lost to Smith in the affluent precincts of the urban Piedmont. In short, parallel to 1898 and 1900, a white elite successfully mobilized white voters to defeat an economic reformer. The issues of Communism and race were used to thwart a candidacy sympathetic to both economic and racial equality (Lubell 1964).

For North Carolina Democrats like Governor Scott who were not strongly opposed to gradual racial change, Graham's defeat was sobering. Smith's victory indicated that, for a majority of voting Tar Heels, racial and economic reform was too threatening, even in the person of "best-loved" Frank Graham.

The 1950 election also highlighted the emerging conflict for Tar Heel Democrats. North Carolina's moderate racial reputation had always been predicated on no serious challenge to the racial status quo (Key 1949). Graham's lifelong commitment to racial change made him an unacceptable symbol to many white Democrats. But to others the party should have been heading in that direction. More than any other issue, race would tear apart the party in the decades to come. During the 1950s and 1960s, racial segregation faced a growing challenge from blacks even as the other key aspect of Democrats' ideology—an activist, procorporate state government—encountered only occasional opposition from Tar Heels.

2 Competing Ideals in North Carolina Politics

Beginning in the 1960s and continuing until the present, North Carolina's politicians and business leaders have chosen policies consistent with one of two competing ideologies: modernism and traditionalism. In other southern states, from Virginia to Texas, similar ideological battles have been waged. The competing ideals do not correlate neatly with party label. Yet overall a pattern emerged by the early 1980s: southern Democrats tended to be modernizers, while southern Republicans endorsed traditionalism. Arkansas governor and U.S. president Bill Clinton has been a vintage modernizer throughout most of his political career. Southern Republican leaders on Capitol Hill, from U.S. Senate leader Trent Lott of Mississippi to the southern Republican chiefs in the House such as Georgia's Newt Gingrich or Texas's Dick Armey or Bill Archer, have relied on traditionalist ideology for their successes. Southern preachers such as Jerry Falwell and Pat Robertson, both of Virginia, have also built their political successes on traditionalist values.

The modernizer ideal in North Carolina and elsewhere in the South has emphasized the importance of economic expansion. Social changes that accompany economic growth, such as suburban sprawl, traffic congestion, or shortages of public school buildings and day care centers, are viewed as less worrisome than missing the opportunity for economic expansion. The traditionalist ideal, skeptical of modernization because of its reliance on a big and free-spending government and its potential for disruption of the small-town, Baptist-based social order, has found considerable merit and political gain in promoting the status quo and the superiority of a mythical ideal past.

In North Carolina in recent decades, modernizers and traditionalists have fought hard for control of state politics. Governor and U.S. Senator Terry Sanford throughout his political career and Governor Jim Hunt during his first two terms, from 1977 to 1985, were prime promoters of modernizer ideology. U.S. Senator Jesse Helms's lengthy political career epitomizes the traditionalist ideal. Helms, at one time a southern Democrat, became a Republican shortly before running for the Senate in 1972. Besides most Republicans, some rural or small-town Democrats, especially whites from eastern North Carolina, appeared committed to traditionalist policies into the twenty-first century.

A third political ideal in North Carolina and across the South, economic populism, has had a checkered history since its evolution over a century ago in the 1880s. In North Carolina in the 1990s, economic populism enjoyed some support among black and white state legislators but was anathema to the state's big-business elite. Economic populism has stood in marked contrast to modernism and traditionalism in insisting that government policy should directly benefit the middle- and low-income majority rather than large corporations and the wealthy.

Traditionalism

Traditionalist ideology is rooted in the Baptist-based culture of North Carolina's small towns and rural areas. Economically, traditionalism has been associated with tobacco production and historic industries such as textiles, apparel, and furniture. This relationship is not accidental. Traditionalists have not opposed economic change but have preferred economic growth that could reinforce the established social order. In the early twentieth century, for example, cotton mills with their adjacent mill villages were desirable because they provided workers continuity with the small-scale rural communities from which they had migrated (Pope 1942; Hall et al. 1987). In the 1980s and 1990s, traditionalists were unsympathetic to the arrival of high-tech industry in North Carolina for several reasons. First, high-technology firms, often lured to the state with tax incentives, would probably pressure existing firms to raise wages to remain competitive for workers and thereby could threaten the profitability of existing industry. Second, high-tech industry tended to bring large numbers of outsiders to North Carolina. Two conflicts of the 1990s illustrate for traditionalists the problems caused by high-tech in-migration. Multinational firms such as IBM and Glaxo in the Research Triangle part of Durham began offering to same-sex partners a benefits package traditionally limited to married couples. Charlotte, which with the growing national prominence of banks such as NationsBank and First Union had been gaining a reputation as the South's leading city after Atlanta (Applebome 1996), was politically torn apart in 1997 by cultural conflict. A traditionalist majority on the Mecklenburg County Commission—four white Republicans and an openly antigay black Democrat—on a close vote ended county funding for a series of local and visiting arts programs. The stated reason was the excessive homosexual content of arts programs (*Charlotte Observer* 1997b).

Traditionalism's ideal community is rooted in the Baptist and other fundamentalist Protestant denominations that permeate North Carolina. Although African American and white native-born Tar Heels are equally likely to have fundamentalist roots, it is white Baptists whose social values have shaped North Carolina's political realities. According to traditionalists, a deferential relationship should exist both between employer and employee and between husband and wife. Traditionalists consider labor unions and collective bargaining disruptive of the workplace. Even though high percentages of North Carolina women are in the low-wage labor force, the ideology of patriarchy, not feminism, remains paramount. For some traditionalists, blacks should never have challenged white authority. Gains of the civil rights movement have forced traditionalist ideology to tolerate racial desegregation. But traditionalists stand firmly opposed to affirmative action programs, whether for African Americans or women.

The implications of social traditionalism for North Carolina politics are many. First, for either traditionalist elites or their mass followers, egalitarian social movements promoted by blacks, women, gays, or labor organizers are anathema because they challenge the established order. Second, a political candidate who runs against specific manifestations of these movements—such as the Equal Rights Amendment (1970s), the paid holiday honoring Dr. Martin Luther King Jr. (1980s), or gay rights (1990s)—can be assured of a certain core support. Third, the strength of traditionalist deference among working-class whites in North Carolina (Botsch 1981) makes the campaigns of either populist politicians or union organizers more difficult, because a certain percentage of the white population does not believe in challenging any authority.

Traditionalist ideology is both antitax and anti–big government. According to the traditionalist ideal, government should not actively promote economic development by subsidizing investments in North Carolina by out-of-state corporations. As legislators, traditionalists usually vote against tax increases. Even though they rarely say so publicly, traditionalists question privately whether more government spending for primary and secondary schools will solve social and economic problems. Ideologically, traditionalists hold that responsibility for learning lies more with the parents than with the state.

Traditionalists believe, finally, that the state does not need to regulate corporations or government agencies to protect the consumer. Such notions of consumer rights imply an economic conflict that traditionalists believe does not, or should not, exist (Black and Black 1987, chap. 2).

North Carolina traditionalists have promoted an antichange ideology in both economic and social policy. But because of North Carolina's legacy as an activist state, going back to Governor Charles B. Aycock's education spending program of 1901, traditionalists have enjoyed more political success in the General Assembly implementing their social views. In response to student activism during the early 1960s, primarily on the Chapel Hill campus of the University of North Carolina, traditionalists in 1963 imposed the Speaker Ban Law. This statute prohibited state-supported colleges from allowing as a campus speaker any Communist, any advocate of the overthrow of federal or state government, or anyone who had "pleaded the Fifth Amendment to the Constitution in refusing to answer any question with respect to Communist or subversive connections or activities." In 1968 a federal court declared the speaker ban unconstitutional (Lefler and Newsome 1973, 699–701). But traditionalist influence continued well into the 1990s. Defeat of the Equal Rights Amendment in six General Assembly sessions between 1973 and 1982 (cf. *Greensboro Record* 1977), strong antipornography legislation (1985), restrictions on sex education in the public schools (1995), and prohibitions in many counties on liquor-by-the-drink or beer and wine sales all suggested the sustaining power of social traditionalism.

One social-traditionalist issue, the symbolic importance of the Confederate battle flag, has not been a major issue in North Carolina. In the mid-1990s the Democratic governor of Georgia, Zell Miller, and South Carolina's Republican governor, David Beasley, both failed in their efforts to reduce the visibility of that Old South symbol (*News and Record* 1996a; 1996d). Tar Heels probably avoided the conflict because no part of the Confederate flag is embedded in the North Carolina flag.

Modernism

Modernizer ideology values individual economic achievement, whether as an entrepreneurial or a corporate activity. By promoting growth, modernizers envision prosperity for all through an expanded economic pie (Elazar 1972; Cobb 1984; Applebome 1996). Unlike traditionalism, modernism places no special value on existing social relations. Indeed, economic change is presumed to alter the old social order, but modernizers do not assume that change means loss of economic or political control (Luebke 1980; Black and Black 1992, 270). North Carolina modernizers continually seek to diversify the state's economy. In particular, in contrast to traditionalists, they have been committed to reducing the state's dependency on low-wage industries such as textiles or apparel (Goldman and Luebke 1985).

Modernizer ideology is more secular than traditionalism, and it is rooted in the major cities of the North Carolina Piedmont. People who relocate in the Tar Heel state, especially those in business, are far more likely to be modernizers than traditionalists. These nonretiree newcomers have disproportionately settled in the Research Triangle area (Durham-Raleigh-Chapel Hill) and metropolitan Charlotte. Modernizer politicians are usually North Carolina natives, often graduates of the University of North Carolina at Chapel Hill or North Carolina State University. The faith in public education is high, and the commitment to improve education is mandatory for a modernizer politician.

Like traditionalism, modernizer ideology has been shaped by educated and affluent white males. Yet, unlike traditionalism, modernism does not reject demands from blacks, women, or unions out of hand. In the interests of social stability and economic gain, modernizers seek an accommodation with such groups. Significantly, modernizers have been more willing to accommodate the demands of middle-class African Americans and women and more hostile to organized labor and any citizen groups that challenged the privileges of the prevailing power structure (Goldman and Luebke 1985). As elsewhere in the South, North Carolina's modernizers recognized the necessity of sharing some power with women and blacks. Both historical out-groups across the South have taken advantage of the political potential in the aftermath of the egalitarian movements of the 1960s and 1970s. In Virginia, Mary Sue Terry, a white lawyer, was elected to a four-year term as attorney general in 1989 (but lost the 1993 race for governor), while Douglas Wilder, an African American attorney, was elected to the office of lieutenant governor (1985) and, later, governor (1989). Two brothers of the Campbell family of Raleigh also exemplified the openness of the white-modernizer establishment to African Americans. In 1993 William Campbell was the third black to be elected mayor of Atlanta, Georgia (he presided over the 1996 Summer Olympic Games), while younger brother Ralph won the North Carolina position of state auditor in 1992. Ralph Campbell was the first nonjudicial black candidate to win a statewide election in North Carolina.

Issues important to women and blacks have constituted a significant point of conflict between modernizers and traditionalists. The King holiday, the Equal Rights Amendment, and abortion rights have illustrated the controversy. Modernizers acknowledge the necessity of some affirmative action policies for blacks and women, even if modernizers themselves would not initiate such policies. Modernizers do not see the need to maintain the deferential social structure preferred by traditionalists. Their ideal society is dynamic and growing.

To fuel the "growth machine" (Molotch 1976), modernizers want an active state government. For existing businesses to expand or new national or international capital to invest in North Carolina, the state's infrastructure of public schools, community colleges, universities, highways, airports, and sewer and water lines must also be expanding (Black and Black 1987; Fleer 1994). Consequently, modernizers believe in taxation. Even though traditionalists in principle are antitaxation, if a tax increase seems essential, the traditionalist usually joins the modernizer in preferring a regressive tax such as a sales tax or a flat fee. Both modernizer and traditionalist politicians have contributed in recent years to a shift in North Carolina's tax burden away from business and toward the middle- and low-income majority (Whitman 1997, 70–74). How state politicians have levied or cut taxes provides an example of what the two ideologies share—in contrast to a third ideology, economic populism.

Economic Populism

A century ago, both in the South and across the Midwest, farmers organized against what they viewed as the monopolistic power of the large banks, railroads, and other economic forces (Goodwyn 1976). Although ultimately unsuccessful, economic populism challenged the dominant political-economic elite with the counterargument that the marketplace should not be unfairly controlled by a few large corporations. Government's job, according to populist ideology, was to ensure economic fairness for the "little guy" (Clotfelter and Hamilton 1972).

In North Carolina the Populist movement in the 1880s and 1890s was strong enough to elect a U.S. senator. Aligned with blacks in the Republican Party, the Populist Party challenged the power of the Democrats who constituted the establishment party. Indeed, Democrat Charles Aycock's turn-of-the-century education reforms were taken in response to political challenges from Populists and Republicans.

In recent decades economic populism has emerged on occasion as an alternative to the Democratic Party's moderate-conservative strategy that embraced the goals of big business. Just as it was a century ago (see Chapter 1), economic populism in the United States is most frequently championed by politicians from the Midwest and the South. While the populists formed their own party in the 1880s and 1890s, populists in the recent past have constituted a left wing within the Democratic Party. Nationally, populist Democrats in 1993 opposed President Clinton's successful battle to approve the North American Free Trade Agreement (NAFTA). Indeed, although not all anti-NAFTA congressional Democrats would have labeled themselves populists, the notion that NAFTA helped multinational corporations more than it helped average workers is typical of populist ideology. Populist Democrats similarly opposed the Clinton administration's effort in 1997 to win "fast-track" trade authority from Congress.

In the 1990s Paul Wellstone of Minnesota was elected twice to the U.S. Senate as a populist Democrat. (Wellstone had a Tar Heel connection; he received a B.A. and a Ph.D. in political science from the University of North Carolina at Chapel Hill.) In the House, Democratic minority leader Dick Gephardt of Missouri and minority whip David Bonior of Michigan frequently invoked economic populism to criticize not only Republican Speaker Gingrich but also fellow Democrats President Clinton and Vice-President Al Gore. The Congressional Black Caucus, since its inception in the 1970s, has advocated in the House a platform that, beyond its call for racial justice, is at its core economic populism. Democratic populists oppose tax breaks for the wealthy and big corporations and advocate more direct tax benefits and government spending for middle- and low-income citizens.

Economic populism has had fewer advocates of late from the South. Radio commentator Jim Hightower, who previously was elected to the statewide Texas office of agricultural commissioner, began in the mid-1990s to make political hay over the airwaves on behalf of the little guys and gals (Hightower 1997; Solomon and Cohen 1997, 145). Three times between 1969 and 1977 Virginia attorney Henry Howell ran for governor, scaring the state's establishment as he came close to winning, especially in 1973. Howell, previously elected lieutenant governor in 1965, was a strong advocate for the majority against the poll tax that restricted black and white working-class voting, high utility rates, and of course corporate tax loopholes (*Richmond Times-Dispatch* 1997a). In 1972 the populist bug spread across the state line into North Carolina. Wilbur Hobby, president of the state AFL-CIO (American Federation of Labor–Congress of Industrial Organizations), ran for governor borrowing Howell's slogan: Keep the big boys honest. But in a crowded Democratic primary that included an African American dentist who won the allegiance of many black voters, Hobby managed just a fourth-place finish.

In North Carolina, corporate leaders, whether traditionalists or modernizers, have opposed economic populism as "unneeded" (Luebke 1981b; Whitman 1997). Because of their long-standing ideological alliance with big business, the modernizer politicians who have dominated the state Democratic Party have consistently sought to soft-pedal any populist positions in their statewide campaigns. But if economic populism has not blossomed in the Tar Heel state, neither has it altogether withered. In recent years urban Democrats, especially from the statehouse, have challenged tax breaks for big banks and other multinational corporations and stressed the importance of cutting the sales tax on groceries (the so-called food tax).

The success of house Republicans in winning control of the state house in November 1994, the first Republican majority in the twentieth century, ironically increased the influence of North Carolina's Democratic populists. On a variety of issues, from cutting the food tax to challenging state government subsidies for incoming corporations that promise to create jobs, house Democrats crafted an "unholy alliance" with principled traditionalist Republicans. The two groups, from the left and right sides of the political spectrum, agreed that government should increase tax relief to the middle- and low-income majority and that government should not dispense handouts to big corporations.

The Confusing Liberal-Conservative Terminology

It is tempting to view traditionalism and modernism as synonymous with conservatism and liberalism, but that is inaccurate for several reasons. First, although traditionalists can usually be termed conservatives, modernizers are not in fact liberals on either economic or social issues. Especially concerning taxation and ties to big business, modernizers are at best moderate conservatives. Economic equity, a key element of liberalism closely associated with Democrats since Franklin Roosevelt's New Deal, has not been important to modernizers. Indeed, America's foremost modernizer during the 1990s, Bill Clinton, at a 1996 Texas fund-raiser symbolized the departure of national Democrats from the ideology of New Deal liberalism. Clinton apologized to the assembled "fat cats" (Domhoff 1972) for having raised their tax rates so high in his 1993 attempt to reduce the federal deficit. At the same time, modernizers, whether in North Carolina or across the South, regularly speak out on the need for increased fairness for racial minorities or women. In 1997 Clinton named world-renowned historian John Hope Franklin to head a national task force on racial reconciliation. Just weeks following Franklin's appointment, North Carolina's Legislative Black Caucus members, with support from white legislative leaders, invited Franklin to address a joint session of the General Assembly. Franklin was the first African American in history to address the North Carolina legislature (Franklin 1997).

On race and gender issues, a white liberal, in contrast to a modernizer, would most likely work closely with African American legislators to initiate change. By contrast, Tar Heel modernizers, almost exclusively white males, have been open to change but likely to undertake it only when pressured by blacks or feminist women.

In the 1990s the resistance of modernizers to economic populism and organized labor's initiatives, even while they heaped praise on African American scholars such as John Hope Franklin, was ironic. The modernizer Democrat-controlled state senate actively resisted populist tax relief that benefited the lower end of the economic ladder. These modernizers seemed to be unaware that support for populist tax relief for the less-affluent majority and opposition to tax benefits for the wealthy were central to the values of Dr. Franklin (Franklin 1947; Franklin 1994).

In recent North Carolina history key statewide elections have accentuated the prominence of traditionalism and modernism. Jesse Helms's first election to the U.S. Senate in 1972 underscored the power of traditionalism, while Jim Hunt's 1976 and 1980 gubernatorial victories affirmed the appeals of modernism. Helms's bloody battle with Hunt in 1984 as well as hard-fought campaigns in 1990 and 1996 against former Charlotte mayor Harvey Gantt exemplified the political conflict between traditionalists and modernizers. Republican Jim Martin's election as governor in 1984 and 1988 and Democrat Jim Hunt's second set of gubernatorial terms both demonstrated the political appeal of a blend of traditionalist and modernizer ideologies.

The Traditionalist Politician: Jesse Helms

During the late 1960s, left-leaning student activists at the University of North Carolina at Chapel Hill and Duke University found little more amusing than to spend five minutes each weekday in front of the television at 6:25 P.M. At that time—and of course there were no VCRs to tape the show for later viewing—both students and nonstudents in the Raleigh-Durham-Chapel Hill area could take in the daily political musings of WRAL-TV's commentator Jesse Helms. For the students, Helms's defense of law and order, states' rights, and the international struggle against communism was a flawed, last-ditch attempt to sustain a dying worldview. But three decades later five-term U.S. senator Jesse Helms was still enjoying a laugh at the students' expense. In fact Helms's editorials, which ran daily from 1960 to 1972 both on television and statewide on the Tobacco Radio Network, had constituted a serious counterattack on the political-equality (civil rights and anti–Vietnam War movements) and radical-culture ("sex, drugs, and rock-n-roll") values of the Carolina and Duke students. Helms understood, even if the student activists did not, that significant percentages of white Tar Heels agreed with his strong traditionalist message.

In the 1990s, as chairman of the Senate Foreign Relations Committee, Helms was taken very seriously by Democrats, Republicans, and world leaders alike. In 1994 Helms created a media frenzy by suggesting that Bill Clinton was so unpopular in the military-rich areas of eastern North Carolina that "he would need a bodyguard" when he visited Fort Bragg. In

1996 Helms forced Clinton to support harsh anti-Cuban trade legislation. Although this Helms-Burton law wreaked havoc for export-oriented corporations in Canada and Europe, Helms did not care if he disrupted world trade with Fidel Castro-led Cuba. Clinton, an ever-pragmatic modernizer, moved toward the traditionalist right because he did not want Florida's key Cuban American voters to label him "soft on Castro." In 1997 Helms flexed his muscle within the Republican Party. He declared Clinton's choice for U.S. ambassador to Mexico, incumbent Massachusetts GOP governor William Weld, unacceptable for his Senate committee's confirmation. Allegedly Weld was "soft on drugs" because as governor he did not oppose medical uses of marijuana. But Helms assuredly also opposed the governor because Weld represented a Republicanism very different from Helms's. Weld was a modernizer Republican sympathetic to big business, but in his Massachusetts statewide campaigns Weld also publicly affirmed his libertarian values and thus his tolerance of gay rights (cf. *New York Times* 1997). For Helms, even tolerance of gay rights was completely unacceptable.

North Carolina Republicanism had transformed the state by the late 1990s. But Republican success was no easy walk. In the early years of Republican struggles following the decisive 1964 defeat of Barry Goldwater by Lyndon Johnson, both nationally and in North Carolina the November 1972 election was a watershed event. Richard Nixon swept the state with 69 percent of the vote against George McGovern. Significantly, for the first time in the twentieth century, voters elected a Republican governor and U.S. senator. Both statewide victors no doubt benefited from Nixon's coattails, but the statewide election of two Republicans, the first such success since 1896, shocked Democrat and Republican alike. Winning Republican governor, Jim Holshouser, and senator, Jesse Helms, ran different campaigns, because they represented important differences in the style and substance of Tar Heel Republicanism. Holshouser, a lifelong Mountain Republican, typified those who had toiled for decades to build a two-party system (Stevenson 1975). His campaign emphasized the inefficiencies of one-party Democratic rule. Holshouser was a Republican modernizer, virtually indistinguishable from his modernizer Democrat opponent, Hargrove "Skipper" Bowles. A quarter-century later, in the late 1990s, Holshouser would still be active in state politics as a lobbyist and as a moderate member of the University of North Carolina Board of Governors. Skipper Bowles's son, Erskine Bowles, would continue the family's political involvement by serving in the late 1990s as presidential chief of staff to Bill Clinton. In the younger Bowles, Clinton found a white southerner-modernizer who had an intuitive understanding of the president's political ideology.

In contrast to Holshouser, Jesse Helms had built his political base among whites in eastern North Carolina. Helms ran as a traditionalist. His message was above party lines. Indeed, he had remained a registered Democrat until 1970, even though he said he had never voted for a Democratic presidential nominee. But because of his sharp media commentary against social equality, his campaign for the U.S. Senate seat received a big boost long before he filed in 1972 as a Republican candidate.

On the air Helms sympathized regularly with Alabama's segregationist governor George Wallace; urged Richard Nixon during the 1968 presidential campaign to stand firm on law and order against "weak-kneed liberals" like his Democratic opponent, Senator Hubert Humphrey; and regularly condemned "pinkos," black militants, and "hippies" as threats to the American way of life. His charismatic style made him a hero in the eyes of thousands of white Tar Heels, who admired him for standing up for what they and he believed was right.

Helms sought to reassure his Tar Heel admirers that it was "the militants"—the liberals, radicals, Yankees, northeastern media, blacks, and, later, women's liberationists—who were off base (Nordhoff 1984, 27). In short, the simple message of the virtues of old-time religion and old-fashioned values struck a responsive chord with white North Carolinians. These Tar Heels felt threatened by demands for racial equality in their hometowns and by calls for other far-reaching changes reported on the nightly national news.

In 1971 Helms's political confidante Raleigh lawyer Tom Ellis convinced him to consider running as a Republican in the upcoming U.S. Senate race. Helms's condition was that Ellis find financial backers. Those business people willing to promote Helms were, not surprisingly, traditionalists, skeptical that big government could do any good. His largest single supporter was Hugh Chatham, scion of a wool-blanket manufacturing family from Elkin and son of a former Democratic congressman, who loaned Helms $50,000. Chatham's ideological commitment to North Carolina Republicanism came at a time when any Republican's statewide candidacy was an extremely long shot. Subsequently many business people from the low-wage textile, apparel, and furniture industries could optimistically support Republicans as an alternative to modernizer Democrats, who emphasized high-tech economic development.

But in 1972 Chatham was a pioneer because Helms was hardly a front-runner. Helms appealed to business on the basis of economic traditionalism. The unfettered free enterprise system needed to be protected from the liberals who sought to hamstring business with regulation. For Helms, liberalism was just a step away from socialism. His traditionalist appeal to business avoided direct references to the social upheaval that had preoccupied him as an editorialist. Helms emphasized economic traditionalism's commitment to low taxes and limited government.

Social traditionalism provided Helms with a broader mass appeal. He promised to say no to busing and other liberal racial reforms. Although Helms in the past had defended segregation, his campaign messages used codes such as "forced busing" that could not be easily tagged as racist. He opposed world communism as a moral threat to Christianity. Thus, his support of the Pentagon took on both patriotic and religious overtones (Helms 1976; Luebke and Risberg 1983).

Helms had the good fortune to run against a modernizer Democrat, Nick Galifianakis, a Durham congressman who had upset aging traditionalist Democrat B. Everett Jordan in the May 1972 primary. Galifianakis symbolized the politics of the fast-growing metro Piedmont, while Jordan, from a tiny textile town near Burlington, represented rural values. In the fall 1972 campaign Helms missed no opportunity to link Galifianakis to Democratic presidential candidate George McGovern, labeling him at times "McGovernGalifianakis" (Bartley and Graham 1975, 176). Further, Helms ran on the ethnocentric slogan "He's one of us," suggesting that Galifianakis was not (Furgurson 1986, 100). Was it Galifianakis's Greek American ethnicity, his non-Baptist religion, or his occasional questioning of Pentagon budget requests that made him an outsider? Helms also ran unabashedly on Nixon's coattails, mailing thousands of would-be supporters a postcard picturing Helms with "Nixon needs him" printed along the bottom. Finally, Helms promised that he would mince no words in the nation's capital; his outspokenness as a TV editorialist would continue on the Senate floor.

In winning comfortably over Galifianakis, 54 to 46 percent, Helms had built a coalition of social traditionalists, economic traditionalists, and straight-ticket Republicans. Once in Washington, D.C., he began a decades-long commitment to heralding traditionalism. In his five terms Helms also strengthened, indirectly but significantly, a traditionalist political agenda at local and state levels. He contributed mightily to the rise of North Carolina Republicanism.

The Modernizer Politician: The Early Jim Hunt

The civil rights conflict of the 1960s forced Tar Heel Democrats to tackle a question many had hoped to avoid: Would North Carolina's white-dominated Democratic Party welcome blacks as equal participants? Leading Democrats by the 1970s saw the change as unavoidable. Whatever their personal beliefs, most white Democratic politicians in the South after the civil rights movement realized that the die had been cast in 1965 when a Texas-born president, Lyndon Johnson, pushed for passage of the Voting Rights Act that would ensure the franchise for African Americans in the South without local intimidation. Beginning with the appearance of civil rights advocate Hubert Humphrey on the 1968 national ticket, North Carolina Democrats became a biracial party. In the November 1968 election a Greensboro attorney, Henry Frye, made history by becoming the first black candidate elected to the General Assembly since the white supremacy movement around 1900.

In the 1970s North Carolina Democrats continued their commitment to an active government sector to promote economic development, but their statewide candidates abandoned their tolerance of racial segregation. In that spirit of a "New South" Democratic Party, Jim Hunt, an energetic attorney with roots in culturally traditionalist eastern North Carolina, won the governorship decisively in 1976. For Democratic businessmen and politicians who had been shocked at Governor Holshouser's election, Hunt's victory constituted what they saw as a return to normalcy.

Jim Hunt typified several strains of Democrat. His father, a populist-leaning New Dealer from Wilson County, inculcated in him the idea of the FDR Democrats, portraying the party as the friend of poor farmers and workers. While somewhat mythological, of course, especially at the level of North Carolina politics, this vision of the party did propel Hunt into the political upper-mobility route followed by countless would-be governors: college Democrats, Young Democrats, and membership on the state executive committee. Such aspiring politicians became "yellow-dog" Democrats, ignoring ideological differences within the party and supporting the entire ticket even if Democratic candidates included, as the saying goes, a couple of yellow dogs.

When Jim Hunt decided in 1970, at age thirty-three, to run for lieutenant governor, he was well positioned ideologically to win. He was one of the youngest modernizer Democrats, who linked the state's future economic development to the gradual elimination of Jim Crow institutions. At the same time, he shared traditionalists' values regarding social issues other than race. For example, he personally opposed abortion and was a teetotaler. Hunt lacked a strong background in state government, but he made up for it by winning the backing of Bert Bennett, a master Democratic power broker. A college classmate of Terry Sanford at Chapel Hill, Bennett played the de facto role of campaign manager of Sanford's successful quest for the 1960 Democratic gubernatorial nomination. Bennett strongly espoused the Sanford-Kennedy link during the fall 1960 campaign. A well-to-do Winston-Salem businessman, he epitomized the urbane, elite orientation of the emerging modernizer Democratic ideology. With Bennett's help Hunt established a coalition based on old-fashioned, county-by-county personal networks, and his 1972 campaign blurred ideological differences between traditionalism and modernism. Hunt won the lieutenant governor's election in 1972 while Democrats were losing both the governor's race and the U.S. Senate seat.

In 1976 Jim Hunt ran a classic modernizer campaign. He pledged to reestablish the Democratic Party as a friend of business investment. In light of the embarrassing fact that North Carolina had fallen to fiftieth place in national industrial wage rankings, Hunt promised to seek new, higher-wage jobs from out of state. Central to Hunt's thinking was the notion of trickle-down, not redistributive, economics. If business prospered, so would workers. But unlike his subsequent 1992 and 1996 campaigns, Hunt's 1976 program at least called for direct wage increases for manufacturing workers, not simply tax relief for corporations that supposedly would help average employees.

As Hunt in 1976 expressed support for civil rights and the Equal Rights Amendment for women, he argued pragmatically with blacks and whites to his left that no other candidate with a chance to win cared as much about their concerns. At the same time, he pitched his media campaign to traditionalist Democrats. In his most memorable TV spot of that year, as the camera zeroed in on the slamming of a prison cell-block door, Jim Hunt promised that he would lock up the criminals. In retrospect it was a precursor to Hunt's "tough on crime" approach of the 1990s.

Hunt's modernizer campaign against three opponents worked well. His 57 percent vote in the August 1976 primary made him the first Democrat in two decades to avoid a runoff by winning an absolute majority. In November he defeated his Republican opponent nearly two to one, while Jimmy

Carter was winning the state with 56 percent over Gerald Ford. Subsequent events would prove 1976, in the aftermath of the 1973–74 Watergate scandal, a high-water mark for North Carolina Democrats.

During his first term Hunt underscored the modernizer commitment to state investment, public-private partnership, and efficient government. One efficiency was his initiative to establish uniform sentencing for criminals. This had the added benefit of alleviating the traditionalists' concern that he might not be "tough enough" on that issue.

Hunt demonstrated his commitment to economic development in three interrelated ways. First, he convinced the General Assembly to place a $300 million transportation—read: highway construction—bond issue on the November ballot. Second, with much fanfare Hunt beefed up the industrial recruitment division of the state Department of Commerce, with the mandate to raise North Carolina's average industrial wage by recruiting high-wage employers into the state. Third, he launched a legislative campaign to improve the quality of public school education by reducing classroom size and establishing minimum competency levels for graduating high school seniors.

Hunt's agenda also focused on gubernatorial succession. He argued, in the name of efficiency, that governors ought to be able to develop a leadership plan for several years without immediate lame-duck status, in contrast to legislators, who were not restricted to one term. Hunt had an interest of course in applying the succession amendment to himself. It meant that he and incumbent Lieutenant Governor Jimmy Green could run for reelection in 1980. Hunt also would have liked at that time to establish a gubernatorial veto, but Democratic legislators agreed to only the former change (Beyle 1981). Voter approval of the succession amendment in November 1977 gave Jim Hunt, a young politician with national aspirations, more time to build a record of achievement as governor and develop a greater set of national political contacts. One of Hunt's protégés among New South politicians was Arkansas governor Bill Clinton (Clinton 1997).

Hunt's support within big business came disproportionately from growth-oriented sectors: bankers, real estate developers, truckers, and executives of multinational corporations. Such capitalists have an unambiguous interest in economic growth and recognize the importance of politicians who believe in government-financed infrastructure such as highways, public schools, and water/sewer lines. At Hunt's 1977 conference on state economic development, held in Charlotte, the keynote speaker was Wachovia bank president John Medlin. In 1979 Hunt organized the North Carolina Council of Management and Development, a who's who of the state's business elite. The council provided Hunt with a sounding board for his proposals and gave key corporate leaders ready access to his office (Hunt 1982, 446–47). It is indicative of modernizer ideology that Hunt developed such close mutual ties with big business, but that labor leaders or environmentalists usually would not enjoy such a close relationship with the governor.

Hunt's first-term agenda, contrasted with the positions taken by Helms, set the stage for their subsequent modernizer-traditionalist encounter along party lines. But not all Tar Heel Democrats and Republicans fall neatly into these categories. Many Democratic legislators, especially from outside the metro Piedmont, are traditionalists. A few metro Piedmont and Coastal Republicans are modernizers. Most importantly, Republican Jim Martin's election as governor in 1984 and 1988 reflected an amalgam of traditionalist and modernizer ideology that was sometimes at odds with Helms's traditionalism. Further, Democrat Jim Hunt of the 1990s took on a strong resemblance to his two-term Republican predecessor, Jim Martin. Hunt acknowledged in a 1992 interview that, following his 1984 defeat by Jesse Helms, his eight years as a corporate lawyer in a major Raleigh firm, including occasional visits as a lobbyist to the General Assembly, had changed his views; he was more in harmony with the political stances of big corporations (*North Carolina Magazine* 1993). Coupled with a general shifting of the national political debate in the late 1980s toward more antigovernment and antitax themes, Hunt's private-sector experiences convinced him to run in 1992 as less of a consumer's friend and more as an ally of tax-leery big business. In short, the "new" Jim Hunt of the 1992 campaign had very much in common with the modernizer-traditionalist blend ideology previously promoted successfully by Governor Martin.

A Traditionalist-Modernizer Blend:
Jim Martin and the New Jim Hunt

Since the political rise of Jesse Helms, North Carolina Republican politicians usually espouse traditionalist rather than modernizer values. In 1980 Jim Hunt's reelection campaign assembled an impressive coalition of political interest groups, from traditionalist business to the AFL-CIO, none of which wished to oppose an incumbent governor. To challenge Hunt, Tar Heel Republicans chose I. Beverly Lake Jr., a former Democratic state senator from Raleigh whose father was a North Carolina Supreme Court justice and had been the Democratic segregationist candidate in the 1960 and 1964 gubernatorial primaries. Lake ran an underfinanced, purely traditionalist race, supported by Helms's National Congressional Club, which attacked Hunt as a big-spending liberal who would assuredly raise taxes. In 1981 Hunt did in fact advocate and receive an increase in the gasoline tax from the General Assembly. To raise sales taxes to provide transportation infrastructure is good modernizer strategy, but a policy that relies on such flat taxes is in fact economic conservatism, not economic liberalism. Yet the Congressional Club's campaign attacks on Hunt had little effect on the 1980 outcome.

Hunt's crucial asset in the 1980 race was the breadth of his coalition, which made him invulnerable to serious attack in either the May gubernatorial primary or the November election. Republican Lake won just 38 percent of the vote, even though Ronald Reagan was carrying the state over Jimmy Carter. But in 1984 the Democratic Party demonstrated anything but unity, as eight candidates, three of whom were well financed, fought bitterly for the right to succeed Hunt as governor.

Sensing opportunity, Jim Martin, a six-term congressman from Charlotte, agreed to run, even though in early 1984 winning that race seemed like a long shot. A GOP gubernatorial candidate would clearly benefit from President Reagan's place on the November ballot, and Helms's race against Hunt assured high voter interest. But Martin, to his credit, ran a strong campaign in his own right. Martin grafted modernizer appeals, both substantive and symbolic, onto the traditionalist base of the GOP. This Republican traditionalist-modernizer blend served Martin well because it attracted moderate Democrats to the Republican Party.

Martin, a Ph.D. chemist who had once been on the faculty at Davidson College, had amassed a strong southern Republican voting record in Congress that won him the admiration and support of big-business political action committees (PACs). In his North Carolina campaign he courted textile, apparel, and furniture industrialists, many of whom had become disenchanted with Governor Hunt's emphasis on out-of-state high-tech economic recruitment. Martin promised these traditionalist business people, who had long been sympathetic to national Republicans but had stuck with Democrats in state elections, that he would end the perceived bias against Tar Heel firms if they would take a chance on his long-shot candidacy. At the same time he assured modernizer business people, such as those in the banking industry, that he would be a pro-growth governor. Thus the Martin campaign made major inroads both among modernizer business people who, four years before, perhaps only pragmatically, had stuck with Hunt, and among traditionalist business people who were increasingly unhappy with the spending programs of state Democrats.

On social issues Martin held two strong cards. First, his 1983 vote against the Martin Luther King Jr. federal holiday (he was the only North Carolina congressman to do so) improved his standing with the National Congressional Club and won him support among white racial traditionalists. At the same time, he took care to develop a modernizer image. For example, when a state GOP direct-mail campaign in the summer of 1984 suggested that whites should vote Republican to send Jesse Jackson a negative message, Martin disassociated himself from the tactic. Cynics correctly noted that the disclaimer never would be seen by the overwhelming majority of traditionalist whites to whom the anti-Jackson mail had been targeted.

Martin's other appeal to traditionalist voters focused on abortion. He promised that, if elected, he would try to eliminate the state abortion fund, a budget item supported by Governor Hunt that allowed low-income women to abort a pregnancy even if they could not afford the cost of the operation. This assured Martin support from right-to-life groups, including recently politicized fundamentalist pastors generally referred to as the religious right. Like his vote against the King holiday, Martin's antiabortion stand provided another link to the Congressional Club. Yet Martin did not highlight his social traditionalism in his television advertising. On the contrary, his media campaign presented him as an urbane, pragmatic modernizer whose strength was not specific issues but rather quality of leadership. Martin's overall image resembled Jim Holshouser's in 1972.

Although his decision to run for governor in 1984 originally was risky, Martin in fact won easily, 54 to 46 percent. (By contrast, in the same election Helms defeated Hunt by just 51 to 49 percent.)

As governor, Jim Martin elaborated on his campaign themes. He highlighted his social traditionalism in 1987 by opposing a paid state holiday to honor Martin Luther King Jr. But his traditional position on this issue did not prevent him from making conciliatory gestures toward blacks. Although there are few black Republicans in North Carolina, Martin appointed some of them to state boards. Further, he participated annually in the voluntary King holiday program for state workers, and he met with Coretta Scott King when she visited North Carolina to lobby for the King holiday.

Martin made good on his promise to fight the abortion fund and to establish an office within the state Department of Commerce to support Tar Heel "traditional industries." His appointments to boards and commissions demonstrated a greater ideological commitment to social and economic traditionalism than to modernism. For example, his nominees to the state Industrial Commission, where workers' compensation claims are handled, were strongly tilted toward management, and all his appointees to the state Day Care Commission voted in 1985 to allow day care centers to use corporal punishment. In the latter instance the commission's Democratic majority, following party lines, voted to prohibit spanking. Here and in the case of the state Social Services Commission, which sought to limit state-funded abortions, Martin tended to appoint Republican traditionalists, whereas Hunt usually named modernizer Democrats.

While Martin played the traditionalist tune on social issues, his economic agenda recognized the realities of an active state sector. Nowhere were Martin's sympathies for modernism clearer than in his support for an increased gasoline tax in 1986. Growth-oriented businesses expressed concern that the state highway fund would soon be bankrupt and unable to provide the road infrastructure they needed. In contrast to the Congressional Club, which always opposed such tax increases, and similar to Hunt's gubernatorial program, Martin advocated higher gasoline taxes and reached a compromise with leading Democrats in the General Assembly.

Public school spending was another area where Martin assumed a modernizer position. He and the Democrats disagreed on specific spending details of the 1985 Basic Education Plan, but Martin resisted the antieducation label that Democrats wanted to affix to him. Finally, Martin energetically involved himself in the recruitment of out-of-state firms to North Carolina. Following Hunt's pattern he traveled to Europe and Asia to promote the state's business climate. Despite his symbolic gesture to the traditionalist textile-furniture sector, Martin was firmly committed to non–North Carolina capital investment.

From 1985 to 1988 Martin continued his partisan assertion that Democrats were thwarting his attempts to lead the state. Democrats, recalling the glory days of one-party domination, did not really believe Governor Martin's condemnation of legislative Democrats would take root with voters. Democrat Lieutenant Governor Bob Jordan, who had presided over the state senate during Martin's first term, thought Martin was easily beatable. In fact, Martin was benefiting from the general popularity of Ronald Reagan among white Tar Heels.

Martin ran an effective two-pronged campaign for the white vote. First, his overall theme of normalcy and prosperity permeated his television advertising, primarily emphasizing the goals of his administration and its alleged record of achievement. This television campaign highlighted Martin the modernizer politician, willing to use government to provide schools, highways, and environmental protection. His ads showed white and black children in classrooms together, as well as shots of the Cape Hatteras lighthouse. An outsider watching the TV spots would have been hard pressed to know whether this sincere-sounding man in his dark suit and red tie was a New South Democrat or a New South Republican.

The Martin campaign neutralized Jordan's accomplishments as lieutenant governor. An analysis of environmental politics during 1987 and 1988, especially of the legislative ban on phosphate detergents, illustrates how the Jordan campaign contributed to its own demise. In 1987 Jordan and other modernizer Democrats in the General Assembly, including lieutenant governor nominee-to-be Tony Rand, supported a legislative proposal to ban phosphates from household detergents. The legislation would have the environmental effect of preventing algae pollution in North Carolina's rivers, the fiscal impact of saving local governments the cost of additional pollution control equipment, and the political benefit to Democrats who supported the phosphate ban of a working alliance with North Carolina's growing environmental organizations (Hall 1988). In addition to the phosphate ban, Jordan and Rand in 1985 had backed a statewide worker and community right-to-know (about nearby hazardous chemicals) law, albeit a weakened version of the Durham right-to-know ordinance enacted by the city council as a result of intense pressure from citizen groups.

Because Governor Martin in 1987 had opposed the phosphate ban and in 1985 had charged that supporters of the right-to-know legislation were suffering from "chemophobia," Democrats believed that they could count on electoral endorsements from the environmental groups. But in 1988 Jordan's campaign did not maintain good communication with the two major statewide environmental PACs, the Sierra Club and the League of Conservation Voters. Although these groups endorsed Jordan's fellow modernizer Tony Rand over Republican Jim Gardner, they were neutral in the governor's race. The Sierra Club and the league had concluded that, regarding issues of water quality and some board appointments in North Carolina, Martin was Jordan's equal in environmental commitment. Further, they recalled that Jordan had established a poor environmental record when he was a state senator, before he became lieutenant governor in 1985. Because political observers generally assume that environmental PACs in the United States endorse Democrats, the North Carolina groups' decision to remain neutral in fact conveyed to the public the impression that a Republican was an acceptable choice for governor.

Martin further helped himself by running TV ads that affirmed his support for the environment. Jordan hurt his chances by declining to air a pro-environment television spot. Thus, despite the reality that Jordan had a stronger commitment to the environment, Martin appeared the better environmental candidate to voters who relied on TV commercials for their political information. A *Charlotte Observer* (1988) poll suggested that Martin's pro-environment ads and Jordan's failure to use them proved beneficial to Martin. By a margin of 39 to 33 percent, most Tar Heels surveyed thought Martin would "do more for the environment."

Martin's first strategy to win the white vote, the campaign that saturated North Carolina's television markets in the weeks before Election Day, emphasized Jim Martin the modernizer governor. The second strategy was less public and stressed his traditionalist side. Throughout 1988 Martin targeted North Carolina right-to-life groups and fundamentalist Protestant organizations that also were strongly antiabortion to remind them by direct mail that he could be relied on to continue his fight against the state abortion fund for poor women.

While Martin was targeting the antiabortion constituencies, the Jordan campaign avoided the abortion issue, fearing that most voters did not agree with the lieutenant governor's 1985 vote to break a tie in the state senate and keep the state abortion fund alive. In fact, poll data consistently indicate that North Carolina voters favor a woman's right to choose an abortion. Jordan's failure to campaign on his pro-choice record left many pro-choice voters with no knowledge that Jordan and Martin had differing positions on the abortion rights issue. Exit polls among white voters in Guilford County (Greensboro) demonstrated what could happen if Jordan's pro-choice stand remained a secret to most of the public. Among fifteen pro-life voters surveyed, 80 percent supported Martin, suggesting that the Martin campaign had successfully alerted the antiabortion electorate. But among thirty pro-choice voters, only 40 percent voted for Jordan. How many additional pro-choice votes might Jordan have won if he had targeted a mailing to, for example, all registered Democratic and Independent women in the six metro Piedmont counties (Luebke and Yeoman 1988)?

Governor Martin's personality and the normalcy/prosperity themes of his reelection advertising were probably the major reasons Republicans did so well in 1988. But another factor was the coattail impact of Martin and presidential candidate George Bush on other Republicans, especially regarding Republican Jim Gardner's narrow 51-to-49 percent victory over Democrat Tony Rand.

The results suggested a Democratic Party in disarray. Jordan won a majority of the November vote only in the eastern Piedmont and on the Coastal Plain, areas that had shown the least population growth since 1972. The modernizer-led Democratic Party was losing key statewide elections time and time again. Across the South, white Democrats wondered how best to respond to the rising southern Republicanism. While African American Democrats insisted that affirmative action and other post–civil rights commitments not be abandoned, their white modernizer allies worried that the Democratic Party was being painted with a broad brush, and that, for white voters in North Carolina and elsewhere in the South, the paint was spelling out that most unpopular political label, liberal.

For these reasons white southern Democrats were disproportionately among the national Democrats who encouraged the formation of the Democratic Leadership Council (DLC). The DLC prided itself on its moderate ideology and stressed its differences with Rainbow Coalition populist Democrats such as Jesse Jackson (Dionne 1997). By 1992 the foremost proponent of DLC moderation was Bill Clinton, simultaneously Arkansas governor, presidential candidate, and Jim Hunt's friend. Jim Hunt did not actively participate in the DLC, as he focused instead on winning handily the 1992 Democratic gubernatorial nomination. But he intended that his shift to the right, the modernizer-traditionalist blend, be noticed by the press and conveyed to the public. The "new" Jim Hunt was a skeptic of government intervention, in contrast to the progovernment enthusiasm of the 1977–85 terms.

Hunt had the good fortune to run against Jim Gardner, who had served for four years as lieutenant governor under Jim Martin. Instead of vying with Hunt, as a Martin clone might have, over whether a Republican or a Democrat could better govern the state with a blend of modernizer and traditionalist views, Gardner concluded that North Carolina wanted a pure traditionalist governor. Consequently, the Gardner campaign lambasted Hunt as a free-spending "liberal Democrat." It was a label that no impartial observer could take seriously about the pro-big-business, culturally conservative Jim Hunt. Although the gubernatorial campaign was heated, Hunt defeated Gardner comfortably, 53 to 43 percent (a Libertarian candidate won 4 percent of the vote).

Hunt illustrated his ideological shift to the right in several ways. First, in early 1994, fearful that North Carolina Republicans were succeeding in depicting him as "soft on crime," Hunt called a special legislative "crime session." During the special session that lasted from February until April 1994 Hunt's crime legislation was noteworthy for its punitive tone. Both in the 1994 crime session and later as Hunt presented his tax-cutting budget to the General Assembly in February 1995, political wags referred to Hunt as North Carolina's "best Republican governor" of the twentieth century. Second, in December 1994, just one month after the house Republicans benefited from the same voter rebellion that helped the Gingrich Republicans in Washington, D.C., Hunt called for massive state tax cuts. This was in marked contrast to his first two gubernatorial terms.

A third example occurred in the spring of 1995. When the house Republicans cut the state abortion fund for poor women from the $1 million appropriated by the house Democrats in the previous year to a new low of $50,000, Governor Hunt used none of his lobbying capital with the Democratic majority in the state senate to restore some of the cut dollars. This was particularly ironic, since Hunt had introduced the abortion fund into the state budget during his first term as governor in 1977.

At the same time, modernizer values remained a key part of Governor Hunt's agenda. During 1993 he proposed the North Carolina Partnership for Children, popularly known as Smart Start, intended to ensure that all Tar Heel children, regardless of race or income, were prepared to enter kindergarten without a high risk of school achievement problems. The Democrat-controlled house and senate in 1993 funded Smart Start to expand day care programs, health check-ups, and immunizations, with the eventual goal of a locally controlled program in all of North Carolina's 100 counties. This quintessential modernizer program, advocating a government-supported preschool program for young children, faced, not surprisingly, fierce opposition from the social traditionalists within the state Republican Party. When the GOP wrested control of the state house from Democrats in the November 1994 election, stopping Smart Start emerged as a major goal of house Republicans. A hard-fought legislative compromise at the end of the 1995 session, crafted by Hunt and his Democratic allies in the senate with the Republican "pro-family" opponents of Smart Start in the house, kept the program alive but forced its reorganization into an independent nonprofit agency that was legally separate from the Hunt-controlled Department of Human Resources. Hunt's modernizer values remained intact in Smart Start, but the house Republican traditionalists, led by state representative Robin Hayes, could claim that they had prevented big-government bureaucracy from interfering with parents' rights to keep their children out of day care.

Hunt's move to the right in the 1990s illustrated the willingness of onetime modernizer Democrats to acquiesce to the pressure of effective state Republican campaigns. It also highlighted the perception of Hunt and other Democrats, especially in the state senate, that North Carolina's white electorate in the early and mid-1990s was demanding a policy shift toward the dominant traditionalist ideology of Tar Heel Republicanism. One area where modernizers, traditionalists, and "blend" candidates such as the new Governor Hunt and former governor Martin shared common ground was in their antipathy to progressive taxation. These politicians clearly indicated, in contrast to the few African American and white Democratic populists, their unwillingness to place any additional tax burden on the wealthy and big business.

The Elite Consensus: Say No to Equity

The differences between modernizer and traditionalist ideology are substantial in their social and economic goals for North Carolina. One key distinction is the importance of government activism and spending and the related significance of taxation and tax cutting. A second variation focuses on the level of tolerance for affirmative action programs to benefit blacks and women. But these ideologies share a common vision concerning equity. Both reject the premises of economic populism that government should promote "tax fairness" for the middle- and low-income majority and should direct disproportionate government benefits toward that majority. Modernizers and traditionalists alike believe in "trickle-down economics": if government ensures that the wealthy and big business prosper, investment by those at the top of the economic structure will also ensure that job opportunities flow downward to the majority. Critics of New Deal Democrat ideology have argued that the actual amount of redistribution to the working-class majority in American politics was limited. Such critics overlook that fundamental to North Carolina politics, in contrast to the historic pattern of public policy in industrial states outside the South, is a bipartisan rejection of redistributive politics that focuses state tax and spending programs on the less-affluent majority (Luebke 1981b; Tomaskovic-Devey and Roscigno 1996).

Modernizer ideology is often confused with economic liberalism. North

Carolina's decision in 1961 to place a sales tax on food offers clear evidence of the economic-conservative tendencies of modernizers. As governor in 1961, Terry Sanford believed that the state needed to invest more in its public school system, including community colleges. Facing resistance from antitax traditionalists, Sanford found that the revenue source with the greatest prospects for legislative approval was the reimposition of the sales tax on groceries. (A 3 percent sales tax on most retail items had become law in 1933, but the General Assembly had exempted groceries in 1941.) The sales tax is regressive because it taxes everyone from pauper to millionaire at the same flat rate.

If Sanford had been an economic liberal, as was often claimed by his political enemies, he might have sought to raise the state individual or corporate income tax, both of which placed relatively greater tax burdens on high-income families and corporations. Alternatively, the legislation might have earmarked the food tax revenues for education and included a sunset provision so that, when certain educational benefits were provided, the tax would be repealed. In fact, Sanford advocated neither. As a consequence the General Assembly's 1961 legislation was still generating unspecified sales tax revenues for the General Fund until 1996, when a 1 percent food tax cut was first implemented. Sanford's defenders claimed that without the food tax none of the educational investment would have been made. That point remains debatable. But undoubtedly reimposition of the food tax was consistent with modernizer ideology. If Democratic or Republican modernizers believe that certain investments will benefit a majority of the state's or a locality's citizens, then such legislative programs are pushed regardless of whether the burden of funding and implementation is disproportionately placed on poor and middle-income citizens.

Such regressive tax policy was typical of New South Democrats in the post–civil rights period of economic growth. Arkansas governor Bill Clinton in the 1970s and 1980s regularly campaigned on cutting the food tax, but such a progressive tax cut never became policy (Luebke 1995; Brummett 1994). South Carolina governor Richard Riley, later secretary of education in the Clinton administration, in the mid-1980s sang a tune from Terry Sanford's songbook by raising the state's sale tax by 1 percent in order to help public education. In both Arkansas and South Carolina the corporations who stood to benefit from a better-educated labor force declined to pay a higher corporate income tax or even a higher individual income tax on themselves.

Investment in the state's future, even if financed by regressive taxes, was a hallmark of Democratic Party policy in the 1970s and 1980s. Under Governor Jim Hunt the modernizer ideology held sway. From the early 1970s to the late 1980s, while Democrats controlled the General Assembly, sales taxes went up and business taxes were reduced. As a consequence the state's tax burden shifted toward low- and middle-income Tar Heels (Liner 1991; Liner 1997).

The traditionalist ideology prefers no new taxes. But faced with a choice of increasing individual income or sales taxes, traditionalists—whether Democrat or Republican—favor the sales tax. Although in principle opposed to new taxes, the traditionalist legislator, who like other legislators makes about three times the income of the average North Carolinian (*News and Record* 1987a), may pragmatically vote on the basis of self-interest. If new revenue were raised via the income tax, the high-income legislator would have to pay a larger share than, for example, a low-income textile worker.

Specifically, the typical North Carolina family that made $35,000 would have paid, according to 1995 state Revenue Department data, twice as much in food tax as a percentage of income as a well-to-do family that earned $100,000. A family earning $13,000 in 1995 was hit even harder by the regressive sales tax. That low-income family paid three times as much as a percentage of income as the family earning $100,000 per year (North Carolina Budget and Tax Center 1997).

The Republican success in controlling the state house after the 1994 elections led to substantial ideological jockeying within the GOP. For the first time in the twentieth century, house Republicans under Speaker Harold Brubaker were a governing party. While Brubaker and other Republicans rode an antitax tide in 1994 to take power, the obligations of governing led some modernizer or modernizer-traditionalist Republicans to speak in favor of increased sales taxes. Two examples from the 1995 and 1997 legislative sessions illustrate the point well.

In 1995 Johnston County Republican Leo Daughtry, seeking a solution for school construction needs in his fast-suburbanizing county southeast of Raleigh, pushed in the house Finance Committee for a local-option sales tax dedicated to public schools. Antitax traditionalist house Republicans joined populist Democrats on the committee to fight the sales tax proposal to a standstill. In 1997, to fund public transit in the fast-growing Charlotte area, a hometown Republican, Ed McMahan of Mecklenburg County, advocated a local-option one-half-cent county sales tax. Traditionalist Republicans and all stripes of house Democrats were lobbied (including personal phone calls from Governor Hunt) to support the tax increase in the name of reducing gridlock in the Charlotte metropolitan area.

Prior to assuming control of the state house in 1995, North Carolina Republicans held a strong card against Tar Heel Democrats. Led by modernizers who favored regressive taxation such as the sales tax in order to fund necessary state governmental infrastructure, Democrats had placed themselves over the decades in the unenviable position of tax advocates. The GOP in North Carolina and other southern states took great pleasure in sticking the "tax-and-spend liberal" label on modernizer Democrats. Once leading Tar Heel Republicans in the state house began advocating sales tax increases, they started to undermine their own reputation as an antitaxation and antispending political party. Especially when most Republicans, whether modernizers or traditionalists, followed party discipline and voted for some tax increases, the GOP advantage in the late 1990s over Democrats was weakened.

On occasion the bipartisan modernizer-traditionalist opposition to economic populism collapsed. Populist Democrats, usually with some support from strongly antitax traditionalist Republicans, at times from the 1970s through the 1990s could defeat legislative proposals of the banking or insurance industries. The reduction of the food tax beginning in 1996 was a prime example of the unholy alliance between Democrats on the left and Republicans on the right. But the unholy alliance was much more the exception than the rule in the state house, and such left-right alliances rarely emerged in the modernizer Democrat-controlled state senate. Typically, the kinds of legislation advocated by well-financed and well-organized corporate lobbies were most likely to succeed, whether Democrats or Republicans controlled a legislative body.

3

The General Assembly:

Two-Party Ideological Conflict

          The social forces that struggle over political goals in North Carolina play themselves out ultimately in the state legislature. The General Assembly divides into the 120-member house of representatives and the 50-member senate. North Carolina's legislature is one of the nation's strongest, even though the governor maintains many significant appointment powers and in 1996 won the right to veto legislation.

For students of North Carolina state politics, November 8, 1994, will stand out as one of the most significant dates of the twentieth century. A sea change occurred on that Election Day, as the house Democrats lost their majority for the first time since 1896. Republicans went from a minority of 42 members to a comfortable 68-to-52 majority. Also on that day, Georgia's Newt Gingrich led congressional Republicans to a majority in the U.S. House of Representatives. But in Washington, D.C., GOP minority status in the House had "only" been in place for forty years, in contrast to the 96 years of Democratic rule in the North Carolina House of Representatives.

The Republican takeover of the state house was the crowning blow in a multiyear rise of GOP fortunes in North Carolina. Its impact was all the greater because it was so unexpected. Although house Democrats after the 1992 elections had held seventy-eight seats, three fewer than after November 1990, no one, including the 1993–94 incumbent Democrat Speaker Dan Blue and the 1995–96 Republican Speaker-to-be Harold Brubaker, believed the Democrats could lose the majority. In retrospect, the Brubaker ascendancy had been foreshadowed by an unusual coalition during 1989–90. In January 1989 twenty dissident Democrats, primarily white male traditionalists from the Coastal Plain, ousted four-term incumbent Democrat Speaker Liston Ramsey by joining forty-five house Republicans who had been elected in 1988 as part of Governor Jim Martin's impressive reelection victory (*Charlotte Observer* 1989b). This bipartisan majority elected Coastal Plain Democrat Joe Mavretic as Speaker, and Mavretic appointed record numbers of Republicans as chairs or cochairs of house committees. Most importantly, traditionalist legislators of both parties held key committee positions that they had not enjoyed during the 1980s under the more modernizer-populist leadership of Speaker Ramsey.

Despite the traditionalist ascendancy in 1989, North Carolina's guiding ideology still was rooted in the policy preferences of the state's largest corporations. These corporations, from their headquarters in the key metro Piedmont cities of Charlotte, Winston-Salem, Greensboro, and Raleigh, preferred an active state government that would fund the infrastructure necessary for economic expansion. In his 1949 classic *Southern Politics*, V. O. Key had explained North Carolina's prominence as the most industrial of the southern states as a consequence of its progressive plutocracy (see Chapter 1). An economic oligarchy prevailed in North Carolina whose interests were often served "without prompting," and those elected to office were "fundamentally in harmony" with the oligarchy's viewpoint (Key 1949, 211). In the 1980s the relationship between big business and the legislature had become more complicated. Competing groups of business people differed on the question of how activist state government should become. Nevertheless a dominant view emerged, similar to Key's findings about the 1940s. Without articulating their ideology explicitly, legislative leaders into the 1990s continued a major commitment to infrastructure development in North Carolina. The purpose of this investment in infrastructure was to meet businesses' needs for transportation, education, and similar amenities. In short, what was good for business was good for North Carolina.

This ideology is conservative in that it argues that direct benefits to business will result in indirect (trickle-down) benefits to a majority, as the majority takes jobs offered by an expanding private sector. The dominant ideology is also modernizing in that it recognizes the importance of government investment to support economic change. The General Assembly, then, could be viewed as committed to conservative modernization (cf. Moore 1966; Billings 1979). This book calls these beliefs "modernizer ideology."

Traditionalist economic ideology, a belief that the legislature should restrict both taxes and expenditures, was rejected in North Carolina through most of the twentieth century. North Carolina's growth as an industrial economy was tied in the 1920s and 1930s to state government spending for highways and the public schools. Indeed, during the Great Depression many county school systems would have gone bankrupt if the General Assembly had not decided to assume funding costs.

Traditionalist ideology, however, fared much better in the social or noneconomic agenda. Such issues as liquor-by-the-drink for years reflected the impact of small-town and rural values in the General Assembly. Modernizing business people who sought to promote North Carolina's "quality of life" were frustrated until the late 1970s by the unwillingness of the legislature to give metropolitan areas the local option for mixed drinks. Also in the 1970s and early 1980s, the General Assembly on six occasions failed to pass the Equal Rights Amendment. These votes reflected the strength of traditionalist values in the noneconomic sphere.

But the house Republican upset of 1994, coupled with a near-upset in the state senate, where Republicans, at 24 to 26, were just two seats short of a majority, placed social traditionalism on a higher pedestal than at any point in the twentieth century. Major grassroots credit for the 1994 Republican success lay with the religious right. Aided by nominally neutral groups such as the Christian Coalition, the religious right mobilized its membership to support Republican candidates, both in North Carolina and nationwide, for an off-year election in which Democrats were singularly unmobilized (Dionne 1997). Republican interest and turnout in the election was relatively high, while many black and white voters who had supported Democrats in 1992 stayed home in 1994. In the Research Triangle area and surrounding counties, for example, Republicans won two congressional seats that had been dominated by Democrats throughout the twentieth century. In the fourth congressional district a little-known GOP challenger, ideologically vague retired Raleigh police chief Fred

Heinemann, upset four-term incumbent David Price. A modernizer Democrat and college professor who had actively brought home plenty of "pork" for his district, Price had been considered a shoo-in for reelection (Smar 1997, 5–6; Worrell 1995). In Wake County, then the largest portion of Price's district, a well-organized Republican Party mobilized traditionalist and even some modernizer voters to "throw the (Democrat) bums out" in legislative and judicial races as well as in the Heinemann-Price congressional election. Republicans in Wake County, in the 1990s by far the fastest-growing of North Carolina's ten largest counties, netted a local judgeship, three state house seats, and most surprisingly, a state senate seat won by an African American man.

In the second congressional district, which included most white voters in Durham County but was dominated by social-traditionalist whites in tobacco-growing agricultural counties east and south of Raleigh, the retirement of six-term Democrat incumbent Tim Valentine created an open seat. Strongly traditionalist Republican David Funderburk, a virtual ideological carbon copy of Jesse Helms, benefited from the general mobilization of the religious right across North Carolina in the 1994 election (cf. Orndorff 1997, 3). But Funderburk also wisely highlighted a long-standing Democratic weakness in the tobacco-growing counties. He labeled the efforts of the federal government to control cigarettes as a prime example of big government "meddling" in the lives of hard-working (white) farmers and others in the second district. Funderburk easily defeated Richard Moore, a young, photogenic modernizer Democrat in the Jim Hunt mold. The importance of Republican voter mobilization versus Democratic voter indifference in 1994 was well illustrated by campaign finance reports. Both Heinemann and Funderburk had been outspent by Price and Moore (Beyle 1997, 13).

Not surprisingly in the light of the religious right's electoral efforts on behalf of the GOP in November 1994, the new Republican majority in the state house in 1995 initially followed an agenda that was heavily shaped by the religious right. The state abortion fund for poor women was effectively eliminated, and a bill requiring teenage girls to seek parental consent before an abortion passed both house and senate overwhelmingly (in previous years, Democrats had kept the bill bottled up in an unfriendly committee). Further, both the state house and the state senate passed "teach abstinence" legislation, in effect restricting what sex education lessons local school boards could select for their high school pupils. Leading the efforts for this social-traditionalist legislation was then—house majority whip

Robin Hayes, who subsequently, in 1996, unexpectedly won the Republican gubernatorial primary against a modernizer Republican, only to lose decisively to Governor Jim Hunt in the fall. Hayes, an heir to the Kannapolis-based Cannon Mills fortune, had been an inactive corporate Democrat before becoming a "born-again" Christian and a religious-right Republican and winning a Kannapolis-area state house seat in 1992. (The house GOP was so talent-thin in 1995 that a two-termer like Hayes could become a party leader, and a first-term Republican lawyer was selected to chair a judiciary committee, a key legislative committee that deals with legal issues.)

The 1995–96 house Republicans had less influence in changing the economic agenda of the General Assembly, in part because on economic issues the difference between Democrats and Republicans had never been as great. Over the decades the procorporate agenda of the General Assembly has been highlighted by the kinds of bills that do not become law. With a minor exception, no Tar Heel public employees have the right to engage in collective bargaining with their employers. Public school teachers and other state employees therefore must accept whatever salaries the General Assembly approves in its annual budget session. Further, North Carolina private-sector workers do not have to join the union that engages in collective bargaining with their employer (the so-called right-to-work law). Anti-unionism is such a fact of life in the General Assembly that the state AFL-CIO has stopped including repeal of the right-to-work law on its legislative wish list.

North Carolina continues to be one of eight states in which compensation from an accident is *not* parceled out by the degree of fault, the doctrine of comparative fault. The General Assembly into the 1990s supported the rule of contributory negligence, the legal course favored by insurance companies and other big business enterprises, which denies individuals all rights to a damage claim if they have contributed in the slightest way to an accident. In short, the procorporate tilt of consumer and labor law has exemplified the ideological hold of business on the General Assembly.

The Evolution of a Two-Party Legislature

The Democratic Party in the South was the party of whites from the turn of the century, when the various states institutionalized white supremacy in politics by restricting blacks' (and some poor whites') right to vote (Franklin 1947), until the civil rights movement of the 1960s. To be sure, the various social classes congregated in the party did not always agree. In

1936, for example, big business's control of the North Carolina party was challenged by Ralph McDonald, a professor and economic populist from Winston-Salem. McDonald lost the gubernatorial primary to Clyde Hoey, but only after a vigorous campaign in which McDonald highlighted how the recently enacted sales tax burdened North Carolina's many poor citizens (Key 1949, chap. 7). But even when corporate Democrats prevailed in statewide primaries, less-affluent Democrats tended to stick with the party. In part this resulted from the strength of yellow-dog consciousness, the Democrat-proud notion that "I'd vote for a yellow dog before I'd vote for a Republican." Another reason, at least during the Great Depression and the following two decades, was Franklin Roosevelt's image as the "poor man's friend." Regardless of the actual ideology of Tar Heel Democratic governors, Roosevelt and the voters' memory of him solidified white working-class support for Democrats in statewide legislative and congressional elections.

By contrast, Republican representation in the General Assembly was primarily regional, centered on districts in the western Piedmont and Mountain counties, where most farmers wanted no part of a North Carolina Democratic Party that they viewed as controlled by the plantation and other wealthy interests (Houghton 1993). Even when, in 1928, a grassroots Baptist rebellion against the Democrats' presidential candidate, the "wet" New York governor Al Smith, led to an electoral college victory for Republican Herbert Hoover, Republicans still won just one-quarter of state house and senate seats. This pattern finally changed when the 1972 Nixon landslide generated both a Republican governor, Jim Holshouser, and fifty GOP legislators. In 1974, however, the Watergate aftermath helped the Democrats reestablish a nine-to-one margin. In 1984 Republicans benefited from the Reagan landslide, also electing a GOP governor, Jim Martin, and fifty legislators. But significantly for North Carolina's evolution into a two-party state, Republicans held their own in the 1986 and 1988 elections. Although the Republican governor had hoped for a voter rebellion against Democratic control of the General Assembly, the two elections did demonstrate that voters in those areas of the state that went Republican in 1984—primarily the western Piedmont, the Charlotte and Triad areas of the metro Piedmont, and the Mountains—were steadfast in their support.

Longtime Democratic control of the General Assembly obscured the many differences among Democrats. Although modernizing ideology shaped the budgetary priorities of the legislature and traditionalism had a major impact on noneconomic items, individual Democratic members could use their position in the legislative structure to pass bills that did not neatly fit the overall trend. One such example was the willingness of modernizer Democrats in the 1980s to support and in some cases promote environmental legislation, at a time before the massive expansion of industrial hog production and the related water pollution problems (cf. *News and Observer* 1995a) had occurred. A growing presence of environmentalists, led by then–Sierra Club and Conservation Council lobbyist Bill Holman, was pressuring legislative Democrats in 1987 to ban laundry detergent phosphates to prevent algae pollution in Tar Heel rivers. In the house, Orange County Democrat Joe Hackney worked successfully for the bill. Meanwhile, in the senate, two Democrats with statewide aspirations, Lieutenant Governor Bob Jordan and Fayetteville state senator Tony Rand, secured passage of the bill, having been convinced both that a phosphate ban was necessary and that environmentalist voters in the 1988 Democratic primaries could help their candidacies (Luebke 1990a, 174–76). Traditionalist Democrats in both house and senate opposed such government regulation of a business product, arguing that consumer choice of a product should be supreme. But this antigovernment perspective lost to the more pragmatic and/or pro-environment Democrats who saw the advantage of winning environmentalists' support.

A review of legislative voting behavior from 1987 through 1997 suggests the importance of region as a factor that leads Democrats to vote in different ways. Specifically, Democrats from the western Piedmont and Coastal Plain were most likely to adopt traditionalist positions. Democrats from the metro Piedmont and from other North Carolina cities tended to support modernizer policies as well as the occasional populist political initiative. Modernizer Democrats hailed from every region of the state, but they were most common in the metro Piedmont counties along Interstate 85. During 1995 about one-quarter of the 52 house Democrats, the minority caucus, voted with the Republican majority most of the time. All 13 were white males; only 1 represented a metro Piedmont district, and 11 of the 13 represented Coastal Plain districts (*Herald-Sun* 1995; Lineberry 1996). Similarly, when 10 house Democrats in 1997 voted for the house Republican version of the budget, 9 of the 10 were from Coastal Plain districts. Only 1 of the 9 "yes" votes from Coastal Plain Democrats was from an African American representative.

The Power of the Small Towns

The Democratic leadership in the state house of representatives for most of the twentieth century stemmed from the small-town, rural areas of North Carolina where Republicans were weak. The reasons for this are understandable. In the two-party regions of the state, Republican challengers were eager to unseat powerful Democrats. In the one-party regions, fellow Democrats at the local level deferred to the successful representatives. For example, house Speaker Liston Ramsey served through the 1990s, having first been elected from his strongly Democratic Mountain district in 1960. His top lieutenant, Billy Watkins, was an eastern Piedmont lawyer who never faced a Republican opponent. In many cases Democrats from the one-party areas had no campaign costs and required no campaign organization, because they faced no opposition in either the primary or the general election.

When Republicans won the state house majority in 1994, they followed the pattern of house Democrats. Their choice for speaker, Harold Brubaker, hailed from a very safe Republican district in Randolph County in the western Piedmont. Brubaker's top lieutenant, rules committee chairman Richard Morgan, represented Moore County, a district made safe for Republicans by the many corporate retirees who had migrated from the North to this nationally known golfing area.

The passage of Jim Hunt's gubernatorial succession amendment in 1977 ensured that power relations would change in the state senate because the lieutenant governor could serve for eight rather than four years. Incumbent Jimmy Green, a traditionalist Democrat from the one-party Coastal Plain region, won reelection and shaped the senate's agenda. Most significantly, as senate presiding officer in 1982 he strongly opposed ratification of the Equal Rights Amendment.

It was less obvious that gubernatorial succession would change power dynamics in the house, but in fact the succession amendment broke the long-held tradition of one-term Speakers. The first multiterm Speaker, Carl Stewart, gave up his seat to run unsuccessfully in 1980 against Green for lieutenant governor. His successor, Liston Ramsey, assumed office in 1981 and served an unprecedented four terms. Coalition Speaker Mavretic, who succeeded Ramsey, would have liked to serve two terms. But house Democrats, who had been badly split during the 1989–90 Mavretic Speakership, patched together sufficient party unity to agree that the 1991–92 Speaker should be a Democrat who had been in the Kennel Club, that is, one who had been in the "dog house" as an opponent of Mavretic and his alliance with house Republicans. An African American lawyer, Dan Blue of Raleigh, out-organized Bob Hunter, a white lawyer from Marion, and Blue served two terms as Speaker from 1991 through 1994.

Beginning in 1985, his first term as governor, Republican Jim Martin criticized the pork barrel legislation approved by the house and senate Democratic majorities. These bills provided funding for pet local projects of Democratic legislators who were loyal to the house and senate leadership. The pork barrel was merely the most visible layer of a decision-making process in which few legislators participated. The eight-member "supersub," three Democratic members of both house and senate plus the Speaker and lieutenant governor, made the crucial choices for the state's $12 billion budget during the hectic closing days of each legislative session.

Subsequently, during the fall 1994 campaign, house Republicans were highly critical of the level of government spending, including public school teacher and state employee raises, that house and senate Democrats approved. Indeed, the slogan "They (the Democrats) spent it all," "it" being the budget surplus of 1994, was seen as one of the most successful weapons in the arsenal of the 1994 house GOP campaigners. But the facts were otherwise. The Democrats had actually saved millions of dollars in a "rainy day" fund, legislative lingo for a savings account that might be needed during the time of a future economic downturn and thus a decline in available revenue. The "spent it all" attack nonetheless appeared to have taken root, because the Democrats lost twenty-six seats.

The irony of the house Republican attack on Democrats for closed decision making and excessive spending became clear during Brubaker's second term in 1997–98. In the budget approved during the 1997 session, there was hardly a difference in dollar terms between the approved house Republican budget and the Democratic budget presented first by Governor Hunt and altered slightly and passed by senate Democrats. Further, the senate Democratic and house Republican budget differences in 1997 were negotiated in such secrecy that longtime legislative observers were reminded precisely of the Democratic supersub that had been so criticized by GOP governor Martin.

From a late-1990s perspective it became clear that pork barrel was popular with whichever political party was able to dispense the millions of dollars in special hometown projects. Tar Heel Republicans had argued in the 1980s and until 1995 that pork barrel was a distinctly Democratic problem; their own record in the state house between 1995 and 1998 suggested that the problem of pork barrel and secrecy was institutionalized in the legislative system. Any party holding a majority in one legislative house became enamored of using that majority position to maximize its advantage over and control of political opponents.

Funding Infrastructure:
The Bipartisan Procorporate Agenda

When Republicans assumed control of the state house in early 1995, the religious-right activists who had been so crucial to the turnout of Republican voters mobilized in the fall of 1994 presumed that their social-traditionalist agenda would prevail. In fact, North Carolina's house Republicans faced the same dilemma as the congressional Republican majority 250 miles to the north: how to reconcile a big-business economic agenda with the demands of less-affluent religious constituencies (Dionne 1997). Just as in Washington, D.C., Tar Heel legislative Republicans found that Democratic state senators (who in 1995 held a narrow majority), Democratic house members, and Democratic governor Jim Hunt (playing a role vis-à-vis Republicans that paralleled President Clinton's in Washington) were in general more sympathetic to the procorporate economic-traditionalist agenda than to the social traditionalism of the religious right. In short, if it was good for big business, house Speaker Brubaker had no difficulty finding support from senate Democratic leader Marc Basnight or from Jim Hunt. Anyone who had watched politics in Washington, D.C., during the early Reagan years, when tax-cut benefits flowed toward the wealthy at a time when Democrats controlled both the U.S. House and the Senate (Greider 1992), was not surprised by North Carolina's bipartisan consensus.

Consumer or environmentalist legislation remained by far the exception rather than the rule. The procorporate tilt of legislative policy was reinforced by a coterie of lobbyists, many of whom were former legislators, who worked hard for their clients (North Carolina Center for Public Policy Research 1986; North Carolina Center for Public Policy Research 1996). Overwhelmingly, these clients were corporations or business associations. At election time the business lobbies supported their favored candidates with contributions from PACs or from individual contributions of up to $4,000 per election. The campaign finance law, in effect until it was restricted slightly by the 1997 General Assembly (Institute of Government 1997, 93–97), permitted, for example, a $4,000 contribution during each scheduled primary election (May and/or June of the election year), even if the recipient politician was not personally on the ballot. Further, minor children could make gifts, and because (unlike federal law) an employer's name did not need to be provided, a corporate employee could be an unofficial "bundler" of contribution checks. Only after detailed computer-based research could Democracy South, a Chapel Hill-based organization that lobbied against the existing campaign finance system, identify in 1997 that corporations such as Guilford Mills, a strongly antiunion textile firm in Greensboro, had, through individual bundled contributions, sent $42,000 to the Jim Hunt Reelection Campaign in 1996. Democracy South asserted that one of the bundlers, Guilford Mills employee Doug Galyon, had been rewarded for his pro-Hunt efforts over the years by receiving a 1993 appointment and 1997 reappointment to the state Board of Transportation (Hall 1997; *News and Observer* 1997f).

Democracy South, via data-sharing relationships with the Durham-based *Independent Weekly* (Yeoman et al. 1992) and the *Charlotte Observer* (1995), documented that these patterns of campaign contributions permeated General Assembly elections as well. The bottom line remained, whether legislators personally agreed or were simply making a more pragmatic response to available campaign cash from well-to-do sources, that the great majority of Democratic and Republican legislators supported the business agenda of either the modernizer or the traditionalist variety. What modernizers and traditionalists have had in common is the belief that government policy should benefit business first (Luebke 1990a, 44–45). This contrasts with the populist view that government's first job should be to help the average citizen, not the large corporation.

Today's modernizers have inherited the mantle of North Carolina's pre–civil rights elite. V. O. Key (1949) called the state a progressive plutocracy because the commitment to progress served the interests of wealthy capitalists. Nowhere is the theoretical distinction between traditionalist and modernizer ideology clearer than on taxation policy. The traditionalist opposes new taxes on principle, seeks to repeal some existing taxes, and believes that the state budget is padded and needs reduction. Such a position collides head-on with the claims of state government agencies from highways to health care.

Governor Martin campaigned in 1984 as a traditionalist, advocating that the combined taxes on groceries, business inventories, and intangible property be cut by $489 million (Betts 1985, 5). By 1986, however, he sounded like a modernizer when he proposed raising the gasoline tax to help the state's ailing Highway Fund. Similarly, in 1995 Speaker Brubaker heralded the tax-cutting agenda of house Republicans. But in 1997 Brubaker quietly allowed metro Piedmont Republicans to win house passage of a public transit bill that raised local vehicle taxes, increased rental car taxes at the Raleigh-Durham and Piedmont Triad airports and surrounding counties, and if supported in a referendum, allowed a half-cent increase in Mecklenburg County's general sales tax (excluding groceries).

Brubaker also signaled a willingness to provide what many economic-traditionalist Republicans labeled corporate welfare, a one-cent general sales tax increase—if approved in a referendum—to fund construction of a major league baseball stadium on the Guilford-Forsyth county line. Baseball advocates hoped to lure the Minnesota Twins to the Triad. House Republicans in 1997 were caught in the same bind Jim Martin had faced in 1986: how to oppose tax increases, as the campaign literature promised Republicans would do, when big-business backers supported a particular tax increase. In the case of Triad baseball, strong opposition from traditionalist house Republican legislators and their similarly antitax county commissioners forced the corporate coalition of Triad modernizers, including heavyweights such as Wachovia Bank (Forsyth) and Jefferson-Pilot corporation (Guilford), to retreat. They downshifted from the one-cent general sales tax increase to be levied in eleven counties surrounding Greensboro and Winston-Salem (a bill that had passed the state senate in May) to a one-cent prepared food tax to be assessed just in Guilford and Forsyth Counties and requiring approval in a referendum. But significantly, Brubaker and numerous other Republicans, especially those from the metro Piedmont counties, had been willing to support even a one-cent general tax increase. The antigovernment feature of traditionalism fares better in more symbolic settings such as the U.S. Senate. Jesse Helms has been able to vote his traditionalist principles as a protest, while recognizing that a majority of the Senate, even most Republicans, will pass the spending bills he opposes. The house Republican willingness to respond to corporate agenda items merely matched what Democratic legislators had done for big business throughout the twentieth century. Significantly, the taxes that business asked Republicans Martin and Brubaker to support were all sales taxes, by definition hitting low-income consumers at a higher rate than the wealthy (cf. Liner 1991).

Modernizer taxation policy begins with the premise that funds must be available to pay for an activist state government. The crucial question is,

Who shall pay for big government? The answer has emerged from the self-interest of modernizer business people. Modernizer ideology, whether espoused by politicians or employers, exists to serve the interests of the growth-oriented business. Consequently, modernizers would prefer to place the burden of taxation on other groups in society besides themselves. Two areas require close examination. First, does the tax fall directly on business or on the consumer? Second, is the tax progressive? Progressive means that the higher one's income, the higher the rate of taxation. It is not surprising, then, that the preferred tax of modernizers in the 1980s and 1990s was the sales tax, paid equally by all consumers regardless of income. Because it is a flat tax, the sales tax is regressive, not progressive.

A gasoline tax (Luebke 1990a, 52–53), a general sales tax, or a local public transit tax are all examples of regressive taxation policy. The impact of such sales taxes was indisputable: purchasing a family's basic necessities such as food and clothing consumes a much smaller proportion of a wealthy family's income than the proportion it takes of a poor family's income. Only through a progressive income tax, increasing the tax rate on those with higher taxable incomes (for example, North Carolina from 1991 on had three rates: 6, 7, and 7.75 percent) and raising the minimum amount on which there is no income tax at all, can a state tax the various income groups equitably (North Carolina Budget and Tax Center 1997).

Although modernizers prefer regressive taxes, they are not inflexible. When spending needs are urgent but the political climate does not permit higher sales taxes, business taxes can be raised. Although this is a position of last resort, it affirms the modernizer commitment to expansion of the state's infrastructure. In 1991 corporate and individual income taxes on the wealthy were raised. In 1987 modernizers raised the state corporate income tax from 6 percent to 7 percent. This was the first increase in fifty-four years. To be sure, the modernizer Democrats also gave business a plum, something traditionalists and some modernizers, including Governor Martin, had been demanding for years: abolition of the tax on business inventories. In effect, a tax increase was exchanged for a tax decrease. Further, the corporate income tax continued to be regressive; the rate was the same for a tiny country store as it was for IBM. Yet business taxes, not consumer taxes, were raised. The major opposition in 1987 to another sales tax increase came from Lieutenant Governor Bob Jordan, who was expected to challenge Jim Martin in the 1988 gubernatorial election. Since the General Assembly had raised the local-option sales tax a half-penny in 1983 and again in 1986, so that sales taxes were 5 percent in all counties, Jordan saw the political risk of facing an opponent like Martin who had successfully campaigned in 1984 as an antitax traditionalist.

During the severe recession of 1991–92, house Democratic Speaker Dan Blue informed business modernizers that, in accord with his commitment to tax fairness, they could not be exempt from raised taxes if the sales tax would as expected be raised from 5 percent to 6 percent. House Finance Committee chairs George Miller and Joe Hackney apprised corporate leaders that the many corporate tax-increase bills that Democrats had introduced left big-business leaders just two basic choices: a general increase in the corporate income tax or a severe slicing back of the various special corporate tax breaks that various sectors of business had won over the years. The modernizer consensus was to accept a corporate income tax increase to 7.75 percent as well as a temporary surcharge (Whitman 1997) rather than to lose the special tax exemptions.

The corporate income tax increases in both 1987 and 1991 emerged from the realization among politician and business modernizers alike that the state's public school programs needed improvement (Luebke 1990a, 46–52). Furthermore, in a recession even corporations have to pay some share toward an otherwise inevitable budget shortfall, or they must expect cutbacks in state government services, especially to K–12, community college, and University of North Carolina system education programs. Although far less fundamental in its implications, the raising of corporate taxes even slightly in lieu of or along with an increased sales tax is somewhat reminiscent of the funding crisis that confronted the legislature during the Great Depression.

When local governments faced bankruptcy during the depression years, the state in 1931 assumed primary funding responsibility for public schools and highways. The individual income tax rates established at the time meant that all but the wealthy were exempt from the tax. Even though the legislature also created a sales tax in 1933, the net effect of the combined business and consumer taxes was progressive. Business taxes accounted for 60 percent of General Fund revenues in 1934–35, while sales taxes made up 31 percent and income taxes 6 percent (Liner 1979, 49). In short, facing a crisis, the state's political leaders forced business and the wealthy to pay a significant share of the costs of state government.

By 1985, when income, property, and sales taxes were combined, all North Carolinians—poor and rich alike—paid virtually the same percentage of their income for taxes (CTJ 1987, tab. 33). In short, the state's tax progressivity had disappeared.

Part of the reason that Tar Heel corporations and wealthy individuals have advocated continued cuts in their share of state taxes has been the reality that, although increasingly inclined toward regressivity, North Carolina's tax system is more progressive than that of most other southern states (CTJ 1996). Tennessee, for example, has no personal income tax and does impose a sales tax, including one on groceries, of 8.5 percent. Florida has a steeper tax on intangible wealth—stocks and bonds—than North Carolina did before the General Assembly repealed the intangibles tax in 1995, but Florida, unlike North Carolina, has no individual income tax. Particularly, recruiters of outside industry, whether at the state Department of Commerce or at individual county chambers of commerce, do not care about possible regressive tax burdens on middle- and low-income North Carolinians. Rather, their focus is sometimes termed "a race to the bottom," in which taxes on corporations and their individual executives need to be lowered, simply because similar taxes in Georgia, Alabama, or Virginia are lower than in North Carolina (CED 1994).

Within North Carolina, even a person interested in state politics is not likely to have known that the state's tax burden in the early 1990s had continued to shift away from business, notwithstanding the corporate tax increase of 1991 (Liner 1991). On the contrary, as a result of continued and effective lobbying by North Carolina businesses, the only policy thoroughly debated by the Democratic legislative majority in the 1980s and the 1990s was whether tax cuts for business and the wealthy were affordable.

Modernizers believed that a good policy goal justified a regressive tax. Terry Sanford, from the time the food tax was reestablished in 1961 through his successful campaign for the U.S. Senate in 1986, argued precisely this point. Modernizers also consistently have looked first for opportunities to lower taxes on corporations and the wealthy. For example, state senate Democrats initially argued, during the 1994 "short session," that Tar Heel education needs meant that legislators could only afford to drop the tax on intangible wealth assets if they passed a replacement tax, for example, a surcharge on income from stocks and bonds. But by December 1994, when state tax revenues continued to rise and, more importantly, the 1994 Republican antitax election campaign themes appeared to have been the reason for big Democratic losses in the senate and the house, modernizer Democrats quickly changed their tune. The senate Democrats, with support from Governor Hunt, put outright repeal of the intangibles tax—without replacement revenue—at the top of their 1995 tax agenda. In effect, the absence of an income tax surcharge on stocks and bonds meant that other, far less progressive taxes would probably have to be raised in the event of a revenue shortfall during the next recession.

The stark difference in tax policy between modernizers and economic populists within legislative Democratic ranks has best manifested itself around the regressive food tax. In both 1995 and 1997, for example, neither the senate Democratic leadership (an amalgam of modernizers and several traditionalist-leaning senators) nor Governor Hunt wanted to cut the food tax. The food tax reductions, both a 1996 1 percent cut effective in January 1997 and an additional 1 percent cut in 1997 to take effect in July 1998, emerged in the house and were supported only reluctantly by the senate. To be sure, senate Democratic backbenchers, both whites and blacks with some populist leanings, had urged Basnight not to resist the food tax cut. But the food tax passed the house only because of the unholy alliance between Democratic economic populists and Republican anti-(every)-tax traditionalists. House Democrats forced a procedural vote on a food tax cut in both 1995 and 1997. Not wanting to appear the defenders of such an unpopular tax, house Republicans regrouped and passed their own version of a one-cent food tax cut, in both 1996 and 1997. Suggesting the political potency of the food tax issue—because it can win votes from both the left and the right sides of the political spectrum—Speaker Brubaker each time allowed a would-be GOP governor to sponsor the bill, majority whip and candidate Robin Hayes in 1996 and majority leader (and putative gubernatorial candidate in 2000) Leo Daughtry in 1997.

The dilemma for the Democrats in the 1990s was that populists and modernizers, who can agree on spending issues such as public education investment or an early childhood program such as Governor Hunt's Smart Start initiative, remained at loggerheads on tax policy. Some house Democrats not only listed food tax repeal as a priority but linked the repeal of such a regressive tax to new revenues that could emerge by closing tax loopholes enjoyed by many Tar Heel big businesses (cf. Luebke and Easterling 1997). For leading senate Democrats the notion of raising taxes on North Carolina's multinational corporations was anathema. The Democrats' house-senate split on tax policy, coupled with Governor Hunt's indifference to a food tax cut, gave legislative Republicans the opportunity to claim that they, not Democrats, were the true foes of the food tax.

Building Infrastructure:
The Public School Policy Debate

Support for public education was a hallmark of the progressive ideology that guided North Carolina into the civil rights era. Although the schools were racially segregated and black schools were underfunded, the General Assembly recognized the importance of elementary and secondary education during the 1930s when it reshaped its tax structure in order to assume primary responsibility for school funding.

But from the 1930s through the 1980s North Carolina placed a relatively high priority on spending for higher education compared with the other forty-nine states, while spending relatively less on K–12 public school education (National Education Association Datasearch 1987, 54, 19; Luebke 1990a, 48). This was partly explainable because over the years the high percentage of Tar Heels in semiskilled manufacturing jobs such as in textile or furniture factories meant that high schools did not have to worry about the quality of literacy or mathematics skills for many if not most graduates. Indeed, North Carolina ranked as the most industrial of the southern states throughout the twentieth century. After the decline of blue-collar jobs in the Midwest and New England in the 1970s and 1980s, North Carolina gained the number one national ranking for having the highest percentage of its employees in manufacturing jobs.

When in the 1970s many of the factories requiring low-skilled workers began to close, and the new factories arriving at the same time or soon thereafter primarily demanded a more literate, better-trained workforce, North Carolina's business leaders and politicians took note. In 1983 Governor Hunt convened a major study commission, with prominent corporate representatives, to examine the relationship between public school quality and economic development. This group, a business-government-educator alliance known as the North Carolina Commission on Education for Economic Growth (CEEG), underscored the commitment of modernizer ideology to both education and growth. Indeed, the CEEG justified its spending recommendations as a cost-effective way to provide acceptable jobs for future generations in North Carolina. It advocated improved teacher training and salaries, an expanded curriculum, and the hiring of more teachers, the effect of which would be to reduce class size.

The CEEG's 1985 recommendations most significantly provided political cover for any legislator, particularly traditionalists, who worried that constituents would object to "big-government" spending on public schools. A similar coalition emerged a decade later in 1995 with the same purpose. The Education Is Everybody's Business campaign, spearheaded by the state's largest business lobby, the North Carolina Citizens for Business and Industry (NCCBI), was directed at spending-shy legislators who wanted business reassurance.

The 1985 General Assembly adopted an education improvement package labeled the Basic Education Plan (BEP). It promised a 34 percent increase in state funds for public education, to be phased in between 1987 and 1996. The money was to be used to provide more teachers and support personnel such as librarians and social workers, reduce class size, upgrade summer school and vocational education, and add other enhancements.

The BEP was a classic example of modernizer policymaking, for it overlooked the question of equity. Did some school districts need state help more than others? The BEP, because it distributed funds on a per-pupil basis, would raise the minimum standards for each of North Carolina's school districts, which numbered 143 at the time. But it lacked an equalization formula to compensate poorer counties and allow them to undertake capital improvements that they could not afford otherwise.

By 1987, however, the issue of school equity did receive attention from the General Assembly. Twenty percent of a ten-year, $800 million package would be earmarked for school districts with critical construction needs. Thus, for the first time, the state was attempting to remedy inequities between the poorer and the wealthier counties. For modernizer Democrats this was a tacit admission that the premise of the BEP—equal funding for all districts—would not address the problems of poor school districts. Without special funding, many of these districts could not build facilities to house the teachers who would come to the district under the BEP. Lieutenant Governor Jordan initiated the critical needs provision. It was unclear whether Jordan had been permanently won over to equity funding for public school districts or whether this was a one-time concession. Undoubtedly, his thinking was influenced by the philanthropic voice of the Democratic modernizer establishment, the Z. Smith Reynolds Foundation of Winston-Salem.

The Z. Smith Reynolds Foundation had created the Public School Forum in 1985 to fill a void caused in 1984 by the dissolution of Governor Hunt's CEEG. Like the CEEG, the Public School Forum brought together key Democratic politicians, corporate executives, and educators to address long-term needs, including the recruitment of future generations of teachers. One of its first projects was a scholarship program to encourage both black and white teenagers to consider careers in the public schools. In 1987 the forum considered the issue of equity and developed a consensus in its membership that school construction needs, including catch-up funds, were critical if North Carolina hoped to generate economic development in the poorer Mountain and Coastal Plain counties.

Interestingly, the Public School Forum relied on research prepared by the Atlantic Committee for Research in Education (ACRE), a Durham-based advocacy group also funded by the Z. Smith Reynolds Foundation. Beginning in 1983 ACRE monitored the various study commissions with a special focus on financial equity. Its reports criticized legislative funding proposals for ignoring the monetary differences among the 143 school districts and thus the inability of some counties to finance school construction. It pointed out that poorer counties had a higher tax rate, not a lower rate, than the wealthier counties. The issue was not willingness, but ability to invest in the future of children.

The major difference between the Public School Forum and ACRE was the political influence of the forum's membership on education policy. In 1987 the forum, using arguments first made by ACRE, persuaded leading modernizer Democrats in the General Assembly to provide some funds toward equalization. Whether modernizer Democrats would continue to move in the direction of educational equity remained an open question, but modernizer business people and politicians were willing to do so during a crisis, much as the General Assembly of the 1920s established a progressive personal income tax.

For modernizers a crisis constitutes a short-term, immediate problem for which equity solutions may be temporarily appropriate. The severity of the education crisis was underscored by the 1986 findings of the North Carolina Commission on Jobs and Economic Growth, a study group of business people and educators funded by the 1985 legislature to develop a Democratic economic development plan separate from that of Governor Martin. Every one of the commission's fourteen recommendations focused on public education and job training. Several of the commission's legislative proposals became law in 1987. The modernizer alliance of business, government, and education was hard at work in the late 1980s. Putting aside partisan politics, leading Democrats were worried about the state's educational and economic future.

Education politics would, however, become more complicated in North Carolina following implementation of the BEP. The primary force challenging the BEP in the early 1990s was the ascendant religious right. Borrowing from the political playbook of Senator Jesse Helms (see Chapter 8) and from policy recommendations of various Washington-based social traditionalist organizations, grassroots fundamentalist Christians, many of whom had been active in the early 1980s in the successful legislative battle against North Carolina's ratification of the Equal Rights Amendment, challenged during the early 1990s the centralized mandates from the state Department of Public Instruction. In Gastonia in the western Piedmont, for example, parents and others fought what they saw as the imposition of a "secular humanist" curriculum, Odyssey, upon their children. After extensive protest the Gaston school board dropped the project. At the legislature, religious-right activists wanted to know why social workers and counselors, and even art and music teachers, were part of the state-funded BEP programming. What, they asked, was wrong with a straightforward curriculum based on reading, writing, and 'rithmetic?

The combination of social-traditionalist criticism and the severe 1991–92 recession and related General Assembly funding crisis knocked the BEP off track. By the early 1990s, even some public school advocates were having second thoughts about the top-down dimensions of the BEP. In 1993, with the notion of local control gaining currency in national and North Carolina public school policy debates, the General Assembly passed a new program, Site-Based Management. Under this proposal schoolteachers would implement specific "building plans," allowing teachers and parents more input into school specifics. In policy terms Site-Based Management was challenging the wisdom of public education ideas that would emerge only from a central office in Raleigh, the Department of Public Instruction, and be imposed on teachers by local school system-based administrators.

For the religious right, however, local control meant much more than the individual school building plans. They called for "school choice," borrowing arguments from a national debate that had been especially heated in Milwaukee, Wisconsin, where some African American parents, frustrated with the public schools' failure to educate black children well, had joined forces with the religious right and traditionalist Republican politicians to implement a school voucher system. With support from traditionalist High Point Republican representative (and future house Speaker pro tem) Steve Wood, a citizen lobby was under way to win a state-funded voucher for each child to use at any school, public or private, that constituted the parents' choice. Key to fueling this effort was the house Republican victory in November 1994 and the comfortable majority that Republicans had in house debates during 1995.

As a consequence, Tar Heel supporters of public schools, like their counterparts in numerous other states, were forced to build defensive alliances that included groups that normally opposed one another. The North Carolina Association of Educators (NCAE), the state affiliate of the National Education Association, for example, had been the premier advocate for teacher and principal salary and benefit increases and a major opponent of merit pay. The NCAE viewed merit criteria as an opportunity for school administrators to "play favorites," while the state School Board Association and business-based groups such as NCCBI believed merit pay allowed school leaders to sort out the "dead wood." However, in order to fight the religious right's voucher proposal, NCAE, the school boards, and the NCCBI worked together. They were joined, in a symbolic manifestation of bipartisan modernizer unity against the religious right, by both Democratic governor Hunt and former Republican governor Martin.

This unusual alliance lasted just long enough to defeat the voucher idea in 1995. Undaunted, Republican voucher-advocate Wood pushed during the 1996 session for charter schools, an idea that had considerably more political support. Charter schools are public schools individually created and controlled by parents and teachers rather than by the usual local school board and administration hierarchy. Free of most administrative restrictions, charter schools nonetheless receive the same state and local appropriation per pupil as do regular public schools. The NCAE, like the National Education Association, opposed charter schools, and the Tar Heel school board association was also unenthusiastic. But NCCBI and business interests in general supported charter schools as a way to light a fire under what they viewed as entrenched schoolteachers and bureaucrats. (Corporate advocates of public school reform generally perceived NCAE as a "teachers' union," even though collective bargaining by public employees has long been prohibited under North Carolina law).

The General Assembly authorized charter schools in 1996 and approved modifications to the original bill in 1997. But Democratic support for charter schools was not a case of "caving in" to the perceived political popularity of a religious-right idea, as was the case with Robin Hayes's "sexual abstinence" bill. Durham Democratic senator Wib Gulley promoted charter schools as a manifestation of "reinventing government" initiatives (cf. Osborne 1992). In particular, funding charter schools was an agenda item of the Washington, D.C.-based DLC, a self-described New

Democrat group, cofounded by then-governor Bill Clinton, to provide Democrats with an organized alternative to a Democratic Party dominated by the national AFL-CIO and racial minorities (for example, Jesse Jackson) (cf. Dionne 1997, chap. 2). For the DLC, charter schools were a way to break down public school bureaucracies. Willing to give the charter school idea a try, Gulley gained senate passage of a Democratic version of Wood's Republican bill, and a compromise became law, effective for the 1997–98 school year. In praise of the charter school initiative, NCCBI's monthly magazine, *North Carolina*, pictured a smiling Gulley and Wood on the cover of the February 1997 issue, accompanied by a sympathetic cover story.

For the average public school teacher, controversies about vouchers or charter schools took a back seat to classroom size, shortage of supplies, and teacher pay. If a teacher were in a low-wealth area, especially in a rural Coastal Plain or Mountain county, these problems were compounded because such counties usually lacked local supplements for teacher salaries or local public education foundations that provided small grants to innovative teachers. Despite increased General Assembly funding for the low-wealth areas, public school officials from these regions were convinced that their schools could never match the quality of public schools in more affluent areas, especially in the six metro Piedmont counties. In numerous other states, poorly funded school districts, whether rural or inner-city minority, had sued and won in state courts, basically on the grounds of denial of poor children's access to an equal education (Kozol 1991, chap. 6). Armed with continuing studies from the Public School Forum, school boards in North Carolina's rural districts sued the state in 1994. Three years later the state supreme court ruled that a "sound basic education" was every pupil's right and remanded the case to a lower-level court for action (*News and Observer* 1997i).

In better-funded urban school districts, teacher pay and related issues remained, regardless of the ultimate outcome of the lawsuit with respect to equity of school funding. Seeking a visible and popular issue for his reelection campaign, Governor Hunt in 1996 embraced the NCAE's goal to have North Carolina reach the national average by 2000. As noted above, Tar Heel average teacher salaries had actually dropped from thirty-second to forty-third between 1985 and 1995. A major reason for the drop was the tendency of poorly paid entry-level public school teachers to switch to other, less-demanding and better-paying jobs after several years. This contrasted to most other states, where both higher entry-level salaries as well as bigger pay increases for experienced teachers led to far less attrition. Since the lower ranks of North Carolina's public school teachers were being depleted faster than those of most other states, it was inevitable that other states that were retaining more teachers and thus paying their average teacher more than North Carolina, would jump ahead of North Carolina in national rankings.

In 1997 Hunt won General Assembly passage of what he termed the Excellent Schools Act, providing large pay increases for every teacher and special increases for those who finish a master's degree or pass a national certification examination (*News and Observer* 1997m). Hunt's lobbying efforts were a textbook case of how to win widespread legislative support, from economic populists on the left to traditionalists on the right. Recognizing that the modernizer-traditionalist corporate consensus would demand more accountability from teachers in exchange for their salary increases, Hunt moved in that rightward direction by giving strong support to the latest public school improvement initiative, the ABC plan. The ABC plan allowed low-performing schools, measured by students' year-to-year test scores, to be placed under state control and to have principals replaced.

But Hunt also recognized that the NCAE teacher advocates would not support what they might see as a punitive salary package that viewed teachers as undeserving and needing to work harder to earn their raises. He deftly crafted a compromise with modernizer-traditionalist house Republicans that they, the NCCBI business group, and the NCAE could, in legislative parlance, "sign off on." Hunt's successful lobbying for the Excellent Schools Act was a masterful how-to-do-it exercise for any would-be centrist politician of either political party. Hunt had crafted a coalition that forced most traditionalist Republicans, ideologically opposed to big-government spending, to support a big-government spending program.

Building Infrastructure:
Transportation and the Environment

North Carolina's reputation as the Good Roads State was the third leg of a three-legged stool that boosted Tar Heels into their position as the South's most forward-looking state (see Chapter 1). The other two legs had been the state's willingness to impose income taxes on both individuals and corporations and a state commitment to investment in public education.

In the 1990s, as noted above, the General Assembly continued to struggle with issues of which taxes and how high and to debate how best to promote public school quality. But in the area of transportation and environmental infrastructure, the 1990s would force a new debate on North Carolinians and, by extension, on the General Assembly and the governor's office. This debate emerged from the conflict between two values, each of which had wide support among political and economic elites and among politically interested citizens. For many North Carolinians and other southerners the value of individualism is even more strongly held than it is generally across American society. Leading students of southern culture (Reed 1990) and politics (Black and Black 1992, 225) have noted the deep resonance in the South for "individual achievement" and the related resistance to big-government regulation.

At the same time that individualism is valued, many North Carolinians, perhaps more so than many other southerners, have valued a positive role for government. Indeed, in the post–World War II period, V. O. Key identified precisely this commitment to government activism as central to North Carolina's relative prosperity among the southern states (Key 1949, chap. 7). Not surprisingly, then, Tar Heel cities took the lead in establishing state-of-the-art water and sewer systems. While state government did not force smaller towns and rural areas to abandon septic tanks, it did set high standards for water quality compared with the other southern states. During the 1980s some traditionalist Democratic leaders in the General Assembly, in the spirit of the Reagan antigovernment "revolution," sought to weaken environmental protections. But most modernizer Democrats recognized a limit to individual rights; they passed legislation in the late 1980s that acknowledged that considerable environmental regulation was both necessary and politically wise, given the growing presence of environmentalists as an organized constituency within the Democratic Party.

The economic growth that North Carolina experienced beginning in the 1970s as part of the post–civil rights New South (Luebke 1991; Cobb 1984) had a predictable but unintended consequence. The metro Piedmont counties, especially around Charlotte and the Research Triangle, as well as resort and retirement counties, notably in the Mountains and along the Atlantic Coast, prospered, while about one-third of North Carolina's counties experienced stagnating economies (see Chapters 4 and 5).

By the late 1980s, traffic congestion in the modernizer Piedmont counties was so bad at rush hour that some politicians and business people began to explore alternatives to the automobile for the area's commuters. These explorations did not primarily address the concerns of the poor, although the poor might benefit from improved public transit established for car-owning citizens. Nevertheless, the desire to build roads was so strong among urban politicians that rural Democrats worried that the urban areas would grab all the highway dollars.

In response to the tendency of more affluent city governments, especially in the booming Piedmont counties, to subsidize state highway projects with local funds in order to speed up the construction timetable, rural Democrats in 1987 unified. Led by Bob Hunter, a Mountain Democrat, they argued persuasively that urban subsidies were inducing the Department of Transportation (DOT) to build city thoroughfares more quickly than rural highways. A Coastal Plain Democrat, Joe Mavretic, spoke a modernizing language that linked highways to jobs and hinted at rural resentment of urban success: "There's only so much money to go around and now it's the turn of other parts of this state to have interstate-quality roads, which in today's society are the prerequisite to development" (*Durham Morning Herald* 1987a).

In the period after 1987 this urban-rural zero-sum conflict struck advocates of highway construction such as construction companies, aggregates providers, and asphalt pavers as unnecessary. Why not, they asked the state DOT, provide more roads for every county in North Carolina? Fortuitously for them, rural roads advocate Mavretic became house Speaker in 1989. Although the intraparty personality squabbles among Democrats following Mavretic's successful coup over former Speaker Ramsey were unending during the 1989 session, road building proved to be a great source of legislative unity. This temporary truce over highways would survive the 1989 session, even though the program, known as the Highway Trust Fund (HTF), required both factions of Democrats as well as newly empowered Republicans to raise new revenue to fund the roads. Virtually every legislator in the state house and senate voted in favor of a substantial increase in gasoline and diesel fuel taxes, as well as in favor of numerous licensing and other regressive fees that would hurt the auto-dependent (because of a woefully inadequate public transit system in North Carolina), lower-income citizen especially hard. Such was the lure of highways.

Only one fly emerged in the highway construction ointment: Triangle-area Democrats George Miller and Dan Blue fought for and won a relatively tiny $5 million appropriation for public transportation. With those funds the public transit division of the state DOT revived once-a-day passenger rail service in both directions between Raleigh and Charlotte. From the perspective of road advocates, even this $5 million in a multibillion-dollar program was a mistake, because it established a precedent for transit funding coming from gasoline taxes.

The 1989 HTF legislation sought to place "in concrete" a multiyear, multibillion-dollar transportation plan that was in fact only a highway construction plan. It affirmed the place of highways as necessary infrastructure to ensure, allegedly, economic growth for all parts of North Carolina. While some critics argued that rural counties needed better public schools far more than they needed four-lane highways, the HTF plans promised specific rural and urban roads as a tradeoff for the higher taxes and fees. By the mid-1990s, however, cracks were growing in the HTF concrete. Most significantly, citizen groups were opposing highway projects in various locales across North Carolina, from the mountains to the sea, but especially in the Triad and Triangle regions. Their opposition raised important but little-debated questions: Had highway construction in North Carolina stopped being a positive force for society? Were new highways in the 1990s providing too many opportunities for autos to pollute the environment, too many chances for developers to eliminate trees and farmland in the name of growth, and too easy an opportunity for the DOT, at least in populated areas, to use powers of eminent domain to destroy existing homes and neighborhoods in order to make way for highways? These questions were raised most vociferously by Raleigh's Umstead Coalition, Durham's No Build Coalition and Eno River Association, and Forsyth County's Citizens against the Northern Beltway.

The DOT under Governor Hunt for the most part refused initially to debate the issue of air pollution. Some top DOT officials even argued that highway construction in urban areas eased air pollution, because cars as a result moved faster. Such self-serving reasoning ignored the obvious point that, especially regarding the HTF plans for new suburban loop roads around cities such as Charlotte, Greensboro, or Raleigh, highways would generate new shopping centers and subdivisions and thus more polluting automobiles. While the DOT denied that new road construction in urban areas caused new air pollution, stagnant summer air during July 1997 across North Carolina led to the first ozone alerts in the state's history (cf. *News and Observer* 1997h). From a public health perspective, the air pollution problem was obvious. From a public policy perspective, insufficient levels of public discontent meant that the state DOT could overlook its role in helping to create the air pollution problem. (Other aspects of DOT policy did, however, become controversial in late 1997; see Chapter 10.)

Water pollution in the 1990s was, by contrast, an issue that political and business elites as well as much of the voting public thought it understood. Once again the value conflict between individual rights and government regulation came to the fore. To the pleasant surprise of environmental activists, the 1997 General Assembly leaders as well as the Hunt administration took substantial steps against the problem of water pollution, especially in the Neuse River and Cape Fear River watersheds located east and southeast of Raleigh. The major reason was the exploding growth of industrial hog production in the Coastal Plain, especially in and around Duplin County (Thu and Durrenberger 1994). Between 1990 and 1997 the number of hogs processed in North Carolina grew from less than 500,000 to more than 10 million. Initially, the issue avoided public scrutiny because the 1991 General Assembly had exempted such hog factories from local government zoning as an agricultural activity. After the fact, the legislative conflict of interest in pursuing that exemption became obvious: the state senate initiated the measure at a time when Wendell Murphy, chief executive officer of Murphy Farms and one of America's largest hog producers, was a member of that body. But the amendment that would help Murphy expand his hog operations without local government control over their siting was a classic legislative rider. Attached to another piece of legislation, the rider amendment passed with most legislators unaware that they had voted on this significant exemption from government regulation.

It helped that Murphy was a well-respected member of the modernizer Democrat establishment (*News and Observer* 1995a). He made big donations to North Carolina State University's athletic foundation, the Wolfpack Club; was a financial backer and personal friend of Governor Hunt (the *News and Observer* published a file photo of Murphy and Hunt chatting while sitting next to each other at a North Carolina State basketball game); and ingratiated himself with some of his fellow legislators by flying them around in his corporate jet.

While Murphy Farms was not the only corporate hog producer, it was the largest. As recently as the spring of 1995 the political clout of the North Carolina Pork Producers Association was enough to thwart environmental regulation efforts. Combining major campaign contributions to key legislators with the predisposition of even modernizer Democrats not to regulate ("If it ain't broke, don't fix it"), the Pork Producers appeared poised to stop reform, just as those corporations with a self-interest in highway construction were fending off their environmental foes. But then it rained hard on the Coastal Plain for a few days; the result was leaks in the euphemistically termed "hog lagoons," actually massive lakes of hog urine and feces. The leaks led to a major fish kill downriver in Onslow County, near the Atlantic Coast. The fish kill and resultant headlines (for example, *News and Observer* 1995b) ignited much of the public and North Carolina's growing tourism industry to demand regulation of industrial hog production. The resultant legislation was minor; most attention focused on a tripartite "blue ribbon" study commission (six appointees each from the governor, the house Speaker and the senate leader) whose mandate was to make recommendations in 1996.

As they began their work in early 1996, the eighteen commission appointees as a group reflected the relative power of the pork producers and the weakness of environmentalists. For example, only one of Governor Hunt's six appointees, an African American attorney associated with a group to preserve landownership among rural (primarily Coastal Plain) blacks, could be termed a consumer or environmental advocate. The Republican house and Democratic senate appointments similarly were tilted toward the large-scale hog production industry. Business-as-usual received a jolt, however, from committee chair and retired second district congressman Tim Valentine. When the committee majority moved to kill any serious attempt to recommend further hog regulation, such as reducing hog odor or increasing setbacks from existing homes and businesses, Valentine refused to go along and indeed chastised his fellow members (*News and Observer* 1996a). Valentine insisted that the commission majority recognize the citizen frustration in Duplin and other big-hog counties. The majority should also have noticed, according to Valentine, that the public across North Carolina had little sympathy for Murphy Farms and other industrial-style producers. Significantly, the legislative leaders and the governor would have been content to accept antiregulation recommendations, had Valentine not blown the whistle.

Once expressed to the press, Valentine's stand became hard for Hunt, Brubaker, or Basnight to oppose publicly. Environmental activists had expected a tough fight in the 1996 short session to push for more antihog measures. But one political leader standing up to the procorporate majority made environmentalists' lobbying job much easier.

Having won reelection by a comfortable majority in November 1996, Governor Hunt took note of public opinion that appeared closer to the outspoken views of Valentine (himself a Hunt appointee) than to the pro-industry foursome whom Hunt had also appointed to the blue ribbon commission. In early 1997, however, Hunt found himself outflanked to his left by an unlikely new friend of the environment, Brubaker confidante and Moore County state representative Richard Morgan. During 1995–96 Morgan, as Rules Committee chair, had opposed even the reform efforts of a fellow GOP legislator, Duplin County representative Cindy Watson, who sought to regulate the stench and flies that had quickly transformed the country life of many of her constituents who lived near the hog production factories (*News and Observer* 1998a). In those years Republican Watson's supporters were primarily pro-environment Democrats from the metro Piedmont.

Morgan's conversion occurred in 1997 because a big hog producer had sought to build a "factory swine farm" near one of the Moore County golf courses that had made the Pinehurst area a mecca for affluent (mostly Republican) retirees from the North. His supporters, some of whom were retired corporate executives, ironically demanded government regulation to protect themselves from a big-business hog operation (*News and Observer* 1997m). When the issue hit his district, Morgan suddenly realized the problems inherent in the no-zoning provision of 1991, as well as in the absence of odor control and of setback requirements. To Morgan's credit, he supported legislation to help all big-hog counties rather than be content with an apology and withdrawal of plans just from his Moore County district. Faced with a house bill stronger than they liked, the pork producers sought to convince friendly senators to attach provisions to force municipal water and sewer systems, which also polluted, to have higher standards.

Despite an expensive television advertising campaign by Farmers for Fairness, a group funded by the hog industry that sought to suggest to Tar Heel viewers during the 1997 legislative session that city sewer spills were as bad as or worse than lagoon spills, most legislators, regardless of party label, remained unconvinced. The compromise bill that passed in fact placed greater regulation on municipalities but was also a bitter regulatory pill for the hog industry to swallow. Besides county zoning and mandatory setbacks from homes, churches, and businesses, the industry also faced a two-year moratorium on new construction. Although Governor Hunt signed the bill without hesitation, he had been relatively uninvolved because his political coalition included both pork producers and environmentalists. In an unexpected twist the 1997 General Assembly's environmentalist of the year was a big-business Republican.

Despite the landmark legislation, the Hog Roundtable, a biracial coalition of low- to middle-income Coastal Plain citizens, remained uncertain about how long the newly converted environment-oriented legislators would maintain a critical stance toward the industrial hog operations. The Hog Roundtable, which had fought a largely unsuccessful war until Morgan entered the battle, noted skeptically that the compromise bill had a greater setback requirement for golf courses than for drinking-water wells (*News and Observer* 1997o). The Roundtable's criticism again raised the uncomfortable observation that modernizer elites, in both politics and business, seemed to recognize little need to respond to grievances if average citizens were the plaintiffs.

Beyond issues of class and race, North Carolina continues to face key regional differences. Indeed, the notion of two North Carolinas, one prospering, the other not, is a recurring discussion in policy circles. The next chapter presents an overview of the recent socioeconomic change in the Tar Heel state that underlies political change.

A Socioeconomic Portrait of North Carolina

The politics of North Carolina reflect, as shown in earlier chapters, the relative strength of conflicting political parties, interest groups, and ideologies. But political battles do not occur in a vacuum. Rather, they emerge in part from the demographic and economic structure that undergirds society. This chapter examines changes in North Carolina's population and economy in the past quarter-century and demonstrates that these changes have reshaped the state's politics. It also compares the differing economic circumstances of the state's three major regions.

For most of the twentieth century, North Carolina ranked tenth in population among the fifty states. Since 1980 the state has vied with Georgia for tenth place in the nation and for third place in the South, after Texas and Florida. The 1996 U.S. Census estimate was 7.3 million, reflecting a 15 percent growth rate during the 1980s and early 1990s (OPR 1997). This growth rate was above average both for the South and for the United States. It resulted in North Carolina's gaining back in 1992 a twelfth seat in the U.S. Congress that had been lost in 1960 because of relatively large out-migration of blacks during the 1950s. Demographers expected North Carolina to approach 8 million in population in 2000.

During the 1980s and 1990s parts of North Carolina enjoyed unprecedented growth, while a handful of counties actually lost residents. The Tar Heel state has become a mix of economic boom and stagnation. Its population growth mostly reflects in-migration from other states. Indeed, North Carolina's birthrate in the 1980s was the ninth lowest in the nation, while its in-migration level was the sixth highest (Calhoun 1988, 4). This population increase has been concentrated in counties with three kinds of characteristics: either an emerging high-tech economy, in which research and development and related services predominate; growing settlements of affluent retirees; or an economic boom at the beach along the Atlantic Coast. Numerous counties illustrate these trends. In both the 1980s and the 1990s the Research Triangle area, especially Wake County, and Mecklenburg County (Charlotte), accounted for more than one-third of North Carolina's population growth. Both regional economies benefited from their reputations as hospitable to high-tech, service-sector corporations such as IBM (both areas) or NORTEL, the Toronto-based electronics firm (Research Triangle Park area). Retirees increasingly moved to Mountain counties such as Henderson (Hendersonville), Macon (Franklin) and Watauga (Boone); a golfing area such as Moore County (Pinehurst); or northern Chatham and southern Orange Counties (the Chapel Hill area). Beach counties such as Brunswick (between Wilmington and Myrtle Beach, South Carolina), New Hanover (Wilmington), and Dare (Nags Head) had the state's fastest growth rates in the 1980s and 1990s (OPR 1997).

Geographically, North Carolina is both large and diverse. The distance from Nags Head on the northeastern coast to Murphy in extreme southwestern North Carolina is 500 miles, farther than from Nags Head to New York City. Murphy lies much closer to Georgia's state capital, Atlanta, than to its own capital city of Raleigh. Schoolchildren learn to divide North Carolina into three regions: the Mountains, the Piedmont, and the Coastal Plain. Relying on topography, which does not coincide precisely with county lines, geographers usually place the state's twenty-three most western counties in the Mountains (see map) and the forty-one most eastern counties in the Coastal Plain. The remaining thirty-six counties constitute the Piedmont. This book follows those distinctions. In 1994 13 percent of Tar Heels lived in the Mountains and 31 percent on the Coastal Plain, while

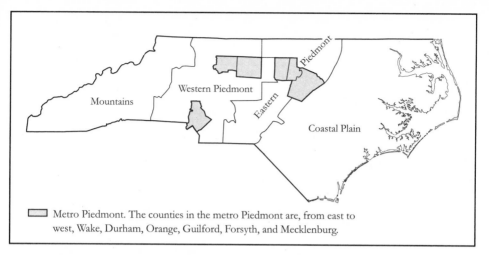

Metro Piedmont. The counties in the metro Piedmont are, from east to west, Wake, Durham, Orange, Guilford, Forsyth, and Mecklenburg.

The Regions of North Carolina

the majority lived in the Piedmont. Analysis of Tar Heel politics requires further refinement of the Piedmont region into three areas: metro, western, and eastern Piedmont.

The notion of a metro Piedmont reflects the cultural power that emanates from the six counties along Interstate 85 that are not even geographically contiguous: Mecklenburg, Forsyth, Guilford, Orange, Durham, and Wake (see map). The essence of modernizer values—that economic prosperity requires an activist state government prepared to invest in transportation, education, and the like—permeates the thinking of political and economic leaders in these counties. North Carolina's most influential daily newspapers are published here. These newspapers circulate, of course, in less-metropolitan counties whose leaders are less sympathetic to a big-budget government. The metro Piedmont is also the home of the state's most prestigious research and liberal arts colleges and universities. Thus, although one-third of all Tar Heels live in this area, its influence on state politics is disproportionately high. Growth-oriented corporations, such as banking, insurance, the media, and high-technology firms, have joined academics and state government leaders in efforts to modernize North Carolina's economy.

The western and eastern Piedmont areas share cultural support for traditionalist values. Leaders of these counties are skeptical of change, especially if it is engineered or mandated by big government—for example, racial equality or abortion rights. The small-town, rural values of the western and eastern Piedmont also pervade the less-urban counties of the Mountains and the Coastal Plain. In fact, the modernizer values of the metro Piedmont often stand in sharp contrast to the small-town culture that remains strong across most of the state's 100 counties.

The distinction between the western and the eastern Piedmont derives from the relative importance of agriculture and the level of black population. The black percentage is below the state average of 22 in all eighteen western Piedmont counties, and at or above 22 in all but one of the twelve eastern Piedmont counties. Similarly, agricultural employment in most western Piedmont counties is below the state average of 2 percent, but agricultural work in eastern Piedmont counties averages 4 percent.

Historically, race has mattered in North Carolina. Blacks and Native Americans have received less education and lower incomes, and they have suffered more unemployment and health problems. Twenty-two percent of Tar Heels are black, the eighth highest proportion in the country. One percent are Native American, the thirteenth highest total. In 1990, for the first time, Asian Americans exceeded 1 percent of the state's population. By the late 1990s, Hispanic residents were a noteworthy part not only of the state's agricultural areas, where they had lived as farm laborers for decades, but also in the larger towns and the cities of the metro Piedmont.

The regional concentration of the state's black population reflects the historical dependency of plantation owners on slave labor. After the Civil War, blacks generally remained in the same areas where they had been forced to live as slaves. Consequently, few blacks live in the western part of the state, where small, independent farmers were the norm. For example, just 6 percent of the Mountain population and 13 percent of the western Piedmont are black. By contrast, eastern Piedmont counties are 32 percent black and the Coastal Plain is 30 percent black. On the Coastal Plain the black population is small in the counties along the Atlantic Ocean, which have relied over the years on seafood (and today, tourism) rather than agriculture for their livelihood. Poor blacks have moved from rural counties to the metro Piedmont in search of greater economic opportunity. More recently, out-of-state black professionals have begun migrating to North Carolina, especially to the metro Piedmont counties. Currently, one-fourth of the metro Piedmont's population is black.

The North Carolina Economy:
The Manufacturing Sector

North Carolina, like the forty-nine other states, is in transition away from manufacturing and agriculture and toward service employment. Throughout the twentieth century North Carolina has ranked as the most industrial southern state. By the 1990s North Carolina held a national record of which few Tar Heels were aware: of the fifty states, North Carolina had the highest percentage of its labor force engaged in manufacturing. This occurred because so many long-established factories in the "rust-belt" states of the Northeast and Midwest closed, while North Carolina as well as other southern states were still gaining new manufacturing jobs.

In 1920 53 percent of the state's labor force worked on farms, and 24 percent were employed in manufacturing (Hobbs 1930, 65). In the following quarter-century until after World War II, employment patterns changed little. In 1947, for example, 42 percent of North Carolinians worked in agriculture, compared with 28 percent in manufacturing (Hammer and Company Associates 1961, 12).

The massive shift in North Carolina's economy occurred between the late 1940s and the 1970s. Between 1947 and 1970 the percentage of Tar Heels employed in agriculture dropped from 42 to 8, while the percentage in manufacturing rose from 28 to 40. Between 1966 and 1976 only two states, Texas and California, exceeded North Carolina in the number of additional manufacturing jobs (Mahaffey and Doty 1979, 6). During the 1960s and 1970s these new jobs fell into two categories. The first included the traditional labor-intensive and low-wage industries—textiles, apparel, and furniture; employment in this category tended to increase, especially in counties where agricultural unemployment was high (Wood 1986, chap. 3). A second category of new industries was more capital intensive and paid higher wages—among them, fabricated metals, paper and rubber production, and machinery (Luebke, Peters, and Wilson 1986, 317). Such firms were more likely to settle in nonagricultural, industrial counties, especially in the metro and western Piedmont.

Between 1970 and 1990 both agricultural and manufacturing employment declined as a percentage of total jobs across the state. As elsewhere in the United States, employment gains in North Carolina have occurred in the tertiary sector, where the distribution of goods and services prevails. The percentage of Tar Heels employed full time in farming dropped from 8 to 2. Among nonagricultural workers, the number in manufacturing decreased from 40 percent in 1970 to 27 percent in 1990 (U.S. Department of Labor 1990; U.S. Department of Labor 1970).

Between 1970 and 1995 the state's labor force nearly doubled to 3.5 million persons. Eighty percent of the new jobs were outside manufacturing. Within the manufacturing sector the kinds of factory jobs changed significantly. North Carolina absorbed many industrial corporations that previously had located all or almost all of their factories outside the South. Firms related to motor vehicle production, such as Dana Corporation, Freightliner, and Eaton, opened industrial plants, especially in the western Piedmont region. The state's reputation as a nonunion if not antiunion environment was attractive. In addition, the related opportunity for corporations to offer wages and benefits that were lower than in their unionized, nonsouthern plants remained a key inducement in the late 1990s. North Carolina's reputation remained such even as some firms such as Freightliner lost a union-organizing battle with the United Auto Workers (UAW) at its Gaston County plant. Especially in the 1980s and 1990s, multinational corporations based, for example, in Japan, Britain, and Germany all increased their manufacturing investment in the Tar Heel state. Unlike the state's historic industries—the production of textiles, apparel, furniture, and tobacco products—all of which had fewer employees statewide in 1995 than in 1970, these new manufacturing jobs tended to be part of the core rather than the periphery of the national economy.

Core industries are noted for capital intensity, high productivity, a high degree of monopoly, high profits, high wages, and relatively high levels of unionization (Tolbert, Horan, and Beck 1980). In the terminology of this book, core business people are usually modernizers. Peripheral industries are noted for labor intensity, low productivity, national and international market competition, low profits, low wages, and lack of unionization. Peripheral industrialists are usually traditionalists. Core industries include construction, utilities, finance, and most forms of manufacturing, among them machinery, transportation equipment, rubber and paper products, and metal fabrication. North Carolina's mainstay industries of textiles, apparel, and furniture are examples of the peripheral sector. Between 1970 and the mid-1990s the structure of North Carolina's economy shifted from a dependency on peripheral industries to a greater balance between core and periphery (Luebke, Peters, and Wilson 1986, 316–17; Noland 1998).

In 1970 39 percent of all Tar Heel manufacturing jobs were in the textile industry, compared with less than 20 percent in 1990 (U.S. Department of Labor 1970; U.S. Department of Labor 1990). But even in the 1990s, textiles employed more North Carolinians than any other manufacturing industry. In the United States, textiles are a low-wage industry, and its continued dominance in North Carolina seemed likely to ensure that the state would retain the dubious honor of appearing last or close to last in national industrial wage rankings in 2000.

As a peripheral industry, textiles have been extremely vulnerable to competition from foreign- and U.S.-owned corporations paying far lower wages in the Third World, primarily in Central America, the Caribbean, and Asia. Wage competition and dusty, antiquated machinery were two major reasons textile employment declined after 1970. In the late 1970s and early 1980s, as textile workers and the federal government demanded cleaner factories and import competition required greater productivity, the industry responded with major investments in new machinery. The irony of textile workers' successful effort to force healthier working conditions was that it expedited textile corporations' decisions to purchase more productive machinery; fewer workers were thus needed to manufacture the same amount of goods. Offshore wage competition continued to pressure both textile and apparel firms in the 1990s. Greensboro's first major industrial employer, Cone Mills, in 1970 still produced denim and related products in ten plants inside the city limits or within twenty-five miles of the city. In 1998 only three factories were still open.

The apparel and furniture industries have shared with textiles a labor-intensive production process and low wages. But unlike textiles these industries have been less vulnerable to imports. Since 1970 the number of both apparel and furniture workers has increased, although the industries' share of the total labor force has declined. While the textile industry has become increasingly capital intensive, thus producing fewer jobs, the apparel and furniture sectors have expanded jobs with a relatively low capital investment. For example, during 1987 each additional job in apparel required a $9,000 investment and an additional job in the furniture industry averaged $19,000, while in textiles each additional job required an $82,000 investment (NCDOC 1988, 32). The value added per employee remains far less in apparel and furniture than in most other Tar Heel industries, and they consequently are even lower-wage sectors than textiles. They remain a steady component of North Carolina's manufacturing base. In both 1970 and 1995 apparel and furniture each provided about 10 percent of the state's manufacturing employment.

The manufacture of tobacco products, primarily cigarettes, has been declining in North Carolina. Cigarette manufacturing is often mistakenly viewed, even by North Carolinians, as a major part of the state's economy. In fact, just 4 percent of industrial workers in 1970 and 2 percent in 1995 produced cigarettes. The confusion occurs because tobacco farming has remained a key component of North Carolina's agricultural economy. Cigarette production today is primarily located in the three cities where major manufacturers have plants: the Winston-Salem area, Greensboro, and Concord, northeast of Charlotte. Durham, the historic home of American cigarette manufacturing because of the late nineteenth-century factories established by the Duke family, witnessed the closing of American Tobacco ("Lucky Strikes") in 1987 and the virtual shutdown by 1998 of the remaining Liggett and Myers factory.

As a high-profit and mostly unionized industrial sector, cigarette manufacturing in the 1990s still paid North Carolina's highest hourly wages. But the number of workers producing cigarettes fell to just 12,000 in 1997, a 50 percent drop in ten years. Despite a lingering national stereotype of North Carolina as dominated by cotton mills and cigarette plants, the Tar Heel manufacturing future lay with core industrial corporations that were once associated with midwestern and northeastern states such as Ohio and New York; Firestone, Kelly-Springfield, Dow-Corning, and Campbell's Soup are just a few of the examples. While usually paying somewhat less than R. J. Reynolds or Philip Morris, these new firms offered wages much higher than those of the historic sectors such as textiles, apparel, and furniture (Hughes 1982, 32–34).

Arguably the most embarrassing manufacturing growth sector in North Carolina was poultry processing. The preparation of chickens and turkeys for the consumer market both in the United States and for export is a low-skill, low-paid job. Firms such as Perdue and Carolina Turkey have mostly located in the eastern Piedmont and Coastal Plain, where the poorer infrastructure, including lower-quality K–12 public schools, has discouraged higher-skill, higher-wage core corporations from settling. A spin-off of poultry processing, breaded chicken nuggets, was the product of Imperial Foods, whose locked fire exits led in 1991 to the death of twenty-five workers when an explosion occurred on the plant floor. The surviving workers in Hamlet, a former railroad center in the eastern Piedmont that had not gotten a fair share of North Carolina's new well-paying core industrial jobs, explained after the fire that they hated both the low pay and the harsh working conditions (Davidson 1996, 172–73). But they needed the income because of family obligations, and because of the residents' low levels of formal education, the Hamlet area offered no alternative to Imperial Foods.

The North Carolina Economy:
The Tertiary Sector

The tertiary sector is the formal term for all nonagricultural (primary sector) and nonmanufacturing (secondary sector) employment in an economy. Eighty percent of North Carolina's employment growth between 1970 and 1987 took place in the tertiary sector. Seventy-five percent of Tar Heels outside agriculture worked in the tertiary sector in 1990, compared with 60 percent in 1970. While nonmanufacturing work is less physically taxing and less dangerous than manufacturing employment, its disadvantage is that wage rates are often comparable to the low incomes in peripheral manufacturing and are usually lower than wages in core manufacturing. Consequently, for most North Carolinians, the economy's shift to the tertiary sector has not necessarily meant a rise in living standards. Retail trade, the state's largest single employment category in 1990, grew from 18 percent of the labor force in 1970 to 30 percent in 1990. Its average weekly wage was also the state's lowest (Employment Security Commission 1990, 10–14). Whether as cause or effect, such low retail trade wages explain why the median income of Tar Heel women remains far below that of men.

The other major growth area within the tertiary sector has been the service industry, which expanded from 12 percent to 20 percent of the labor force between 1970 and 1990. Jobs in government, finance and real estate, and transportation and utilities increased in absolute terms between 1970 and 1990, but their share of total state employment did not grow. Overall, employment expansion in the tertiary sector both responds to existing economic growth and can itself be a source of growth. In North Carolina, tertiary sector employment has increased primarily in metro Piedmont counties and other urban centers such as Asheville, Fayetteville, and Wilmington. It has expanded secondarily in smaller cities. The establishment of shopping centers and malls across the state in the 1980s and 1990s was a good example of low-wage tertiary sector employment.

The North Carolina Economy:
The Agricultural Sector

Until the quarter-century after World War II, farming was North Carolina's leading occupation. In 1925, although tenth in population nationally, North Carolina ranked second in the number of farms (Hobbs 1930, 89). It was then and has remained a state of small farms. Between 1945 and 1970 thousands of white and black Tar Heels migrated from the land either to the North or to North Carolina's cities. But many discouraged farmers also remained in rural areas to work in factories, many of which first came to North Carolina in these postwar years. Consequently, the state's rural population, the nation's sixth largest, has a higher percentage at work in non-agricultural jobs than is the case in most states. Indeed, in 1990 North Carolina ranked first in the "rural nonfarm" employment category but twelfth in the number of farms (73,000) (NCDOA 1990). Farms continued to be small; the average size of 142 acres in 1980 ranked forty-fourth in the nation and, after Tennessee, was the smallest of the eleven southern states (NCDOA 1990).

Farmer indebtedness and prices for farm commodities have contributed to economic uncertainty in agriculture. Total farm income for crops, livestock, dairy, and poultry products fluctuated slightly between 1982 and 1995 but, most importantly, did not increase. Although tobacco has remained North Carolina's leading cash crop, and although North Carolina leads the nation in tobacco production, tobacco's percentage of total farm income in the Tar Heel state fell from 30 in 1982 to below 20 in 1995.

By the 1980s, raising poultry had become North Carolina agriculture's second most important area. In 1985 the cash value of broilers and turkeys was nearly as large as that of the state's tobacco crop. But in the 1990s the agricultural product that threatened to make tobacco less controversial was pigs. Centered on the Coastal Plain in Duplin County, about sixty miles southeast of Raleigh, industrial hog farms expanded from 250,000 pigs in 1990 to more than 10 million in 1998. Objections to the fast-growing hog production industry led the General Assembly in 1997 to pass a series of restrictions (see Chapter 3). But by then hogs had replaced tobacco as North Carolina's largest cash crop. This contrasted with 1985, when tobacco was the top product in annual farm income and hogs ranked seventh (NCDOA 1986, 7). But tobacco was still more labor intensive than hogs. In the mid-1990s one-third of the state's farm labor force was directly working in tobacco. These farmers produced nearly 37 percent of all tobacco grown in the United States in 1995, making North Carolina the leading tobacco-producing state in the nation. Income from hogs gave the state the 1994 ranking of second among the fifty states; preliminary rankings for 1998 suggested the state had achieved the distinction of having taken over first place from Iowa. But North Carolina's farm economy in the 1990s also produced leaders and contenders in several other categories beyond to-bacco and hogs. It ranked first nationally in sweet potatoes and turkeys, second in broilers and cucumbers (the latter primarily for pickle produc-tion), and third in peanuts (NCDOA 1997).

Agriculture is not evenly distributed across North Carolina. Indeed, in the mid-1990s the eastern Piedmont and Coastal Plain regions were three times more likely than any other part of North Carolina to have farmers and farmworkers in their labor force. Seven of the ten top-ranking counties in terms of farm income were on the Coastal Plain. One more indication of the surge of hog-based income is that Duplin County, in the heart of the Coastal Plain and home to Murphy Farms, led the state in farm income in the 1990s (NCDOA 1997). Although agriculture is least important to the economies of the metro Piedmont and the western Piedmont, the rapid ex-pansion of broilers in two western Piedmont counties (Wilkes, northwest of Winston-Salem, and Union, southeast of Charlotte) moved them onto the top-ten farm-income list in the mid-1990s. This was a shift from the previous decade, when tobacco production, disproportionately grown in eastern North Carolina, was relatively more fundamental to North Caro-lina's farm economy and all top-ten agriculture counties lay east of Raleigh.

The difficult economics of independent small farming had an impact on the racial and ethnic composition of North Carolina agriculture. Under-capitalized small farmers were, not surprisingly, likely to stop farming in the quarter-century between 1970 and 1995, and these lower-income farm-ers were disproportionately African American. One factor contributing to the greater land loss among black farmers was the racial discrimination that had been practiced, and was acknowledged in a 1990s federal court settle-ment, by white county agricultural agents who were employed with state and federal funds. Wage laborers in farming, especially in labor-intensive areas such as cucumbers and tobacco, were increasingly likely by the 1990s to be Hispanic. On the Coastal Plain, Spanish-language store signs had become commonplace in agricultural centers such as Newton Grove and Faison.

Regional Differences:
Occupations, Unemployment, and Income

North Carolina's per capita income ranked thirty-seventh of the fifty states in 1990. Primarily two factors account for the difference between the state's moderately low ranking in per capita income compared with its nearly rock-bottom standing in average manufacturing wages. First, some of North Carolina's jobs, especially professional work, pay salaries close to the national norm. Second, a higher percentage of Tar Heel adults participate in the labor force than in most states, and the state unemployment rate is lower than the national rate (4 percent versus 5 percent in 1997).

The statewide and national data leave an impression that North Carolina's lower income is compensated for by a lower unemployment rate. But a breakdown of the state's economy by region indicates that this is not the case. The incidence of well-paying jobs and low unemployment correlates positively. During the 1980s and 1990s, for example, the Research Triangle area consistently enjoyed one of the lowest unemployment rates in the United States, often second only to the Stamford, Connecticut, area outside New York City. Meanwhile, per capita income in Wake (Raleigh) and Durham Counties ranked among the state's highest, comparable to that of other metro Piedmont areas. Less than fifty miles to the north, however, eastern Piedmont counties such as Person (Roxboro), Vance (Henderson), or Warren (Warrenton) had more than twice as much unemployment and only two-thirds of Raleigh-Durham's per capita income (OSBM 1997).

Manufacturing employment is another example of the uneven distribution of jobs in North Carolina. Statewide, 27 percent of Tar Heels held manufacturing jobs in 1990. But in the western Piedmont, the state's industrial heartland, 39 percent of the labor force worked in manufacturing. That area historically relied on textiles, apparel, and furniture but in the 1990s also benefited from an influx of higher-paying jobs from the core industrial sector. In 1990, per capita income in the western Piedmont ($12,500) was 11 percent above the state average, and 1997 unemployment (4 percent) was normal for the state. Although the area has been hit by plant closings, out-of-state employers find it attractive because of its centrality in the state and its location along Interstates 85, 40, and 77 and near the Norfolk Southern main rail line. For policymakers the western Piedmont is not in crisis.

The Mountain counties, by contrast, are a problem region. Unemployment (6.5 percent in 1997) has remained above average, and per capita income ($10,800 in 1990) has been below average. Although 31 percent of the labor force was in manufacturing, a disproportionate number of employees worked in low-wage industries. When a Democratic-backed bill to provide tax credits for employers who established new jobs in "distressed" counties became law in 1987, eight of the region's twenty-three counties were eligible.

The eastern Piedmont shares many of the economic problems of the Coastal Plain. As noted above, they are North Carolina's most agricultural regions, the heartland of flue-cured tobacco and hog production. But agriculture employs few persons full time (4 percent in the eastern Piedmont and 7 percent on the Coastal Plain). The eastern Piedmont has a larger manufacturing base than the Coastal Plain, but both rely on low-wage industries such as food products, textiles, and apparel. Unemployment (7 percent in 1997) has been highest in the state in these regions, and per capita income ($11,000 in 1990) has remained below the state average. In 1987 three of the twelve eastern Piedmont counties and nine of the forty-one Coastal Plain counties became eligible for employer state-tax credits for distressed areas.

The metro Piedmont is the center of the state's expanding economy. Based heavily on the provision of services and information, this area is leading North Carolina's transition from manufacturing employment. Agriculture is barely visible in the six-county area. Its manufacturing level is comparable to the Coastal Plain's, but the kinds of nonmanufacturing jobs are vastly different. The large number of professional jobs in the metro Piedmont, compared with the rest of the state, has led to a huge difference in per capita income ($16,100 versus $11,500 in 1990). The unemployment rate in 1997 was 2 percent, compared with the statewide rate of 4 percent. During the 1990s the Research Triangle counties around Raleigh, Durham, and Chapel Hill as well as Mecklenburg County (Charlotte) prospered more than the Triad counties of Forsyth and Guilford (Winston-Salem, Greensboro, and High Point).

Educational Levels

The dilemma facing North Carolina policymakers centers on manufacturing and nonmanufacturing employers' increasing preference for a better-educated labor force. For potential employers this correlates with larger cities offering good roads, airports, and a variety of cultural activities. Consequently, North Carolina increasingly resembles a dual economy, in which economic prosperity seems predictable in the metro Piedmont but much of the rest of the state is left behind. To be sure, within the other regions urban centers with skilled labor forces, transportation, and an active cultural life are more likely to prosper than in nearby rural counties. Examples include Buncombe County (Asheville) in the Mountains, and New Hanover (Wilmington) and Cumberland (Fayetteville) Counties in the east.

Nevertheless, the regional educational differences are striking. Whereas less than 11 percent of western and eastern Piedmont residents were college graduates in 1990, 32 percent of adults living in the metro Piedmont had college degrees. Sixty-four percent in the western Piedmont and 62 percent in the eastern Piedmont were high school graduates, compared with 81 percent in the metro Piedmont. Statewide in 1994, 17 percent of the residents were college graduates, and 70 percent were high school graduates.

The regional differences in the growth of the number of college graduates among the population over age twenty-five—the metro Piedmont changed from 22 percent to 32 percent between 1980 and 1990, while the western and eastern Piedmont's median formal education level barely changed (10 percent in 1980 and 11 percent in 1990)—led to greater cultural gaps between the metro Piedmont and the rest of the state. The data help explain the political battles waged in the late 1990s by traditionalist North Carolinians, primarily native-born Tar Heels, in metro Piedmont counties such as Mecklenburg and Guilford to restrict funding for the allegedly "pro-homosexual life-style" arts programming (see Chapter 2). They viewed the modernizer-supported arts advocates as arrogant (college-educated) outsiders who threatened their cultural values. In areas where traditionalists were heavily outnumbered by modernizer and urban-populist supporters of the arts—for example, Durham and Orange Counties— Broadway-on-tour plays such as *Angels in America*, with open presentation of gay and AIDS issues, were staged without public controversy. This contrasted markedly with Charlotte (Mecklenburg County), where the production of *Angels* sparked the 1997 decision by a social-traditionalist majority on the county commission to cut arts funding, and with Greensboro (Guilford County), where a similar funding cut occurred in 1997 as a result of citizen protest against *La Cage aux Folles*.

Finally, the in-migration of the 1980s and 1990s also changed the religious composition of North Carolina, most discernibly in the metro Piedmont. The number and/or size of Roman Catholic parishes in all six metro

Piedmont counties grew, leading to increased demands for Catholic elementary and high schools. Vietnamese and Hispanic newcomers joined U.S.-born northerners and midwesterners in swelling the number of Catholics in North Carolina. In Durham a Jewish day school opened in the late 1990s to accommodate children from Durham and nearby Chapel Hill.

The gap between the various high-growth counties and the rest of North Carolina grew rather than declined in the decade between the late 1980s and the late 1990s. This reflected, first, North Carolina's loss of labor-intensive manufacturing jobs to settings outside the United States. Second, corporations offering higher-paid, core-sector manufacturing employment and higher-income, high-tech, service-sector jobs tended to locate in the western Piedmont for the former and in the metro Piedmont for the latter. How politicians and big-business leaders sought to make North Carolina attractive to outside investors, from the 1950s, when Governor Hodges helped launch the Research Triangle Park, to the 1990s, when the park maintained its lure, is considered in the next chapter.

5 The Politics of Economic Development

Economic development policy in the southern states, beginning with Mississippi's BAWI (Balance Agriculture with Industry) plan of 1937, had generally included a heavy dose of tax abatement as the best way to lure northern corporations (Cobb 1984). North Carolina prided itself as an exception to the rule. Corporations could and would come to the Tar Heel state without special tax breaks because of an available workforce and an infrastructure that excelled by southern standards (Wood 1986).

From the 1950s through the 1980s North Carolina pursued an economic development strategy based on recruitment of out-of-state employers. The premise of this strategy, the so-called Buffalo Hunt, was that any out-of-state "game" could be no worse, in terms of average industrial wage and working conditions, than North Carolina's core industries of textiles, apparel, and furniture. Individual communities, however, could not afford to be choosy about wage levels, and many rural counties, especially in the Mountains and on the Coastal Plain, became home to low-wage companies. In effect, even firms paying at or near the minimum wage, including textile, apparel, and furniture plants, were welcome in North Carolina.

By the mid-1980s the flow of new industry to North Carolina had slowed considerably. North Carolina joined other southern states in arguing that the era of the Buffalo Hunt was over. The state turned inward, spending more on K–12 public schools and community colleges (see Chapter 3), in hopes that a better-educated labor force could lead North Carolina-based entrepreneurs to invest in manufacturing and better-paid service-sector jobs. The recession of 1990–1991, however, undermined efforts at internally generated jobs. The economic revival beginning in 1992 and 1993 included two features that had been absent in the past: significant tax subsidies provided by city and county governments to in-state or out-of-state corporations who agreed to locate in that specific jurisdiction, and the winning of professional sports franchises with the aid of both local and state subsidies. The latter shift would lead to major-league basketball, football, and hockey franchises all playing in North Carolina by 1998. While not all Tar Heels agreed that major-league sports was important, it allowed state and local politicians and corporate leaders (for example, Charlotte-based NationsBank, which helped finance new sports stadia and arenas) to proclaim that North Carolina had literally become a "big-league" state. It was also a development that few in North Carolina would have predicted just a decade earlier.

From the 1950s to the 1970s

The decline of North Carolina's agricultural economy in the 1950s provided industrial employers with a ready supply of workers who expected wages far less than what northerners were demanding. Unemployment, and thus available labor, was greatest in the rural counties of east and west. Because many farm owners and workers migrated into cities, labor was also available in the urban areas (Mahaffey and Doty 1979; Mahaffey and Doty 1981, 228; Wood 1986).

A major advantage North Carolina had over other southern states was its commitment early in the twentieth century to an active governmental role in the provision of infrastructure (see Chapter 2). For example, the state assumed fiscal responsibility for highways in 1921 and accepted primary responsibility for public school funding in 1931 (Wood 1986, 125–28). Prospective investors found a state government eager to cooperate to ensure a profitable venture. Further, the state adopted an unfriendly stance toward unions. In 1947 North Carolina was among the first southern states to pass right-to-work legislation, which outlawed mandatory worker membership in unions even if a union was the legally recognized collective bargaining agent with management.

In the 1950s Governor Luther Hodges typified the state's simultaneous antiunionism and prodiversification strategies. He worked with private developers beginning in 1955 to establish a research and development park in the area between Durham and Raleigh; the park's lure would be the research links to the University of North Carolina at Chapel Hill, Duke University in Durham, and North Carolina State University in Raleigh. When the project appeared near collapse in 1958, Hodges endorsed the proposal of Wachovia banker Robert Hanes to establish a nonprofit corporation to buy out the original investors. Fellow Wachovia banker and state senator Archie Davis undertook the task of raising the money, which he found surprisingly easy. The connections between growth-oriented business and a supportive state government, coupled with ties to universities, were attractive to public-spirited and affluent North Carolinians. Today the highly successful Research Triangle Park rivals any research and development center in the world. But at the time the good name of Governor Hodges was key to legitimizing the idea (Vogel and Larson 1985, 243–48; Hodges 1962, chap. 9).

After the 1960 election, in which Terry Sanford had been the only southern candidate for statewide office willing to tie his campaign openly to John F. Kennedy's, Kennedy selected Hodges as his secretary of commerce. He repaid his political debt to Sanford, who became governor at the same time that Kennedy assumed the presidency, by agreeing to locate the National Institute for Environmental Health Sciences in the Research Triangle Park. That federal decision and IBM's selection of the park in 1965 for a large corporate expansion were watershed events in the park's success (Vogel and Larson 1985, 254–55).

Simultaneous with his commitment to a new economic development plan for North Carolina, Governor Hodges in 1958 sided with traditionalists in a bitter labor dispute at Harriet-Henderson Yarns, located in the eastern Piedmont town of Henderson. The textile mill sought to break its fourteen-year-old labor contract with the Textile Workers Union of America, and the union went on strike. Hodges sent the National Guard and the Highway Patrol to Henderson, and they allowed strikebreakers to cross a weakened picket line (Hodges 1962, chap. 10; Frankel 1986; Clark 1997).

Antiunionism coupled with low wages and few strikes made North

Carolina a low-cost production location. The state enhanced its attractiveness to business in the late 1950s with the establishment of customized industrial training. One of the first states to develop made-to-order job training in 1957, North Carolina through the 1990s maintained one of the nation's largest budgets to meet employer requests for trained workers. Customized industrial training has constituted a direct subsidy to industry, in which the state's community college system pays instructors to provide specific job training for prospective employees of a new firm. The training service is available for any firm that provides at least twelve new jobs.

The message from the 1950s on was clear. North Carolina promised relatively low wages, few unions, and few strikes. Moreover, it was willing to subsidize employer costs through on-site training. Wanting to keep jobs in the nonmetropolitan areas, the state's industrial recruiters emphasized the virtues of decentralized manufacturing (Mahaffey and Doty 1981, 228). A 1957 *New York Times* advertising supplement on North Carolina was headlined "Labor Ready, Willing and Able." Governor Hodges stressed the stability of the rural labor force and its accessibility due to the state's highway network. According to Hodges, industry could "locate away from congestion and at the same time . . . draw upon a large and industrious labor supply that is mostly rural." As Hodges's successor in the early 1960s, Governor Sanford spoke of Tar Heel workers' willingness to provide a "full day's work for a full day's pay" (quotations from Wood 1986, 163, 242).

Until the 1970s the state's recruitment program to bring industry to both urban and rural North Carolina was successful. Both urban and rural North Carolina won new jobs, and core industries such as machinery or bus production paying higher wages than the state average were more likely than ever to locate in the state (Doty and Mahaffey 1979, 7–9). The labor-intensive industries that settled primarily in rural counties required little skill from workers. Industrialists in these areas did not worry about residents' educational attainment levels, literacy rates, or quality public schools (Rosenfeld 1983, 2).

As long as the wages of prospective firms were competitive with prevailing wages, no local conflict emerged. In the 1970s, however, the question of whether communities should welcome a firm that paid above the local average erupted into numerous debates across North Carolina. In general, traditionalists said no and modernizers said yes. How Tar Heel business divided itself—into traditionalist and modernizer perspectives—has provided an understanding of the ideological conflict surrounding North Carolina's economic development.

Ideological Conflict over Development Policy

Until the 1970s the issue of wages did not loom as a major source of conflict among North Carolina business people. But after a vigorous debate among academicians during 1975 as to why North Carolina's manufacturing wage rates were fiftieth in the nation (Malizia, Crow, et al. 1975; Morse 1978; Stuart 1981, 248–49), gubernatorial candidate Jim Hunt decided in 1976 to make the raising of industrial wages an explicit plank in his campaign platform. Hunt introduced an issue that had not previously been seriously discussed in North Carolina political campaigns, even though higher wages, like apple pie, was hardly a matter that politicians wanted to oppose publicly. Subsequently, in his 1992 and 1996 campaigns for governor, Hunt would adapt to the more probusiness mood in the nation and in North Carolina by soft-pedaling any interest in real wage increases for workers. But in 1976, seeking to take the governor's office away from Republicans, Hunt campaigned on and his corporate backers supported, if not enthusiastically, his calls for improved wages (*North Carolina Magazine* 1993).

Who were Hunt's major financial supporters? Would they be likely to resist higher wages in North Carolina? The presumption behind campaign contributions is that donors gain access to candidates and that candidates' political programs bear some resemblance to the political values of financial supporters. If this is true, then Jim Hunt the modernizer politician par excellence of the 1970s and 1980s should have been backed by modernizer business people. Similarly, traditionalist business people should have contributed disproportionately to a traditionalist politician such as Jesse Helms.

The clearest indication of the financial supporters of Hunt and Helms emerges from campaign reports of their race for the U.S. Senate in 1984, and of each candidate's contributors during the 1970s. The 1984 contributions are from the $26 million campaign that was at the time the most expensive in U.S. Senate history. The analysis examined in-state contributors only.

Modernizer businesses have a self-interest in economic growth and change. Traditionalist businesses fear the competition that might result from widespread economic growth. Construction, transportation, and real estate firms are typical modernizers. Textile, apparel, and furniture firms, which historically have relied on lower wages and lower levels of capitalization, are typical traditionalists. If these businesses indeed followed their self-interests, modernizer firms should have backed Hunt more strongly and traditionalists should have supported Helms.

A comparison of Helms's contributors in his first two Senate races (1972 and 1978) with Hunt's supporters in his campaigns for lieutenant governor in 1972 and governor in 1976 shows a striking difference in economic base. Forty percent of Helms's dollars came from the textile and furniture industries, while just 5 percent of Hunt's came from those industries. Twenty percent of Hunt's money came from the construction and transportation industries, compared with 3 percent for Helms (Luebke, Peters, and Wilson 1986).

Examining $1,000 contributors during 1983 and 1984, the data reveal clear contrasts among three business areas: manufacturing, construction, and real estate. Helms received 60 percent more funding from manufacturers than did Hunt. But in the change-oriented fields of construction and real estate, Hunt received two and one-half times the amount of money raised by Helms (Hall 1985a).

A similar pattern emerged in a study of contributions to Helms and Hunt in their separate campaigns during the 1970s (Luebke, Peters, and Wilson 1986; Luebke 1990a, 74). This clear disinclination of business modernizers to support a traditionalist like Helms was less evident in the 1990s, partially a consequence of the rightward shift of national and state political debates. For example, WRAL-TV and Durham Bulls owner Jim Goodman contributed $1,500 in 1996 to Senator Helms's reelection effort and did not send a contribution to challenger Harvey Gantt. Higher wages, no tax cuts, and a supportive stance of the role of government—the essence of both Gantt's 1990 and 1996 campaigns and Hunt's 1976 campaign for governor—were no longer attractive to most Tar Heel corporate leaders in the late 1990s.

The causality of the relationship between business sector support and candidate ideology was not clear. But the campaign contributions of the 1970s and 1980s revealed an ideological distinction. "Growth machine" business people backed Hunt, since they were not threatened by a booming economy and a related call for higher wages for industrial workers. By contrast, the textile and apparel industrialists who were more likely to support Helms had reason to fear economic development, because a labor shortage that resulted from a job surplus could force them to raise their local wages. Unlike the realtors or contractors who were more sympathetic to Hunt, textile and apparel leaders were often competing with labor markets in Third World societies where wages were extremely low.

Modernizers versus Traditionalists: The Late 1970s to the Late 1980s

The industrial recruitment division in the North Carolina Department of Commerce faced slightly different political environments under Jim Hunt's first two terms from 1977 to 1985, Jim Martin's two terms from 1985 to 1993, and Hunt's final two terms beginning in 1993. The early Hunt administrations wanted the Commerce Department to hug the middle ground between traditionalists on one hand and Hunt's "left-wing" supporters—the pro-union populists—on the other. Modernizers did not seek to overturn North Carolina's long-standing reputation as an antiunion, low-wage, and probusiness state. But they did wish to welcome all new firms, regardless of their wages or collective bargaining arrangements with unions. Like other industrial recruitment offices, North Carolina's sought to match counties with industry needs. Beginning in the early 1970s under Governor Bob Scott, state officials had encouraged counties, towns, and cities to develop a local recruitment office that cooperated with the state Department of Commerce (Friedlein 1986, 48).

Martin differed from the early Hunt in his open opposition to organized labor. In 1987, for example, at the annual luncheon of the NCCBI, whose members have always constituted a who's who of Tar Heel big business, Martin expressed his concern that North Carolina with increased unionization might "lose the confidence of business decision-makers" by creating an "anti-business climate" (Luebke 1990a, 88–89). Interestingly, even the later Hunt, while slipping away from the commitment to higher wages that he had made in his first term as governor, would never engage in the hardline antiunionism of a Republican. His decade-long support from the state AFL-CIO meant that he, like almost all Democrats running for statewide office, would not blatantly oppose unions (see Chapter 6).

One economic recruitment controversy during Hunt's first term took place in Person County, an eastern Piedmont county just north of Durham. State Commerce Department officials in 1977 were showing Brockway Glass, a Pennsylvania-based corporation with unionized plants, a site in Roxboro, the county seat. When the local economic development commission learned that Brockway's unionized wages were 30 percent above the county's prevailing wage, it passed a resolution "disinviting" Brockway (*News and Observer* 1977a). For the commission majority it was better to pass up several hundred jobs than risk the disruption of social and economic relations (Luebke, McMahon, and Risberg 1979). A local banker declared that the only problem with the Brockway episode was that it had become public. The state recruiters expressed a desire to avoid such conflicts in the future by redlining those counties whose business and political leaders did not want higher-wage industry (Wood 1986, 167–68).

A similar incident occurred in December 1977 in Cabarrus County, northeast of Charlotte, where Philip Morris had selected a site to build a cigarette-manufacturing factory. When it became known that the tobacco firm intended to pay unionized wages high above the county average, the management of Cannon Mills, located in the nearby company town of Kannapolis, objected to the new plant, fearing wage competition (*News and Observer* 1977c). But public opinion in Cabarrus County had been mobilized in favor of the new jobs. In a western Piedmont traditionalist county where political demonstrations were rare, 4,000 citizens turned out for a profactory rally. In this case Cannon was unable to muster sufficient support on the economic development commission to overturn the majority endorsement of the Philip Morris investment. Symbolically, Jim Hunt made a much-publicized phone call to Philip Morris's chairman to urge the company not to withdraw from the county (Luebke, McMahon, and Risberg 1979; Wood 1986).

The essence of traditionalist fears of unions became apparent when business people in and around Roxboro were interviewed in 1979 about the prospect of unionization in their individual counties. Universally, the local elite felt that unions, often labeled "militant labor organizations," were a disadvantage to the community. In one businessman's view, unions represented an outside power base that would give the county a bad reputation in future recruitment efforts. The belief that unions might challenge the status quo was key. The local elite ignored the probability that unionized jobs would increase workers' wages and, through a multiplier effect, benefit the county economy and even produce additional jobs. The emphasis on social stability rather than social change is common to traditionalist ideology (Mahaffey and Doty 1979, 80–82). Highlighting this issue, a Charlotte-based antiunion consultant told a 1970s university audience that allowing unions in a plant was like letting the fox guard the chicken coop (Dowd 1976).

While recognizing that Governor Martin was openly antiunion and Governor Hunt was neutral on the question, the state Department of Commerce learned to steer clear of conflict by allowing a local county to turn down firms whose wages were too high. But under either governor the department remained true to its job to foster economic growth by refusing to turn down an out-of-state unionized firm out of hand. The department merely sought to find an accepting location.

Guilford County provided an example in the early 1990s of a metro Piedmont county whose business leaders were not unanimous on the virtues of high-wage industry. A modernizer-oriented county commission was pleased to learn that United Air Lines was considering placing a major maintenance operation at the Piedmont Triad airport. Both the Greensboro–High Point area (Guilford) and nearby Winston-Salem (Forsyth) had lost numerous manufacturing jobs in the 1980s. Unlike both the Research Triangle area and Mecklenburg County, the Triad counties did not enjoy an influx of high-tech, high-wage research and development jobs, so most elected officials believed that employing well-paid unionized mechanics at United's maintenance center would be an obvious plus.

But a High Point-based employer group felt differently about the possible pressure from such United employees upon nearby lower-paid Guilford County workers. To the dismay of local and state economic recruiters, the High Point traditionalists wrote to United headquarters in Chicago asking the airline to take their high-paid union jobs to another state. United obliged, establishing the maintenance center in Indianapolis. In all likelihood the antiunion letter was less crucial than the substantial package of tax incentives that Indiana offered United. For local modernizer officials worried that Greensboro was not growing fast enough (*News and Record* 1997b), the traditionalist objection reflected insufficient understanding of how high-paid union jobs could have a positive multiplier effect on economic growth in the Triad.

In the early 1990s still another political conflict over economic development emerged between traditionalists and modernizers. Following the 1990–91 recession Forsyth County and Winston-Salem officials, worried about the loss of both manufacturing jobs (for example, R. J. Reynolds in cigarettes and Hanes in apparel) and office headquarters (R. J. Reynolds/Nabisco had relocated to Atlanta) in their county/city jurisdictions, started to offer local subsidies for both out-of-state and in-state corporations if they would select Forsyth/Winston-Salem for expanded operations. Among the beneficiaries of local government subsidies were Pepsico, for a large warehouse and distribution center, and Southern National Bank, a mid-sized North Carolina bank that relocated its corporate headquarters from Lumberton, a small regional town along Interstate 95 on the Coastal Plain. The subsidy strategy soon was adopted by neighboring Guilford County and Greensboro. While the subsidies were often relatively small, such as $50,000 or $100,000, some citizen voices were raised as to why such "sweeteners" were being offered at all. The conflict became more open when local corporations such as the Khoury Company, which owned the Four Seasons Holiday Inn and the adjoining convention center, asked for a $2 million subsidy to expand its operations in Guilford County (*News and Record* 1993).

Interestingly, the local subsidies initially were restricted to counties, it appeared, that were in the circulation areas of the *Winston-Salem Journal* and the *Greensboro News and Record*. Local news coverage in one county seemed to encourage county commissioners in a neighboring county to try their hand at subsidies as an economic recruitment tool. Feeling the pressure to bring in jobs, some counties offered subsidies even when their county commissioners, ideologically traditionalist, had serious philosophical objections to the practice. The issue came to a head when a Winston-Salem trial lawyer, arguing the traditionalist objection that such subsidies amounted to welfare for big corporations, claimed in a 1993 lawsuit that the tax breaks also violated the North Carolina state constitution. William Maready cited the constitution's clause that tax dollars had to be spent on a "public purpose" (Manuel 1997).

Maready won his case in lower court. But in 1995 the state supreme court disagreed, in an unusual decision that pitted the state's five Democrats against the two Republicans. The majority sounded like modernizers in ruling that such tax subsidies, whether from a local government or the state, were a defensible expenditure. The minority, in the language of traditionalists, said that government should not use tax dollars to provide direct benefits to a private enterprise (Manuel 1997, 30).

The Maready decision had the effect of encouraging local subsidies in all of the state's regions. Cabarrus County, site of the 1977 battle over whether to welcome Phillip Morris's cigarette factory, in 1996 made one of the state's most controversial decisions in attracting a new factory from multinational corporation Dow-Corning. The county agreed to pay back to Dow-Corning over a five-year period the equivalent of the corporation's property taxes. Because Dow-Corning was actually paying its taxes, observers believed this unusual arrangement would, in the light of the supreme court's Maready decision, meet constitutional muster (McLaughlin 1997).

Under the third Hunt administration the state Department of Commerce began repositioning North Carolina in the national Buffalo Hunt that was growing more costly for states competing with one another for national or international investment. Arguing that other southern states, especially South Carolina and Virginia, were winning the hunt for new corporate investment, Hunt argued that investment subsidies needed to be available in all 100 North Carolina counties. Tax credits that had initially been developed for the state's most distressed counties in 1987 (see below) were expanded via a tier system. The legislation was termed the Bill Lee Act, in honor of the late Duke Power executive who had been a member of Governor Hunt's Economic Development Commission. As part of the 1996 legislation the Commerce Department developed a complicated methodology for determining economic well-being and placed each county into one of five tiers. In the metro Piedmont counties, the core of tier five, the state's subsidy to investors was small; in the tier one counties, located either on the Coastal Plain and in the eastern Piedmont or the Mountains, the state's tax credit per new job in some cases exceeded $12,000. In 1997 the General Assembly expanded the Bill Lee Act to make administrative offices in places such as the metro Piedmont also eligible for subsidies.

Critics of this Hunt administration policy were primarily in the state house: traditionalist Republicans who opposed the subsidies on principle, and populist Democrats who believed government subsidies should be directed toward the less-affluent, not big corporations. But most legislators, including traditionalists in both parties, seemed persuaded that North Carolina had little choice but to become a big player in the subsidies game. Some out-of-state legislators, notably a Republican state senator from Ohio, sought to organize a national campaign against such programs, arguing that corporations were simply blackmailing states and playing one state against another. The Corporation for Enterprise Development (CED), a national research group with a North Carolina office, agreed and suggested that state government would do better to invest in infrastructure, especially improved public schools in the low-wealth counties, rather than to provide direct tax breaks to corporations (CED 1994). This CED report criticized North Carolina and other states for a scattershot policy that failed to ask two basic questions: Was a specific dollar subsidy to a for-profit firm the best way to ensure that residents of all the state's regions would have access to well-paying jobs? Would the firm not have invested in North Carolina anyway, without that certain amount of taxpayer subsidy (CED 1994; Whitman 1997)?

The Problem of Rural Economic Development

During the fall of 1986 Republicans and Democrats alike took steps to attack the issue of economic decline, especially in the Coastal Plain, eastern Piedmont, and Mountain regions. Governor Martin's Republican administration, through the state Department of Commerce, issued its report in September 1986. Secretary of Commerce Howard Haworth, whose background as a furniture executive symbolized Martin's commitment to traditionalist values, drafted the Republican report, known as North Carolina's blueprint for economic development. Lieutenant Governor Jordan, in effect speaking for the state's Democrats, established the Commission on Jobs and Economic Growth, whose work paralleled that of the Commerce Department. Chaired by Jim Melvin, a modernizer Democrat, banker, and former mayor of Greensboro, Jordan's commission released a second, more comprehensive analysis, full of specific legislative proposals, in November 1986. Because the Democrats dominated the General Assembly, Jordan's rather than Martin's proposals became law in 1987.

The two reports shared a common understanding of the economic problems facing the state's rural areas. Further, they both emphasized investment in education, transportation, and water resources as the key to economic development of these areas (O'Connor 1987b). The reports differed in what role the state should play in such an effort. The Democrats recommended the creation of a North Carolina rural economic development center, to be funded by the General Assembly, which would seek to shepherd economic growth in rural North Carolina. The Democrats also proposed a tax credit for businesses that located jobs in any of the state's twenty distressed counties. The eligible list would vary from year to year but would be based on unemployment rates and average wage rates. For 1987 the eligible counties were disproportionately on the Coastal Plain and in the Mountains.

Reflecting a greater commitment to traditionalist "free enterprise" ideology than Jordan's proposal did, Martin's recommendations did not call for either a new state agency or specific tax credits. Rather, they emphasized traditionalism's antitax philosophy by seeking abolition of the taxes on inventory and intangibles. Labeling these two taxes on business and the wealthy "intrinsically counterproductive," the Republicans argued that economic development would result from a less-restrictive tax environment. Finally, the Republican report placed more emphasis on local initiatives and less on state action (NCDOC 1986, 1, 10).

Both Democratic proposals became law during the 1987 session. In supporting the recommendations of Jordan's commission, the General Assembly merely followed party lines. In fact, policymakers disagreed on whether the greater state action promoted by the Democrats would provide better results than the Republican plan (Luger 1986, 214). But the two reports reflected the difference between the application of Democratic modernizer ideology and the blend of modernism and traditionalism that characterized the mainstream Republicanism of the Martin administration.

A decade after its inception, the Rural Economic Development Center continued to receive funding from the General Assembly. In 1997–98, for example, the center received a $7 million appropriation, most of which was to be funneled to local economic development organizations. But the millions in appropriations over a decade could not overcome the fundamental differences in infrastructure quality between the six metro Piedmont counties and most of the higher-wage western Piedmont industrial counties, on one hand, and the rural counties of the Mountains, eastern Piedmont, and the Coastal Plain, on the other hand (McLaughlin and Skinner 1997). Besides their location near major airports and interstate highways, the metro Piedmont counties had qualitatively better public schools, as well as nearby major universities and colleges. The urban/suburban quality of life arguably matched that of any nonsouthern city, and concerns about crime were probably less than in other non-South city settings.

Meanwhile, the western Piedmont was full of long-standing industrial towns, so that literally generations of residents were used to the discipline of the factory (cf. Botsch 1981). In any western Piedmont community a core industry such as truck manufacturing or chemicals could replace a peripheral-sector cotton mill, but the labor force was nonetheless well socialized to the requirements of factory production. This gave the western Piedmont an important advantage over other small-town and rural regions of the state, even though, in terms of years of formal education, western Piedmont residents did not appear that much better educated than other (non–metro Piedmont) Tar Heels. Further, manufactured products could be quickly moved along trunk rail lines or along any of three interstate highways, and virtually every western Piedmont county was within a two-hour drive of a major airport.

Over the years North Carolina had also begun offering various indirect subsidies to corporations. Because a corporation could benefit from these subsidies by locating in any of the state's 100 counties, the effect of these government programs was to reduce the likelihood that any corporation would locate in a "poorer infrastructure" county. For example, customized job training by community colleges has meant that the Tar Heel taxpayer, not incoming corporations, has paid for workers' on-the-job skill building. Second, industrial revenue bonds, first authorized by the General Assembly in 1977, allowed localities to float industrial bonds for business investment. This enabled the corporation to pay lower interest rates via the tax-free locality than if the corporation tried to sell the bonds directly. Third, corporations often directly benefited from water and sewer lines, an access road, or even an interstate highway interchange that local or state government was willing to build in order to attract the would-be investor. A visible example of such subsidies is the state DOT's construction for the Carolina Panthers of an access road from their stadium to Charlotte's uptown highway system. Less obvious to the public is the fact that the city of Charlotte donated the downtown property on which the Panthers football franchise built its stadium.

The Business of Major-League Sports

One of the clearest areas in which rural North Carolina has stood virtually no chance to attract economic investment is major-league sports. The exception has been NASCAR racing sites. Professional sports are of course big business. But within North Carolina the issue of subsidies for these corporations has generated much more controversy than the various tax breaks available from the state Commerce Department to nonsport corporations. For modernizers, tax breaks to sports franchises are an unambiguous plus because of the multiplier effect, including the subjective benefits of an area like Charlotte or the Triad becoming "major league." For strong traditionalists on the right and populists on the left, sports subsidies are unmitigated corporate welfare (cf. Glasberg and Skidmore 1997).

The initial excitement surrounding Charlotte's winning of a National Basketball Association franchise in 1989 was so great that the city's construction of a basketball coliseum and a lease very favorable to the team owner generated no controversy whatsoever. In Durham, meanwhile, the owner of the Durham Bulls, a successful class-A farm team for the Atlanta Braves, insisted in the late 1980s that the city-owned Durham Athletic Park was too rundown. He convinced the Durham County Commission to hold a March 1990 referendum for a new $10 million stadium. Possibly a precursor to later controversies about subsidies for professional sports teams in North Carolina, a majority of Durham voters opposed the bonds. In 1992 the city of Durham nevertheless agreed to build a stadium for new team owner Jim Goodman, who also owned WRAL-TV. The issuance of bonds through certificates of participation was legal, even though it violated the spirit of the 1990 referendum result. New stadium advocates believed that Goodman would move the team out of downtown Durham and even out of Durham County unless the new stadium was constructed. Opponents would have dared him to try, unwilling to believe the city's political-economic future depended on a government subsidy for a sports stadium. While the Durham Bulls Athletic Park was an immediate success when it opened in April 1995, referendum opponents received some satisfaction in the prior 1993 city election by defeating the mayor and city council member most responsible for the construction project.

The Carolina Panthers' arrival as a National Football League franchise in 1995 was accompanied by the indirect state and city subsidies mentioned above. The citizen reaction in Charlotte against professional sports did not materialize until early 1997, when George Shinn, owner of the Charlotte Hornets basketball team, declared that the city-owned coliseum, built before the advent of high-profit luxury boxes, was no longer an acceptable home court. Shinn reasoned that his net profit was too small after paying the Hornets players their large salaries. He suggested that the city build a new arena in uptown Charlotte, near the headquarters of NationsBank and First Union Bank and the Panthers' football stadium. When local government, with support from modernizer business leaders, tentatively agreed to support such a proposal, the reaction from many citizens and some elected officials was swift and negative. The view that millionaires did not deserve taxpayer subsidies primarily came from Republican-leaning traditionalists, although some Democratic populists joined in the protest as well. The criticism of the new public arena as corporate welfare persisted in Charlotte even as continued private-public negotiations led to a new possible agreement with an increased private share and a reduced taxpayer share. Frustrated with the public opposition, Shinn finally withdrew his uptown proposal (*Charlotte Observer* 1997a).

Modernizer business leaders in Raleigh received an ambivalent public re-action when, also in early 1997, they sought to build enthusiasm for a large combination basketball-hockey arena that would allow a National Hockey League franchise to come to the capital city. Because of a pattern similar to Charlotte's, in which traditionalist Republicans opposed to government subsidy led the charge with support from populist Democrats, modernizer politicians were forced to build a more modest arena. But subsidized major-league hockey did come to Raleigh (*News and Observer* 1997e).

The third sports-as-economic-development controversy of 1997 came in the twelve-county Triad region over the issue of major-league baseball. Modernizers in Winston-Salem (for example, at Wachovia Bank) and in Greensboro (for example, at Jefferson Pilot insurance) were convinced that an available new baseball stadium could convince an existing major-league franchise in one of the low-profit, small-market cities such as Pitts-burgh or Minneapolis to relocate to the Triad. Their plan was that all residents of the two metro Piedmont and the surrounding ten western Piedmont counties should support the stadium construction with a tem-porary six-month, one-cent increase in the general sales tax, from 6 percent to 7 percent.

The Triad case also suggested, as seen above in the Charlotte and Raleigh examples, the gap in economic development thinking between modernizer corporate leaders and politicians on one side and, on the other side, the many citizens and elected officials, especially county commissioners, who adhered to economic traditionalism. Interestingly, each group tended to label itself conservative, and most of the actors on both sides of this value conflict were usually part of the growing Tar Heel Republican electorate.

In the western Piedmont counties on the periphery of Forsyth and Guil-ford, a stampede of county commissioners began voting to remove their re-spective counties from any referendum. While the general sales tax propo-sal to subsidize a baseball stadium had sailed through the state senate with only limited if vocal opposition from some traditionalist GOP senators, the bill immediately hit rough waters at the house Finance Committee. Opposi-tion from a bipartisan coalition of antitax traditionalist Republicans and anti-sales-tax (as a regressive tax) populist Democrats stalled the measure. Ultimately, the state house passed and the state senate accepted a watered-down tax bill: a twenty-five-year, 1 percent increase in the prepared food tax for Forsyth and Guilford Counties only. If the proposal passed in a May 1998 bicounty voter referendum, then the prepared food tax revenues plus a fifty-cents-per-ticket surcharge would provide the revenues for a $140 million taxpayer subsidy of a $210 million Triad baseball stadium. Symbolizing the bicounty modernizer commitment to the major-league baseball project, the 1997 legislation required that the stadium be constructed on the Forsyth-Guilford line, just west of the Piedmont Triad airport. In fact, voters in both counties decisively defeated the tax proposal in the May 1998 referendum.

The Reality of Two North Carolinas

The late-1990s commitment by the Hunt administration to expand economic subsidies even in the metro Piedmont had the backhanded effect of making it less likely that corporations would invest in those rural counties in western and eastern North Carolina that most desperately needed good-paying jobs. It did not seem to make sense for a major investor with high-paying, high-tech jobs to settle, for example, 100 miles northeast of the Research Triangle area in a poor Coastal Plain county, when the state would subsidize job creation in the Triangle counties or elsewhere in the metro Piedmont.

Only specially crafted, costly tax-incentive packages, the sort that North Carolina historically had been unwilling to offer to individual firms, could likely induce major employers to settle in the poorer counties. Perhaps over time, public education improvements as well as other infrastructural advances, such as natural gas or sewer lines, might make rural North Carolina counties more attractive to investors—without the state providing each prospective large employer with a customized tax break. But in the short run the preference of most out-of-state corporations for selecting areas of the state that already benefited from better infrastructure and low unemployment appeared to ensure the reality of two North Carolinas for long into the twenty-first century.

Organized Labor:
Still Not a Major Player

V. O. Key's 1949 comprehensive study of southern politics, even though it was written a half-century ago, has provided a major benchmark against which to compare the present. One of Key's major predictions was that further southern industrialization would lead to an eventual breakdown of Jim Crow racial segregation but would also lead to increased strength for organized labor. As the southern state in the late 1940s with the highest percentage of employees in manufacturing, North Carolina should have been, in Key's view, fertile ground for unionization (Key 1949). A fifty-year retrospective on southern politics leaves no doubt that Key was correct on the first point but wrong on the second.

Consider, for example, North Carolina politics from 1972 to the present. When state government officials in North Carolina undertake long-range planning, the business community is automatically included as a planning partner. But this is not so for labor. Whether under Democratic or Republican governors, modernizer or traditionalist ideology, organized labor has not succeeded in winning a regular seat at the table. During Jim Hunt's four terms a token labor representative would sometimes be included on commissions otherwise dominated by corporation executives, politicians, university professors, and other politically active upper middle-class citizens. The denial of equal status to North Carolina unions contrasts sharply with other major states outside the South. Even though unions nationwide lost members in the 1980s and 1990s (*Durham Morning Herald* 1988; Applebome 1996), planning at the federal level or in states such as Massachusetts, Illinois, or California still follows the pattern established in the heyday of organized labor following World War II (Goldman and Luebke 1985). There the policy players have been business, government, and labor. In North Carolina the third seat has usually been assigned to the state's major universities.

Labor's status as outsider is regularly evident in the weeks before a North Carolina general election. In October 1996 incumbent GOP congressmen David Funderburk and Fred Heinemann, who had benefited from the national pro-Republican voting of 1994 and had won upset elections in the two Research Triangle-area congressional districts, sought to hold on to their seats by slamming their Democratic opponents as beholden to "corrupt labor bosses" (Smar 1997). In the 1984 Helms-Hunt U.S. Senate race, Jesse Helms sought to prove that Jim Hunt was a "closet liberal." He made his point by running a 30-second TV spot that simply scrolled across the screen the names and amounts of labor union contributions to the Hunt campaign. Borrowing from a pro-union advertising campaign of the International Ladies Garment Workers Union, the Helms piece ended with the line, "Look for the union label."

These two political events—quiet planning meetings in a state office building and high-stakes negative campaign advertising—have more in common than meets the eye. Both presume that organized labor has no legitimate place in state politics. Unlike regions of the United States where union power is institutionalized and where, indeed, unions are sometimes viewed as part of a power elite that opposes political change, North Carolina is ruled by the belief that unions are an unnecessary disruption of the routine affairs of business and government.

Traditionalist business people, still a key force in the state's textile, apparel, and furniture industries, question whether unions have ever served a useful purpose in American or North Carolina history. Their emphasis on individualism leads to the conclusion that unionism constitutes inappropriate interference in the employer-employee relationship. Free enterprise flourishes best when unfettered by "third party interference" (Judkins

1986, 164–66). Traditionalists feel strongly that unions should stay weak in North Carolina.

Modernizer business people in the Tar Heel state disproportionately represent capital-intensive (and usually high-profit) industries such as cigarette production or paper products, as well as nonmanufacturing growth sectors such as banking or biotechnology. These modernizers, like traditionalists, also dislike unions, but their logic follows a different route. They see unions as anachronistic in today's era of enlightened management. Further, in the 1980s and 1990s, modernizers recognized an opportunity to fight off unions in North Carolina because of labor's weakened position nationwide. However, unlike traditionalists, modernizers have developed a pragmatic attitude toward unions in the workplace. If workers insist on union representation, modernizers accept the union as a necessary part of doing business (Goldman and Luebke 1985).

Traditionalists, by contrast, have fought unions hard. In some cases the National Labor Relations Board (NLRB) has ruled decisively that Tar Heel industrialists flagrantly violated federal labor law (*Charlotte Observer* 1997h). For example, after Fieldcrest-Cannon in Kannapolis and nearby plants in the long-standing western Piedmont textile region narrowly defeated a union drive (3,312 to 3,210) in 1991, the textile workers union filed numerous complaints about unfair labor practices against the company. Although the union (renamed UNITE in the interim) needed five years to take the challenge through the NLRB legal process and subsequent Fieldcrest-Cannon appeals, the federal courts ruled in 1996 that workers' rights to a fair organizing election had been violated. The courts ruled that workers were entitled to a new election, with restrictions placed on the company's behavior. Specifically, UNITE representatives were allowed unimpeded access to all workers in the multiplant bargaining unit, and Fieldcrest-Cannon was required to read aloud to all plant workers their admission that the company had violated federal labor laws in the 1991 election.

Fieldcrest-Cannon once again narrowly defeated UNITE in September 1997. But when the company shortly thereafter sold its Kannapolis-area plants to another firm, Pillowtex, some workers who had opposed UNITE began to have second thoughts. UNITE in December 1997 asked Pillowtex to agree to another union election (*Charlotte Observer* 1997h). It remained a classic labor-management conflict in the North Carolina textile industry.

The biggest North Carolina labor battle of the 1960s and the 1970s involved J. P. Stevens, a major textile industrialist subsequently bought out by West Point-Pepperel. UNITE's predecessor union, the Amalgamated Clothing and Textile Workers (ACTWU), won an election in August 1974 at Stevens plants in Roanoke Rapids, a small eastern North Carolina town off Interstate 95 just south of the Virginia line (Mullins and Luebke 1982). Not until 1980 did the union finalize the contract with Stevens. ACTWU won the six-year battle after filing unfair collective bargaining charges against Stevens before the NLRB and organizing a national consumer boycott against the company's products. One of ACTWU's clever slogans was "Don't Sleep With J. P. Stevens," a reference to the company's product line of bed sheets and pillow cases. But the union contract was not signed until 1980, after ACTWU undertook a "corporate campaign." The union persuaded sympathetic institutional stockholders and other pro-union advocacy groups to demand that outside Stevens directors change the no-contract position of Stevens's top management. The resultant pressure, increased by press accounts naming the recalcitrant directors, forced Stevens to settle (Mullins and Luebke 1984).

But the Stevens victory did not lead to a string of successful organizing drives across North Carolina. On the contrary, the unpublicized understanding between traditionalists and modernizers—that the Tar Heel state prospers best if unions remain weak—held sway in the 1980s and 1990s. Throughout this period North Carolina ranked forty-ninth in level of unionization among private-sector workers. Paralleling the national decline in union membership, the percentage of Tar Heel unionized workers dropped from 9 in 1982 to 4 in 1994 (Troy and Shaeflin 1985; Applebome 1996). To be sure, one reason for the decline is that job growth in North Carolina and in the United States is heavily in the service sector, such as retail employment. Especially in the South, hardly any retail employees work under union contracts. But whether in 1982 or 1994, North Carolina's ranking placed it forty-ninth, ahead of only South Carolina. Even Mississippi had a somewhat higher percentage of unionized workers than North Carolina.

The strength of unions is concentrated in large corporations that have branch plants in North Carolina. The leaders of these companies tend to be modernizers rather than traditionalists. For example, utilities (Bell South), breweries (Miller), paper mills (Georgia Pacific), cigarette manufacturers (Lorillard), truck producers (Freightliner), and grocery chains (Kroger) are the most heavily organized sectors of the North Carolina economy. While executives of such firms may not like unions, they are, in most cases, accustomed to labor-management agreements in other states.

Unionized firms are disproportionately located in larger cities. In many rural counties of North Carolina not a single business is unionized. Two factors help to explain the urban concentration. First, the types of large firms least hostile to unions are more likely to locate in metropolitan rather than rural areas because they wish to be close to population centers (for example, breweries or supermarkets) or because they desire easy access to airports, interstate highways, and railroad trunk lines. Second, in metropolitan areas, employers have less direct social control over their workers. The argument that a union will damage a local economy irrevocably by raising wages or by ruining a town's reputation for harmonious labor relations is simply less persuasive to workers who live in the city (Wood 1986, 164). Such antiunion sentiments are common in the small-town newspapers that dot North Carolina. But few if any of the state's major metropolitan newspapers (Luebke 1987b) ever take blatant antiunion stances, even though newspaper management is surely grateful that newspaper unions no longer exist in the state. (Before the Knight-Ridder chain bought the afternoon daily, the *Charlotte News*, its reporters were members of the American Newspaper Guild).

North Carolina's industrial recruiters, part of the state Department of Commerce, have continued to remind national and international investors that unions are few and far between. A 1986–87 industrial recruitment report, produced while Republican Jim Martin was governor, used clear if coded language to discuss the state of unionism: "North Carolina's labor force is one of the most productive in the nation. . . . Labor-management relations are harmonious, and work stoppages are rare" (NCDOC 1986–87, 6, 8).

As a concession to the AFL-CIO that endorsed him each of the six times he ran for statewide office between 1972 and 1996, Governor Hunt's Department of Commerce has been more cautious about putting such realities about Tar Heel unionization in print. But America's corporate leaders continue to admire North Carolina's business climate. A 1985 national study of such leaders found that low wages and low level of unionization were North Carolina's chief attractions (*News and Record* 1985b).

Within the state, organized labor has so little public clout that decision makers do not appear to give much thought to state rankings on union and wage questions. According to a 1985 study of North Carolina's political

and business leaders, a majority was unaware that the state's average indus-
trial wage had stood close to fiftieth, near that of Mississippi and South
Carolina, for almost a decade. Similarly, most did not know that North
Carolina ranked forty-ninth among the fifty states in level of unionization
(Baker 1986).

The Rise and Fall of the Labor Education Center:
A 1970s Vignette

In 1976 modernizer Democratic gubernatorial candidate Jim Hunt, seeking to strengthen his ties to the populist wing of the party, sought the
endorsement of the state AFL-CIO. The AFL-CIO did endorse Hunt, both in
the crucial first primary, when he needed an absolute majority to avoid a
runoff election, and in the November general election, when he faced weak
Republican opposition. In exchange Hunt agreed to encourage University
of North Carolina President William Friday to find a home on one of the
university system's sixteen campuses for a labor education and research
center, modeled after similar centers in two dozen other states, including
six southern states (Adams 1981).

By April 1977 Chancellor Albert Whiting of historically black North
Carolina Central University had agreed to house the center at his campus in
Durham. The curriculum, designed like those in other states especially to
help unionized workers, was to include courses in collective bargaining,
grievance procedures, labor history, and occupational health and safety.
Governor Hunt's office approved temporary staff with federal funds available under the Comprehensive Education and Training Act. The expecta-
tion was that regular funding would follow after routine approval from the
University of North Carolina Board of Governors.

Institutionalizing a union-oriented program into the university system
was, however, hardly a routine activity. The Board of Governors consisted
primarily of business people and professionals, both traditionalists and
modernizers, who had little sympathy for unions or other manifestations
of political activism. Modernizers differed from traditionalists in their willingness to listen to a pro–labor center presentation from President Friday.
He argued that such a center followed precedents in other southern states
and provided services appropriate for a state university, comparable to
applied programs in law, medicine, banking, business, public education,
agriculture, and the arts.

Traditionalists lost an early round in October 1977 when the board's planning committee approved the labor center proposal, but traditionalists pressured board members in November to reexamine their support. Their arguments centered on their belief that North Carolina's prosperity depended on antiunionism. They harped on a private AFL-CIO eight-year organizing plan, accidentally left by a union official in a Raleigh motel room, which showed the labor center as part of a larger union plan to increase its power in North Carolina (Adams 1981, 362–63). The traditionalist opposition was led by board members from the textile and furniture industries who feared that an active labor movement would endanger their low-wage businesses. Board member and textile company president Daniel Gunter spearheaded the fight against the AFL-CIO's right to appoint a majority of the labor center's board. Although this provision was dropped from later drafts, planning committee member and furniture industrialist Harley Shuford argued candidly, "I am opposed [to the center] because I think it would strengthen the cause of organized labor in our state. I feel organized labor is detrimental to both the quality of life and economic development in our state" (*Durham Morning Herald*, February 18, 1978, quoted in Goldman and Luebke 1985, 26). Republican businessman-legislator Cass Ballenger, who was subsequently elected (1986) to Congress from a western North Carolina district, had these blunt words in the heat of the battle: "The first thought of most industries moving out of the North is the antiunion attitude of the workers in the state of North Carolina. It's an attraction. So why is the state going to try to change the attitude of the workers?" (*Charlotte Observer*, December 31, 1977, quoted in Goldman and Luebke 1985, 26). In fact, Tar Heel workers' attitudes toward unions are far more favorable, if complicated, than Ballenger believed. But in the labor center debate, the traditionalist arguments were taking root.

Significantly, on the Board of Governors itself, no member spoke strongly for the proposal. Friday and other university staff, as well as editorial writers of the state's major daily newspapers, were the only advocates. The university administration argued for the case on technical grounds. Only the newspapers made the case that, inasmuch as unions appeared to be a permanent structure in North Carolina, labor-management relations would be more stable if union members could benefit from university course work. But the one modernizer politician who could have turned the day for the labor center, Jim Hunt, chose not to act. The AFL-CIO itself appeared to acquiesce in defeat, deciding that to try to mobilize its members to pressure either the governor or board members would only encourage traditionalists to fight harder. The Democratic Party's "black and (white) liberal" wing is usually credited with influencing at least 30 percent of a primary vote and 25 percent in a general election. But in the labor center case, these various constituencies, including blacks and campus groups, hardly raised a protest.

Governor Hunt's moves as a modernizer politician were completely predictable. Modernizer ideology can tolerate unions if necessary. In the labor center case, a firestorm of protest came from traditionalist business people, while from the populist wing of the Democratic Party hardly a murmur was raised. It taught Jim Hunt and other modernizer politicians of the day that the North Carolina AFL-CIO and its allies may be reliable for some votes on Election Day, but in a direct confrontation with traditionalists, antiunionism wins hands down. When Hunt subsequently ran for reelection in 1980, the U.S. Senate in 1984, and twice for governor in the 1990s, he deemphasized his advocacy of higher worker wages, seeking to avoid the label of a prolabor politician. The lesson was clear: labor remained illegitimate in North Carolina politics.

The defeat of the labor center coincided with a major defeat for the AFL-CIO at the national level. Also in 1977, a nascent coalition of big business interests calling itself the Business Roundtable was able to defeat in Congress the attempts of organized labor to strengthen the National Labor Relations Act. The Business Roundtable was successful despite a Democratic majority in the U.S. Senate and House of Representatives and Democrat Jimmy Carter in the White House (Goldman and Luebke 1985). For those business interests trying to stall any gains by organized labor, both in North Carolina and across the United States, 1977 was a watershed year.

Hard-Line and Genteel Antiunionism: Politicians at Work

As part of his defense of free enterprise, Jesse Helms made unions a favorite whipping boy in his efforts to strengthen the traditionalist political agenda for North Carolina. His staunch antiunionism was adopted by the state Republican Party and remains a strong component of the ideology of many Democratic politicians as well. Allegations of communism and corruption were central to Helms's attack.

This traditionalist stance was rooted in both fact and fiction. It was a fact that a Communist-oriented union sought to organize workers at the Loray Mill in Gastonia in 1929, but it was fiction to suggest that North Carolina textile industrialists would have accepted the union had it lacked leftist ties.

Indeed, when the non-Communist UTW organized workers in Marion the same year, it too faced massive resistance from the elite. The reality of some Communist influence in many CIO unions of the 1930s and 1940s, including the food and tobacco workers' local at R. J. Reynolds during and after World War II, provided traditionalism with a favorite point of attack. If unions could be labeled socialist, then they could be criticized both as anticapitalist and anti-Christian. The fact that leftist influence was minimal was beside the point (Marshall 1967; Luebke 1991).

Similarly, the corruption unearthed in national unions during the 1950s, associated especially with the Teamsters, constituted another building block in hardline antiunionism. Within North Carolina the 1982 conviction of former AFL-CIO chief Wilbur Hobby for misuse of Comprehensive Education and Training Act funds confirmed the traditionalists' view of unions as inherently corrupt.

A kind of antiunionism by omission permeates many of North Carolina's social institutions. Schoolteachers in Detroit are unionized and view the UAW as part of the Michigan landscape; in other words, union membership is normal. In North Carolina, teachers are far more likely never to bring up unions. Similarly, unions as important organizations of working people are rarely mentioned in the North Carolina media, in contrast to Michigan coverage of union Fourth of July picnics, Labor Day solidarity parades, or UAW participation in United Way fund-raising. News coverage in North Carolina is usually restricted to the conflict surrounding a strike or a union election. In their contrasting behavior, teachers and editors in Michigan and in North Carolina can help shape the long-term probability of unions' winning representation elections several decades into the future.

Desperate for new jobs, small towns in the Coastal Plain raised few questions when antiunion traditionalists were willing to open low-wage factories. Town leaders of Hamlet, a once-thriving railroad town on the Seaboard Railway (now CSX) with many unionized workers, did not object when Emmett Roe wanted to open a chicken-processing plant on the poor side of town (Davidson 1996, 171–73; Applebome 1996, 198–99). Low-income blacks and whites with little formal education worked at Imperial Food Products (a fitting name for a company that imposed Third World working conditions and literally showed the door to any employee who protested). During the first shift on September 3, 1991, the day after Labor Day, a hydraulic line on a deep-fat fryer broke and caused an explosion and fire. Twenty-five persons died, primarily because owner Roe had illegally locked all fire-exit doors. Roe's rationale had been that workers were using the fire exits to steal chickens. But North Carolina state government was complicitous in the employees' deaths. The state-run Occupational Safety and Health Administration (OSHA) had not inspected Imperial Foods even once during the company's eleven years in Hamlet. Behind a veneer of government-corporate cooperation alleged to ensure worker health and safety, North Carolina's Department of Labor, headed by an elected Democratic commissioner with strong modernizer credentials, was severely shortchanging Tar Heel industrial workers. As excellent reporting in the *Charlotte Observer* (1991a; 1991b) and the *News and Observer* of Raleigh (1992) revealed, the political reality was that the Labor Department had, without public protest, acquiesced in inadequate legislative appropriations. It was guaranteed that many North Carolina factories, whether sweatshops like Imperial or corporate operations with higher self-imposed health and safety standards, would never be subject to an OSHA inspection.

Perhaps more significant than the blatant antiunionism of traditionalist ideology has been the subtle opposition to unions within modernizer ideology. The actions of Terry Sanford illustrated this genteel antiunionism. In his 1986 and 1992 U.S. Senate races, Sanford accepted contributions from union PACs. As governor in the early 1960s he commuted the sentence of a textile union organizer who had been convicted in a state court of conspiracy charges on very dubious grounds. But as president of Duke University in the late 1970s, Sanford agreed to the hiring of an antiunion consulting firm that helped the Duke University Medical Center defeat a vigorous organizing drive by the American Federation of State, Municipal, and County Employees.

Sanford's predecessor as governor, Luther Hodges Sr., similarly opposed unions while seeking to modernize the state's economy. In the same years that Hodges endorsed the concept of the Research Triangle Park, he called out the National Guard to police a 1958 textile workers' strike in Henderson, the effect of which was to weaken and ultimately defeat the union's efforts at Harriet-Henderson Yarns (Frankel 1986; Clark 1997). Hodges's interest in the modernization of North Carolina's economy, especially to reduce its reliance on textile manufacturing, went hand in hand with a preference to decrease, not increase, collective bargaining (Billings 1979, 227–28). Yet Hodges avoided blatant antiunion statements. Like Sanford, he demonstrated the substance of genteel antiunionism, evidenced less by strong words and more by deliberate action.

Jim Hunt's tenure as governor, especially in his first term, provided another clear example of genteel antiunionism. The case of the North

Carolina labor center illustrated Hunt's unwillingness to take a major political risk on behalf of unions.

A final manifestation of genteel antiunionism lies with many national corporations themselves, which have unionized plants in other parts of the country but have chosen to fight the union when they build new plants in North Carolina. Oftentimes the suggestion to resist unionization has come from traditionalist business people, who have not wanted to give unions a foothold in the community. One example was Dana Corporation, organized by the UAW elsewhere in the country, which defeated the union at a 1982 representation election in Gastonia (*News and Observer* 1981a; Mullins and Luebke 1984, 26). Similarly, when truck manufacturer Freightliner came to Gaston County in the late 1980s, it too resisted the UAW organizing drive. In the Freightliner case a majority of workers in 1990 supported the union, primarily because management was viewed as playing favorites. Freightliner, a subsidiary of Mercedes-Benz, only reluctantly signed the union contract in 1991, even though its plants elsewhere in the United States had long been unionized.

The North Carolina General Assembly has been dominated by a mix of both hardline and genteel antiunionism. But as in the case of the ill-fated labor center, the traditionalists' hard line usually has prevailed. In stark contrast to the situation in northeastern and midwestern industrial states, North Carolina state law prohibits collective bargaining for state and local employees. While state employees and teacher groups certainly lobby the legislature for benefits, no public employee group can bargain with a local school board, city or county officials, or any agency of state government for a union contract. Once again, a traditionalist-modernizer alliance has affirmed the illegitimacy of unionism.

Why Unions Lose Elections:
The Culture of Antiunionism

Throughout the 1980s and 1990s, unions in North Carolina won only about one-third of the nearly 300 representation elections that have been held at private-sector workplaces subject to the jurisdiction of the NLRB. One reason for this relatively low success rate has been the national sentiment toward unions. Beginning in the 1980s, the decline of the manufacturing sector; increased competition within that sector, especially from overseas; and a less-cordial attitude toward unions under President Ronald Reagan (epitomized by the ill-fated 1981 air controllers' strike) contributed to an environment hostile to union advances. Throughout the United States, workers worried about losing their jobs were less likely to go on strike or, if unorganized, less likely to support a union drive.

But North Carolina's reputation as weak in unions has had its roots in additional factors. The most important has been the strength of institutional opposition to organized labor. As illustrated above, both traditionalist and modernizer ideologies within government and business have been unsympathetic to unions. This lack of sympathy carries over into other institutions as well. Public school teachers are prohibited from collective bargaining, so they rarely debate the case for unionism. No newspaper or radio or television station in North Carolina is organized, so unions are perforce presented in the media as somebody else's issue. Judges generally respond favorably to corporations' requests to limit the number of picketing strikers to a handful. Baptists, North Carolina's predominant Protestant denomination, have no tradition of support for organized labor. This contrasts especially with the frequent expressions of support for unions from Roman Catholic priests in northern cities. A Decatur, Illinois, priest joined the picket line in 1995 in unions' ultimately unsuccessful strike against Caterpillar and the Staley Corporation. In the lengthy mid-1990s newspaper strike against the *Detroit News* and the *Detroit Free Press*, both owned by national chains Gannett and Knight-Ridder, respectively, workers were supported by the Detroit-area Roman Catholic diocese.

In sum, unlike nonsouthern industrial regions, the Tar Heel state lacks any strong institutional base for a positive presentation of unionism. On the contrary, the dominant institutional message, as illustrated throughout this chapter, is that unions are at best superfluous and at worst evil. It is no surprise that unions win few elections.

Some observers argue that unions' defeats are linked less to institutional opposition than to the strong tradition of rugged individualism that permeates the state's culture. But contrary to popular thought, surveys of North Carolina workers have consistently found support for trade unions (Leiter 1986; *Greensboro Record* 1979). Attitudes toward unions have depended on employees' perceptions of the fairness of their working conditions. Union support has been highest among those who feel that their pay and work situation are unsatisfactory. Younger, lower-income, and black workers have been most likely to support unions, and gender makes no difference (Leiter 1986; Zingraff and Schulman 1984). The traditionalist view that North Carolina workers do not want a "third party" to represent them in negotiations with management has not been supported in recent research (Leiter 1986; Schneider 1985; Tomaskovic-Devey and Roscigno 1996). Many workers, especially blacks, seek greater power on the job (Goldman and Luebke 1985; Zingraff and Schulman 1984). Why, then, do unions not win more representation elections? The answer lies in the complex web of factors that intervene between workers' responses to a survey and their actual vote in a union election.

Some of these factors are practically constants. For example, workers who express pro-union attitudes to researchers have usually not been confronted by the counterarguments that elite institutions raise when an actual union organizing drive is under way. In a normal North Carolina setting, politicians, business people, and newspaper editors are likely to raise the issues of lengthy strikes and thus loss of pay, violence, and the possibility of a plant shutdown to avoid higher labor costs and union grievance systems. Workers typically are asked if they know how their union dues will be spent and why they think their grievances cannot be met with direct appeals to management (cf. *News and Observer* 1977c).

Unions are more likely to lose elections if their organizing team is weaker than the consultants whom virtually every firm today will hire during an organizing drive. Although companies may well have retained an out-of-state antiunion consultant, they will no doubt hit unions with the charge that they are bringing in outsiders. Further, unions that have not solidified a strong interracial team of in-plant workers will find companies sowing seeds of dissatisfaction among either black or white workers.

These specific company strategies, undertaken against the backdrop of North Carolina's antiunion culture, put the burden on the union to convince workers that they should undertake the risk of a pro-union vote. However bad pay, benefits, or working conditions might be, workers in North Carolina have few positive precedents to lead them to conclude that the benefits of a pro-union vote outweigh the risks.

The Brown Lung Association: A Successful Occupational Health Movement

As long ago as 1942, Britain identified cotton dust as an occupational health hazard, but well into the 1970s the American Textile Manufacturers' Institute continued to maintain that no such risk existed in the United States. A movement of North Carolina textile workers, most of whom were retired and in poor health, assisted by a bevy of energetic community organizers, forced textile companies in the late 1970s to begin providing compensation

(Conway 1979). In addition, effective lobbying of Governor Hunt and the General Assembly led in 1982 to the state's elimination of certain regulations that restricted mill workers' eligibility for workers' compensation.

The Carolina Brown Lung Association (CBLA) is one of the few instances where workers defeated corporations in the halls of the General Assembly. The movement succeeded both because it marshaled significant resources within a short period and because the workers—homegrown Tar Heels who were white, sickly, elderly, and nonunion—constituted a difficult target for textile companies to discredit. The CBLA's victory instructs because of the contrasts with union organizing attempts. First, in the early 1970s, federally funded researchers had identified cotton dust as a probable source of occupational disease. Ralph Nader had publicized the problem as brown lung, a spin-off term from the black lung disease that coal miners contracted from coal dust. Second, OSHA, in response to the research findings, was developing a cotton dust standard that would force textile manufacturers to reduce the amount of cotton dust inside a mill. Third, various liberal foundations were willing to fund CBLA staff to go into mill villages in Greensboro, Erwin, and Roanoke Rapids, for example, to organize brown lung victims into an active community force. Fourth, the workers themselves, prototypes of the employees who constituted the backbone of the state's cotton-textile economy for decades, were sympathetic figures, especially for television and newspaper reporters. How could one deny that these ailing workers were entitled to compensation?

The CBLA had to fight for compensation because of state laws requiring workers to file a claim within a short period after leaving employment. The workers argued that, inasmuch as their employers denied that their respiratory ailments had anything to do with cotton dust, how could workers possibly know they could file? All of these factors led to a public perception that greatly favored the CBLA, an organization of low-income and sick retired mill workers in a David versus Goliath battle against the insurance companies of some of the country's major textile firms, such as Cone Mills, Burlington Industries, and J. P. Stevens. Over an eight-year period, from 1974, when the CBLA was founded, until 1982, when the General Assembly eased the regulations for workers' compensation, the CBLA successfully captured the positive symbols of a sympathetic underdog. Brown lung victims, after all, had played by the rules of traditionalist North Carolina, working hard for the free enterprise system, and now the textile companies, holding to the letter of the law, sought to deny these workers decent compensation in the last years of their lives.

CBLA's victory for ailing cotton mill workers also contrasts with the difficulties of union organizing. Unionism's dominant symbols in this state are negative, far different from the appeals of the CBLA. At a minimum, modernizers see unions as a bureaucratic layer that is no longer needed in these days of enlightened management, and more fundamentally, traditionalists oppose unions as a leftist-influenced and corrupt interference in the prerogatives of management. In contrast to their support for the brown lung movement, the federal government is not a sympathetic ally of union organizers, and few foundations are underwriting union drives. In short, healthy workers pushing for unions may simply be viewed as selfish.

Making the Best of a Bad Situation

After the Republican victories in 1984, it became apparent that even the token recognition that modernizers such as Jim Hunt granted organized labor would be missing during the terms of Jim Martin. For the state AFL-CIO the question was how to respond to the increasingly negative situation. To state president Christopher Scott, an English literature Ph.D. candidate turned labor politician, the answer was clear. Scott and other labor lobbyists at the General Assembly moved toward building behind-the-scenes coalitions of friendly representatives and senators. Their goal was to promote prolabor legislation without trying to claim public credit for their activities.

One example of AFL-CIO success was the package of bills, passed in 1992 as a result of the Hamlet tragedy, that gave employees rights to report hazards without fear of firing and required additional OSHA inspections from the Labor Department, especially at workplaces with a history of accidents, worker injuries, or worker deaths. To be sure, this victory received a substantial boost from the house Speaker at the time, Dan Blue. Blue, a plaintiff's lawyer who became Speaker in 1991, was one of the first African Americans in the United States to be elected house Speaker of any of the fifty states. He had grown up in rural Robeson County on the Coastal Plain and arguably brought more economic-populist values to the office than any Speaker in North Carolina's history. Blue's personal observations of and experiences with race and class discrimination made him a strong advocate of pro-worker positions. Facing Speaker Blue, the corporate lobbyists could not gut the post-Hamlet bills but could at most try to weaken them.

Another union effort succeeded in 1985 when the General Assembly passed a right-to-know bill that gave workers and communities the right to information concerning hazardous chemicals in the workplace. The law was modeled on legislation passed in other states. Several incidents in the early 1980s had demonstrated that dangerous chemicals were in abundance in North Carolina. In particular, an explosion at a chemical storage plant in East Durham in 1983 prompted a Durham citizens' coalition to demand the removal of the plant and, more generally, a local right-to-know ordinance.

The AFL-CIO joined the Sierra Club and the North Carolina Occupational Safety and Health Project, a Durham-based statewide organization of union members and health professionals, to lobby for right-to-know in the General Assembly. Harry Payne, a Wilmington Democrat who was sympathetic to these advocacy organizations and who later won a 1992 statewide election as labor commissioner, introduced the bill in the house. Payne, other supportive legislators, and the lobbyists promoted the bill as a public health measure rather than as a labor issue. Although so labeled, the bill was vigorously opposed by various business lobbies. Business argued that the bill would require firms to divulge trade secrets and that these companies should be trusted to care responsibly for their chemicals. Although the legislation was weaker in terms of citizens' rights than Durham's local ordinance and the new law preempted the Durham statute, the 1985 right-to-know statute nevertheless constituted a significant victory for the labor-environmentalist coalition.

In the 1980s and 1990s, labor continued its policy of quiet worker advocacy. Workers' compensation laws (see Chapter 3) were liberalized, maximum unemployment compensation was increased, and the state minimum wage was coupled with the federal wage so that both would increase simultaneously (AFL-CIO Legislative Report 1987; AFL-CIO Legislative Report 1997). In the 1990s, labor lobbyist Scott was a strong supporter of successful efforts to reduce the sales tax on groceries. In all cases the AFL-CIO lobbied privately but never sought to take public credit for the new legislation.

Labor's recent gains in the General Assembly have been real. But they have been achieved only because their proponents maintained a low profile, playing by the rules of North Carolina's political game. In that game labor cannot be a visible public player. Ironically, even as the AFL-CIO joined a small group of like-minded lobbyists and legislators in promoting economic populist legislation in the 1990s, unions remained illegitimate in the eyes of both the modernizer and the traditionalist elite. Labor illegitimacy has been promoted by government and business alike, conveying the message publicly both in the state and nationally that North Carolina prospers in part because unions are so weak.

Only a handful of legislative insiders know that the AFL-CIO lobby has been a small but constant force in the General Assembly. For any citizen relying on the daily press, the probable conclusion would be that unions play no role in state politics. Unfortunately for the AFL-CIO, the perception of unions as both insignificant and illegitimate perpetuates a view that unions serve no useful purpose in today's North Carolina. Like other lobbies promoting citizen power, the AFL-CIO remains an outsider. But much more so than either civil rights or environmentalism, union association remains a stigma. Even prolabor legislators fear being labeled pro-union.

Because prolabor politicians are so outnumbered in the General Assembly, most find it safer to hide behind the cloak of modernizer ideology. Legislators who agree with unions' political priorities pretend publicly that they are more centrist than they really are. The blurring of differences between North Carolina's prolabor legislators and corporate modernizers such as Terry Sanford, Jim Hunt, or Marc Basnight may have made political survival easier for those legislators. But it has also confirmed the dominance of modernizer and modernizer-traditionalist ideology in the North Carolina Democratic Party. The weakness in state politics of labor unions constitutes a major difference between North Carolina and most other industrial states outside the South.

7

Racial and Ethnic Politics:
The Multicoloring of North Carolina

North Carolina through most of the twentieth century maintained its reputation as the southern model of moderate race relations. The Tar Heel state stood, from a national perspective, in welcome contrast to the extreme racial politics characteristic of Deep South states such as Mississippi and Alabama, as well as neighbors such as South Carolina (Franklin 1997). But with the election of onetime ardent segregationist Jesse Helms to the U.S. Senate in 1972, the state's dubious case against ten civil rights activists in Wilmington in the mid-1970s, and the 1979 killings of Communists by Nazi and Ku Klux Klan members in Greensboro, that reputation became tarnished.

From the perspective of black North Carolinians, however, the state's racial moderation was always problematic. To be sure, compared with the Deep South, black Tar Heels had less to fear from lynching and other racial violence. But the moderate path that the white elite chose nevertheless institutionalized and legitimated a segregated society in which blacks could not expect either political or economic equality. The reality was that blacks had little voting strength and even less political power, especially in the state's small towns and rural counties.

By the late 1990s two significant events—one political and the other demographic—had changed the face of race and ethnic relations in North Carolina. First, compared with the early 1960s, African Americans' gains in political power were unmistakable. Without the strong support of black Democrats, hardly a white Tar Heel Democrat could win a statewide election against the rising tide of North Carolina Republicanism. State representative Dan Blue of Raleigh served two terms as house Speaker from 1991 until 1995. (In Virginia, overlapping Blue's tenure, former state senator and lieutenant governor Douglas Wilder was elected governor in 1989—the first African American governor in the United States since a Louisiana black served briefly in the 1870s).

Further, as a result of the required decennial redistricting in 1991, two blacks, Mel Watt and Eva Clayton, were elected to the U.S. Congress, the first persons of color to represent a North Carolina congressional district since 1901 (cf. Anderson 1981). Despite North Carolina's consistent black population of between 20 and 25 percent throughout the twentieth century, the legacy of the 1890s white supremacist Democratic Party (see Chapter 1) was obvious: an all-white delegation of U.S. representatives and senators to Washington, D.C., and an all-white state legislature.

The 1991 redistricting also raised, after the November 1992 election, the number of African American legislators, plus one Native American representative from Robeson County on the Coastal Plain, to a record high of 26 of 170 seats: 19 of 120 seats in the state house, and 7 of 50 seats in the state senate.

But the 1991 redistricting also sparked a reaction from a white Durham modernizer, Robinson O. Everett. A longtime Democrat and Duke law school professor who had opposed Jim Crow racial segregation, Everett was offended by the efforts of the Democrat-controlled General Assembly in 1991–92 to maximize African American voting strength. Ironically, the General Assembly in 1991 had in fact constructed only one majority-black congressional district and relatively few majority-black legislative districts. It was the Republican George Bush administration's Office of Civil Rights that, under its interpretation of the 1982 revised federal Voting Rights Act and subsequent federal court decisions, told the Democrat-controlled General Assembly that more so-called majority-minority districts should be drawn. After the Bush-influenced districts were drawn and Watt and

Clayton won seats in Congress, Everett sued, arguing that such racially in-fluenced and gerrymandered district configurations violated his civil rights.

The resultant U.S. Supreme Court opinions in the two cases brought by Everett, *Shaw v. Reno* and *Shaw v. Hunt*, were landmark decisions. By 5-to-4 majorities the Supreme Court ruled that district gerrymandering was not constitutional if race was the predominant factor in a legislature's draw-ing of district lines. Watt's district, tagged infamously the Interstate 85 district because it at times was only as wide as the highway that stretched 160 miles from Gastonia near the South Carolina line to Durham, was ruled unconstitutional.

Beyond Black-White Relations

Besides the power shifts in biracial politics, North Carolina's race and ethnic relations in the late 1990s had changed, compared with the 1960s, because of the increased diversity of the state's population. In the years following the civil rights movement, Tar Heel African American residents stabilized at about 22 percent of the total. Whites in the 1990s constituted three-fourths of the state's population of more than 7 million. The Moun-tain region was about 90 percent white, while on the Coastal Plain whites were just two-thirds of the population. In a handful of rural Coastal Plain counties, a majority of residents was black.

North Carolina's most significant demographic change occurred among Hispanics, calculated by the U.S. Census as persons of any race who self-identify with Spanish-speaking cultures. In 1994 U.S. Census data, His-panics surpassed Native Americans as the state's third largest racial or ethnic group; they were 1.35 percent of North Carolina's population, com-pared with Native Americans' share of 1.24 percent (OPR 1997). But a more immediate population measure, numbers of Hispanic children en-rolling in the public schools, suggested that the Hispanic migration in the late 1990s was increasing more rapidly than state population experts could gather official data. Most but not all of the Latino migrants ("Latino" and "Hispanic" are interchangeable terms, with Spanish speakers more likely to prefer the former term) were not bilingual and therefore, regardless of formal education, were relegated to unskilled or semiskilled jobs. The migration of the mid- to late 1990s was especially heavy into the econom-ically bustling cities of the metro Piedmont.

Spanish-speaking migrants were first attracted to growing job opportunities during the 1970s in the labor-intensive agriculture sector. Particularly in cultivating and harvesting tobacco and picking vegetables in the Coastal Plain region, white farmers by the late 1980s were heavily dependent on Hispanic workers. For example, in Duplin County, Hispanics dominated the cucumber harvesting essential for the nearby pickle factories in Mount Olive. By the 1990s, Latino culture had become institutionalized in the towns of the Coastal Plain. Grocery stores, video shops, and restaurants as well as law offices with bilingual attorneys filled the storefronts whose businesses had previously served the English-speaking indigenous white and black residents.

In the Research Triangle area, many available manual-labor jobs in fast-growing companies such as construction or landscaping were filled by Spanish speakers, primarily from Mexico but also from Central American countries such as Guatemala and Honduras. But white employers also faced labor shortages in manufacturing. In 1997 Hispanic blue-collar workers were a majority or near-majority in low-wage furniture and textile companies in, for example, Siler City and Asheboro, south of Greensboro (*News and Record* 1997a). In Sanford, 45 miles south of Raleigh on U.S. 1, the labor shortage during the 1990s economic boom was so severe that white employers acknowledged hiring undocumented Latino workers (*News and Observer* 1997j). In Morganton, sixty miles east of Asheville, the owners of a low-wage chicken-processing factory openly recruited Guatemalan workers to take the jobs that indigenous whites were rejecting because the whites preferred nearby better-paying jobs that offered better working conditions.

Not surprisingly, the Latino migration toward available jobs was accompanied by both social and economic conflict. In metro Piedmont cities such as Durham and Winston-Salem the new residents settled in already troubled, low-income neighborhoods. Some of them became easy marks for local thieves. Ethnic tension, particularly between Hispanics and African Americans, was high (*News and Observer* 1997d). In Siler City a parade through downtown that was part of a Latino celebration of the religious holiday of Our Lady of Guadalupe was not well received by native white and black dwellers (*News and Record* 1997a). In Morganton the recruited Guatemalans reacted to the harsh working conditions by voting for union representation (*News and Observer* 1996c).

A third wave of ethnic in-migration was from Asia. State population data from 1994 revealed that 1 percent of North Carolinians were of Asian heritage. But Asians were twice as prominent in the metro Piedmont region for two reasons. First, Asians who had migrated to the United States as a consequence of American involvement in their home country, such as the Vietnamese, as well as the Hmong, settled in the larger cities, in particular in Greensboro (*News and Record* 1997c). Many of these migrants had little formal education. Second, a number of well-educated Asians from countries such as India, Korea, and China moved to metro Piedmont cities and attained professional positions in those cities' universities, medical centers, and high-tech corporations.

For the foreseeable future the additional coloring and diversity of North Carolina's population will have little effect on politics. Many adult immigrants, especially Hispanics, are not citizens. Only as they become citizens and their children turn eighteen are the Latino and Asian populations likely to have a significant impact on local and state elections.

Delaying School Integration:
Tar Heel Democrats in the 1950s

After the U.S. Supreme Court's 1954 declaration, in *Brown v. Topeka Board of Education*, that segregated public schools were inherently unequal and must be eliminated "with all deliberate speed," North Carolina's white leaders faced a dilemma. The state's "progressive" ideology that its governors and corporate leaders followed during the first half of the twentieth century had turned North Carolina into the South's leading industrial state. This same ideology demanded that, despite some tinkering at the edges, the basic caste system of racial segregation was to remain. Yet the U.S. Supreme Court's ruling on that third Monday in May 1954, referred to by most white southern leaders as Black Monday, seemed to demand immediate racial change. The North Carolina solution was to strike a middle ground between the Supreme Court's ruling and the policies of some other southern states (mostly in the Deep South but also including neighboring Virginia) whose politicians had decided on hard-core resistance (Chafe 1981, chap. 2).

To North Carolina's north in 1954, for example, Prince Edward County, a southside Virginia area 75 miles southwest of Richmond, simply closed its public schools rather than open the historically white facilities to black children (Smith 1965). The segregationist Virginia Democratic Party declared "massive resistance" to the U.S. Supreme Court ruling (Bass and DeVries 1976). By contrast, in 1956 the North Carolina General Assembly approved the Pearsall Plan, named after a Rocky Mount legislator and

Hodges ally. Architects of the Pearsall Plan, including Hodges, began with the premise that the North Carolina branch of the National Association for the Advancement of Colored People (NAACP) and other black advocates of desegregation were illegitimately agitating for political change. A typical white Democratic elite, this group of politicians believed that they should determine the speed of school desegregation. Tar Heel Democrats felt the Supreme Court decision had been wrong in the first place; their job was to steer a middle course between the NAACP and the Ku Klux Klan. The mistake in this argument, as historian William Chafe points out, was the assumption that white Tar Heels would not accept school desegregation. In fact, a sociological survey of the Greensboro area in 1956 found that most whites would not actively oppose desegregation if it were implemented. Chafe argues that the progressive elite blamed "rednecks" for requiring a slowing down of desegregation through the Pearsall Plan, when it was Hodges and other white male Democrats themselves who wanted to maintain the segregated status quo (Chafe 1981, 59).

The Pearsall Plan allowed any North Carolina school district to close all or some of its schools if desegregation occurred, and it provided state tuition grants for white students to attend segregated private schools (Chafe 1981, 53). While the Pearsall Plan did not prevent local school districts from establishing a process for desegregation, the entire burden of petitioning for desegregation fell on black children and their parents. The plan nonetheless gave North Carolina the appearance of complying, albeit slowly, with the Supreme Court's ruling. Token desegregation occurred in Greensboro, Winston-Salem, and several other metro Piedmont cities. North Carolina progressives claimed they had moved the state as fast as they could. From the perspective of black parents seeking educational equality, however, the Pearsall Plan illustrated the reality that "North Carolina progressivism consisted primarily of its shrewdness in opposing racial change." An Arkansas school official summarized Tar Heel school desegregation policy as "one of the cleverest techniques of perpetuating segregation that we have seen" (quotations from Chafe 1981, 70).

Two decades after the Brown decision the evolving modernist ideology in North Carolina accepted the value of racial equality as a necessary societal goal. The strength of the national civil rights movement and resultant federal legislation meant that, by the early 1970s, the old Tar Heel progressive ideology, which promoted economic and educational change while sustaining Jim Crow segregation, could not survive. Modernism's importance as a New South ideology lay in its continued commitment to an activist state government and its recognition that, in the civil rights era, blacks had to be offered a minimal level of participation in this activist government. Many white Democrats and some Republicans became modernizers, or at least showed some commitment to modernism. But African Americans' relationship to white Democratic and Republican modernizers has differed.

In North Carolina almost all politicized blacks are Democrats. In 1996, for example, 95 percent of black voters were registered Democrats. This means that most blacks have expected little from Republicans. A Republican governor's appointment of a handful of black Republicans to boards or patronage jobs served two functions. First, it provided a practical reason for upwardly mobile middle-class blacks to gravitate to the GOP. Second, it suggested that Republicans were indeed committed to racial equality. (Jim Martin in his two terms as governor made precisely such appointments of African Americans. Jesse Helms's selection of a black press secretary for his 1984 U.S. Senate race, when Jim Hunt's campaign had no blacks in visible positions, provided him with a public-relations coup, even though few blacks voted for Helms on Election Day.)

Black Democratic leaders can and usually do deliver an overwhelming straight-ticket vote for Democratic candidates. Consequently, they have expected white Democratic modernizers to respond to black demands. This has generated conflict between white modernizers and blacks because the white modernizers have tended to view themselves as representing black interests well. Similar to Luther Hodges's policies of the 1950s, which sought a middle road between racial equality and hard-line segregation, most white modernizers from the 1970s through the 1990s believed that their political decisions had benefited blacks without pushing too many white registered Democrats into the Republican column. On racial issues, however, this frequently meant that blacks felt unrepresented. Tar Heel black leaders often perceived that white modernizers only cared about them shortly before Election Day, when white candidates needed endorsements of the straight-Democratic ticket from local black organizations around the state. Feeling taken for granted, black leaders did not work as hard as they might have for the all-white statewide Democratic ticket, and turnout was lower among blacks, especially poor blacks, than it might have been.

Governor Hunt's decision to call a special crime session of the General Assembly in February 1994, despite a lack of support from Speaker Dan Blue and other populist-leaning house Democrats, illustrated how most

African American politicians and traditionalist-leaning white Democrats differed on an issue such as crime control. Hunt's plan emphasized punitive, tough-on-crime measures that, for example, spent millions on new prison construction and ensured use of the new space by increasing prison terms. During a cantankerous seven-week session characterized by personality differences that overlaid ideological splits, Blue sought to temper punishment with outlays for prevention, that is, by also appropriating monies for after-school programs for latch-key middle schoolers or for drug rehabilitation programs for the incarcerated. Black and populist white Democrats considered it obvious that preventing new generations of school dropouts was a key to reducing crime in the future. (They noted that 92 percent of North Carolina's prison inmates were high school dropouts and 65 percent were abusers of alcohol or other drugs). The modernizer-traditionalist view of Hunt, supported by a majority of the Democrat-controlled state senate, was that the (white) public wanted "results," and that necessitated a "politics of punishment."

Underlying the Hunt-Blue debate was a key difference in political goals. Hunt's intent was to endorse social traditionalism if necessary in order to prevent state Republicans from co-opting the tough-on-crime position. By contrast, Blue and his house Democratic allies wanted a less-punitive program for two reasons: they felt that including prevention was better policy, and they worried that tough-on-crime language had a subliminal message that stereotyped blacks as criminals. The dispute paralleled differences occurring during the mid-1990s between President Clinton and the Congressional Black Caucus. In both cases the Clinton-Hunt endorsement of social traditionalism did not prevent legislative Democrats from suffering major defeats in November 1994. But by November 1996 their Republican-leaning crime positions enabled Clinton and Hunt to win comfortably their respective reelection battles for president and governor. The controversy over how well, if at all, white modernizer Democrats represented black interests lay at the heart of most blacks' discontent with the North Carolina and the national Democratic Party.

Racial Conflict in Greensboro:
A Matter of Perspective

When, on February 1, 1960, four college students from North Carolina Agricultural and Technical State University (A&T) sat down in the whites-only section of Woolworth's lunch counter in Greensboro, the city's progressive business and political leaders believed that such direct action was a mistake. Twenty years later, Greensboro white modernizer leaders had changed their tune. In retrospect, they viewed the sit-ins as forcing long-overdue changes. City fathers even dedicated a historic marker in downtown Greensboro on that twentieth anniversary.

In celebrating desegregation the 1980 ceremony obscured the fact that racial change in Greensboro and elsewhere in North Carolina did not come easily. In the first place the 1960 sit-ins, after months of negotiations, led to only token desegregation of public facilities in the city (Wolff 1970). In the spring of 1963 A&T students demonstrated in much larger numbers in the streets of downtown Greensboro, forcing mass arrests by the police department. White leaders again regarded the sit-ins as disruptive and criticized A&T student leaders, including student body president Jesse Jackson, for making excessive demands. Blacks countered that the white elite should not dictate the pace of desegregation, but black-white negotiations stalled. In fact, despite Greensboro's reputation for moderation, widespread desegregation of public facilities occurred only after the 1964 federal civil rights law required it (Chafe 1981).

The reluctance of Greensboro's political and economic elite to initiate desegregation even after extensive organized protests from blacks highlighted a component of modernizer ideology. Modernizers recognized in theory the legitimacy of racial equality but hesitated to take the necessary steps to achieve it unless they saw no alternative. But they differed from traditionalists in listening more closely to black demands, even if they have not gladly shared power.

The official praise accorded the four A&T demonstrators in February 1980, two decades after the fact, came ironically just three months after a widely publicized event that badly tarnished Greensboro's reputation. Four whites and one black were killed by members of the Ku Klux Klan and the Nazi Party in a black public housing project on November 3, 1979. A small Communist party known as the Workers Viewpoint Organization had scheduled a Death to the Klan rally in the low-income neighborhood to try to gain support among black workers. According to Elizabeth Wheaton, despite much publicity about the rally and advance information that Klansmen and Nazi Party members from outside Greensboro planned to attend, no Greensboro police were present when these individuals drove into the housing project (Wheaton 1987, 165). The Klan and Nazi Party members emerged from their cars in front of the demonstration and, after a brief shoving match, began shooting at the crowd. Eighty-eight seconds later, five persons—all Communists or individuals sympathetic to the party—were dead (Wheaton 1987, 135–51). The national publicity surrounding the killings was negative for both Greensboro and North Carolina. City and state modernizer leaders responded that the criticism was unfair because it implied that segregationist whites were dominant in Greensboro and North Carolina. The leaders had a point. Modernizers, not racial traditionalists, held key positions of power in Greensboro. But how much power did the city's white leaders share with blacks?

In November 1980 an all-white jury in Greensboro found the Klan and Nazi defendants not guilty of all charges. Although Greensboro's white leaders correctly argued that they could not affect the trial outcome, the acquittals sent a symbolic message about the Klan through the city's black community.

The following October a well-organized black voter turnout in the city council primary election raised the possibility that black candidates could win two or even three of the six seats that were at stake in the November general election. Although blacks at that time constituted a third of the city's population, they had never elected more than one black to the six at-large seats. Indeed, this was why black leaders had long advocated reform of the city electoral system.

But blacks found that even trying to win under the existing system evoked white opposition. Many white leaders took the traditionalist view that expanded black political power, under any system, was a threat to Greensboro's future. They hastily organized opposition groups under the ethnocentric rallying cries of "Stand Up for Greensboro" and "the Committee to Keep Greensboro Greensboro." One full-page ad in the *Greensboro Daily News* appealed to white residents with the argument, "The way you vote will affect your home life, your family life, and your job life" (Lavelle 1981, 4–5). With extensive newspaper and radio advertising and a heavy turnout from affluent white wards, the 1981 election had a shocking result: an all-white city council was elected. Greensboro's progressive reputation was once again challenged.

The embarrassment of the racial overtones during the campaign and the all-white outcome forced white modernizer political and business leaders to act. In February 1982 they established a biracial elite commission, the Greensboro Dialogue Task Force Committee, which recommended a compromise 5-3-1 system: five ward seats, three at-large seats, and the mayor. The task force demonstrated the ability of the Greensboro modernizer elite to implement change when it concluded that change was necessary.

By November 1982 the modernizer elite had convinced leaders of the 1981 all-white political campaigns to support the compromise district system. The stated reason was a consensus among white modernizers that "Greensboro's black community feels alienated from the all-white City Council" (*Greensboro Daily News* 1982, November 16). But black political alienation from white political power had certainly not begun in November 1981. An equally plausible reason for the white elite's newly found interest in a ward system was a decision of the U.S. Justice Department that prohibited city annexation of affluent white suburbs. In the light of the 1981 election results in Greensboro, the Justice Department ruled that further annexation of whites would make it more difficult for blacks to win political representation on the city council (*Greensboro Daily News* 1982, June 24).

An obvious remedy was the implementation of the ward system. To avoid further public divisiveness in a referendum, the Greensboro task force recommended that the city council redistrict by ordinance. This request tested the task force's influence, because each of the council members had promised during the 1981 campaign to change to a district system only by referendum. Recognizing the need to establish a new political consensus that included blacks, the all-white city council acted unanimously in December 1982 (*Greensboro Daily News* 1982, December 17). Beginning with the November 1983 election, blacks held two of the nine council seats.

Fifteen years later, institutionalized African American political power had changed at least the color of the public debate in Greensboro. A coalition of blacks with a minority of Greensboro whites who shared the goal of racial and economic fairness elected a white woman, former sociologist and League of Women Voters activist Carolyn Allen, to the mayor's office in 1993. This same coalition also won an at-large seat on the city council for an African American woman, so that in the 1990s three of Greensboro's eight council seats were usually held by blacks. The fact that Allen's election and her reelection as mayor depended on a well-mobilized black vote—dubbed by the organizers themselves as "the Underground Railroad"—ensured that the concerns of black leaders had the mayor's attention. Not surprisingly, the white-dominated Chamber of Commerce also adapted to the new realities of black political power.

But the new politics of Greensboro was not without its ironies. Hoping to improve the chances of African American representation on the board of commissioners of surrounding Guilford County, black Democrats in the General Assembly in 1991 won legislative approval of a district voting plan that made it easier for both black Democrats and white Republicans to be elected, and more difficult for white Democrats. Some whites sympathetic to the Republican candidates then used, in the 1996 county commission contests, an unsubtle racial appeal to try to win support among undecided white voters. They bought an ad in the Greensboro *News and Record* that featured a reprinted photo of Greensboro state representative Alma Adams with a clenched fist (taken by a news photographer at a political rally), reminding readers in the ad that Representative Adams was a leader of the black-Greensboro-based Underground Railroad that had heavily influenced the outcome of the 1995 city elections. Under Adams's picture was the racially tinged slogan "Stop Welfare, Vote Republican." Although the local Republican Party distanced itself from the ad, the anti-black appeal obviously urged whites to vote GOP (*News and Record* 1996b).

A final note on Greensboro racial politics is that African American elected officials showed during the 1990s that they were more sensitive to the middle-class black concern for political visibility than they were to the economic impact of city policies on poor blacks. While Greensboro was surely not the only southern city in which middle-class black elected officials slighted the needs of poor blacks, and while southern whites as well as blacks have shown a middle- to upper-class tilt in their political goals in local or legislative politics, it was nevertheless noteworthy that middle-class black officials were far from the policy radicals that white traditionalist Republicans liked to imagine. For example, when Greensboro's transit authority in 1996 recommended a fare increase for city buses from sixty cents to one dollar, none of three African Americans on the Greensboro city council objected. Lacking an ongoing advocacy organization that worked for poor blacks (as opposed to the Election Day-oriented Underground Railroad), most low-income bus riders were unaware that a fare increase was imminent. Only after the increase was implemented did many bus riders complain to the newspaper, and only then did the black members of the city council express concern (*News and Record* 1996c). Clearly, in the 1990s, racial representation without sensitivity to economic class also left many African Americans without adequate representation. But if the issue of class divisions among blacks was a good example of the complexity of black-white relations in the North Carolina of the 1990s, the 1950s and 1960s by contrast were periods in which many Tar Heel whites were willing to oppose any political power for any blacks, regardless of their social class or sociopolitical values.

The Impact of Racial Traditionalism

The "hell, no" response of racial traditionalists in the Deep South to the idea of public school or university desegregation, among them Governors Orval Faubus in Arkansas (1956), Ross Barnett in Mississippi (1962), or George Wallace in Alabama (1963), was not the North Carolina way (Carter 1995). As noted above, Tar Heel governor Luther Hodges sought a middle ground between civil rights sympathies of the North and the resistance to racial change that turned the Deep South states into a pariah region. But Hodges's moderate-segregationist views were unacceptable to many white North Carolinians, especially in the rural Coastal Plain counties where blacks made up sizable minorities or even absolute majorities. By the 1980s the modernizer value of racial tolerance had become an obligatory position for any aspiring politician, forcing racial traditionalists to use code words to indicate their stand vis-à-vis blacks. Just two decades earlier, however, open opposition was common.

North Carolina's two leading segregationists in the late 1950s and 1960s were TV editorialist Jesse Helms and I. Beverly Lake Sr., a Harvard-trained lawyer who ran in the Democratic primary election for governor in both 1960 and 1964. Helms and Lake shared an outspoken style, stating publicly what many whites would not say aloud. Their favorite whipping boy was the NAACP. After the *Brown* decision in 1954, Lake criticized the Hodges-backed Pearsall Plan for not resisting desegregation more strongly and urged Tar Heel communities to develop whites-only private schools if necessary. Lake ran in the 1960 Democratic primary as a staunch segregationist, denying the legitimacy of the *Brown* decision and blaming the NAACP for North Carolina's racial problems. On the nightly news Helms reminded viewers which politicians were supported by the so-called Negro bloc vote. According to Helms, any white politician whom blacks endorsed, whatever his public position on segregation, was untrustworthy. Helms also condemned black leaders for insisting on rapid racial change.

The impact of southern traditional racism on the state's political debate during that period was formidable. Terry Sanford, for example, while running for governor in 1960 against Lake and two other major primary opponents, adopted segregationist positions (Black 1976, 217–19). At the time no advocate of racial desegregation could have won a statewide election. Sanford demonstrated allegiance to the national Democratic Party by supporting John Kennedy for president, but he covered his racial bases by campaigning as a segregationist. This typified North Carolina's pre–civil rights Democratic ideology, that is, supporting economic change while defending the racial status quo. Sanford's supporters in eastern North Carolina implied that staunch segregationists could count on him, even if his language differed from Lake's (Spence 1968, 11). In a bitter runoff Sanford defeated Lake by a 60-to-40 margin.

During the early 1960s the civil rights movement mushroomed in North Carolina, and Sanford was forced to respond to black demands. He established Good Neighbor Councils to try to maintain racial harmony in communities racked by protest. This conciliatory position did not please Lake supporters. At the same time Sanford angered protesters by criticizing their demonstrations against segregated public facilities (Chafe 1981, chap. 5).

In 1964 Greensboro federal judge Richardson Preyer sought to succeed Sanford as governor and thus become the symbolic leader of the Democrats' progressive wing. But both Lake, who placed third in the May 1964 primary, and Helms explicitly publicized the high level of black support for Preyer in that first election. In the runoff, Preyer's campaign tried to emphasize his opposition to the civil rights bill then before Congress, but Lake and Helms questioned the depth of Preyer's segregationist commitment.

The racial traditionalists easily placed Preyer on the defensive because the civil rights movement from 1962 to 1964 was gaining strength even in Alabama and Mississippi (Dittmer 1994; Salter 1979). In Washington, D.C., the federal civil rights bill to outlaw racial segregation in public places such as restaurants and hotels was finally passing the U.S. Congress. The ability of Helms's and Lake's southern Democratic segregationist allies to stop civil rights legislation had crumbled as a result of unfavorable national and international publicity (Carter 1995). A white, southern-born president, Lyndon Johnson, was urging the passage of the 1964 civil rights bill.

As a last-ditch stand against the Sanford-Preyer wing of the Democratic Party, Lake threw his support to Dan K. Moore, a western North Carolina judge whose racial ideology fell between Preyer's and Lake's. Moore defeated Preyer, 62 percent to 38 percent.

Moore's racial position was certainly not the only reason he won. For example, many business leaders, including executives at both Duke Power Company and Carolina Power and Light, preferred Moore's more anti-government economic views. For most Tar Heel big business, racial desegregation might be inevitable, as the Sanford-Preyer Democrats argued privately. But big business largely took no position on segregation, focusing instead on issues such as Moore's opposition to more government regulation of business.

Lyndon Johnson's landslide election in 1964 led to passage of a second major law, the 1965 Voting Rights Act, that targeted any county in the South in which white local officials appeared to have restricted black voter registration. According to a formula calculating the percentage of unregistered blacks in a county, 40 of North Carolina's 100 counties came under the scrutiny of the federal Department of Justice before any local electoral laws or districts could be changed. The greatest racial change for white and black Tar Heels, however, came in 1971, when the U.S. Supreme Court unanimously ruled in *Swann v. Charlotte-Mecklenburg County* that busing was an appropriate remedy to end public school segregation that occurred because of segregated housing patterns. Thus the era of busing for racial balance began as a result of a black North Carolinian's complaint that the Charlotte-area school board was still resisting genuine desegregation. Once again the federal government—this time, the courts—could be viewed, from a traditionalist perspective, as interfering with race relations that had worked fine for decades.

Certainly candidate Lake and journalist Helms pushed the parameters of the political debate to the right, so that racial equality, into the 1970s, was viewed with suspicion by a significant percentage of white North Carolinians. Of the two, Helms's words took on greater significance because they were heard every day, not just during the campaigns of 1960 and 1964. Lake and Helms both bolstered the cause of resistance as political opponents of desegregation, but Helms also served as a cultural symbol of opposition. As the civil rights movement gained strength and some change appeared inevitable, Helms chose his words carefully. He assailed not so much the goal of equality but the methods that blacks and their allies had allegedly adopted. His television commentary from April 1965, shortly after the Selma-to-Montgomery voting rights march, brought together much of Helms's racial ideology in one place: "The Negroes of America, regardless of the merits of some of their complaints, have recourse through exceedingly sympathetic courts to settle their grievances. They have a president whose ear is constantly cocked to the frequent reminder by civil-rights leaders that he received 95 percent of the Negro vote in 1964. They have a Congress which would tomorrow morning enact Webster's Dictionary into law if someone accidentally threw it into the hopper with a civil rights label on it. And the Supreme Court would stand in applause" (Nordhoff 1984, 41).

Helms effectively summarized the sentiments of states' rights advocates in North Carolina and across the South. Since the federal government actively worked against their values, racial traditionalists wanted state legislators to do what they could to stop change. This antichange perspective manifested itself in North Carolina in various ways, even while state leaders espoused racial moderation. For example, until 1977 a huge Ku Klux Klan billboard along U.S. 70 greeted visitors to Smithfield, a county seat twenty-five miles east of Raleigh. Its message said simply to "fight communism and intergration [*sic*]" by joining the Klan. The sign's existence did not suggest, of course, that all of Smithfield's citizens were Klan sympathizers. Indeed, the twice-weekly *Smithfield Herald* was a leading voice for racial modernism, continually urging residents to reject violent resistance to desegregation. But the fact that the sign remained until the late 1970s suggests the strength of racial traditionalism in eastern North Carolina. Further, the deep roots of racial traditionalism in this Coastal Plain region provided the necessary ingredient to facilitate the rise of Tar Heel Republicanism beginning in the mid-1960s.

After the 1954 *Brown* decision the Democrat-controlled General Assembly sought to keep itself lily-white, even while key state politicians, with the prominent exception of Beverly Lake, avoided the rhetoric of resistance. Because most legislative districts had more than one member, legislators were concerned that blacks might concentrate their votes on one black candidate, who could be elected if whites spread their votes among various white candidates. This process, known as "single-shooting" or "bullet-voting," has historically been the major method that a black must choose to win an election if whites are unwilling to support a black candidate (Luebke 1979). First in 1955 with an anti-single-shot law and later in 1967 with a numbered-seat plan that also precluded single-shooting, the all-white legislature took two concrete steps to keep blacks from holding seats. These civil-rights-era laws were in addition to literacy tests, a mechanism stemming from the turn of the century to keep blacks from even registering to vote.

In 1982 black Greensboro attorney Henry Frye would become the first African American to serve on the North Carolina Supreme Court. In 1956, however, as a college graduate and veteran returning to his small eastern Piedmont hometown of Ellerbe, he had been denied the right to vote by a local registrar who claimed Frye had failed the literacy test. Just twelve years later Frye would be the first black to be seated in the General Assembly in the twentieth century. He was elected from Greensboro, where a coalition of blacks and white modernizers provided the necessary votes. Frye overcame the legislative obstacles to black victories and was for many a sign of hope. But in 1969 he remained the sole black legislator of 170 representatives and senators, even though more than one-fifth of the state's residents were black.

Also highlighting North Carolina's resistance to racial change was a nationally publicized trial following conflict in Wilmington in early 1971 over school desegregation. Ben Chavis was a United Church of Christ minister assigned to the church's Commission for Racial Justice. He went to Wilmington after white-instigated violence sought to undermine court-ordered school desegregation, and a Wilmington Church of Christ minister asked Chavis to help black high school students negotiate their differences with the all-white school board. After the school board proved recalcitrant, Chavis helped organize a nonviolent student boycott, which was met by white vigilante actions. Throughout this period city government refused Chavis's request for a curfew to curb the violence. Several firebombings occurred, including one at a small grocery named Mike's.

One year later, in March 1972, Chavis, seven black male teenagers, a twenty-one-year-old black man, and a thirty-four-year-old white woman were arrested for that firebombing. The "Wilmington Ten," as they became known, were found guilty of arson in November 1972 and sentenced to a total of 282 years in prison. Chavis's 29-to-34-year term was the longest imposed for arson in North Carolina history. The prosecuting attorney urged that the ten defendants receive maximum sentences, describing them in courtroom arguments as "dangerous animals who should be put away for the rest of their lives" (Pinsky 1977, 754; Myerson 1978, 188–89; Fox 1982).

In retrospect, the Wilmington Ten case appeared to be a prime example of prosecutors guided by racial traditionalism. The three major witnesses for the prosecution, two of whom were convicted felons, recanted their testimony in 1976 and early 1977 after a five-year campaign by defense attorneys and political support groups (Pinsky 1977, 755). Nevertheless, the Wilmington Ten's state and federal appeals were exhausted, and they were in jail before the witnesses' recantations became public.

Following extensive publicity about the case from Amnesty International, the Congressional Black Caucus, and CBS's "60 Minutes," as well as criticism of the state's case from dailies such as the *Charlotte Observer* and the *News and Observer*, Governor Jim Hunt in January 1978 felt compelled to act (*News and Observer* 1978a). Black leaders wanted the governor to issue a pardon, but he merely reduced the sentences so that the defendants could be eligible for parole. Hunt's move was consistent with the moderate actions that are central to modernizer ideology. In refusing to pardon the Wilmington Ten, he acknowledged that the case was hurting North Carolina's reputation. Yet he declined to take sides between the prosecution and the defense (*News and Observer* 1978a; W. King 1978).

The Klan billboard in Smithfield, anti-single-shot legislation, and the Wilmington Ten case all demonstrated the strength of North Carolina's racial traditionalism behind a facade of racial modernism. Politically active black Tar Heels in the 1970s had few illusions about the reality of racial politics in North Carolina. Blacks' low voter registration and little electoral success statewide also became evident late in the decade. This lack of success led to a historic voting rights case by black plaintiffs against the Democratic-dominated government of North Carolina. It focused the argument of whether black Democrats should seek political power without relying on an alliance with white Democrats.

Documenting Voting Discrimination:
Gingles v. Edmisten

In 1960 nearly 40 percent of all eligible blacks were registered to vote in North Carolina, by far the highest percentage in the South. In 1980 North Carolina fell to last place in that category, although the number of registered blacks actually increased to 49 percent. In the six other southern states covered by the 1965 Voting Rights Act, federal intervention to prevent harassment of black voters by white registrars sparked major voter registration drives. The most dramatic change occurred in Mississippi, where the percentage of eligible blacks registered to vote jumped from 5 in 1960 to 72 in 1980.

In North Carolina, however, the presence of racial modernizers in the state's political leadership had the apparent effect of reducing the amount of local civil rights activism by blacks. Black leaders acknowledged that North Carolina's moderate reputation influenced blacks' own perceptions of the necessity of political organizing. As NAACP state president Kelly Alexander Jr. said, "Everybody looked at North Carolina as a liberal state. It [the discrimination] was more sophisticated. A lot of blacks themselves had been propagandized into believing North Carolina wasn't Mississippi or South Carolina. . . . We've had to fight a feeling of apathy, complacency" (*News and Observer* 1981e).

But political success was constrained by white resistance as well as black complacency. The major barrier lay in the presence of multimember voting districts. Because of housing segregation, blacks usually lived in a particular part of a county. If electoral districts had only one representative, blacks' chances of election from a majority-black district were enhanced. Multimember districts tended to dilute black voting strength.

The problem of vote dilution became clear in the November 1980 election. In the three metropolitan counties that surround the cities of Charlotte, Greensboro, and Winston-Salem, where blacks constituted more than 20 percent of the registered voters, four blacks (two in Charlotte) had captured the Democratic nomination for the state house. Yet none of the four black Democrats won a seat, even though most of the white Democrats in these counties were successful. Had each of these black candidates campaigned in a single-member district (similar to a ward seat in a city council election), all would have been elected. Electoral analysis showed that many whites in the three counties were unwilling to vote for a black Democrat (Luebke and Feeney 1981).

In 1981, as a consequence of the multimember district and racially polarized voting by whites, only 4 of 170 seats in the General Assembly were occupied by blacks. Twelve years after Henry Frye's historic election to the legislature, progress had been minimal. For blacks to win a General Assembly seat, it appeared that several factors were necessary. First, a substantial minority of whites in a multimember district had to find the black candidate attractive. In Greensboro in 1980, state senate candidate Frye, after six terms in the North Carolina House of Representatives, was popular enough with white voters to defeat the opposition. But fellow black Democrat attorney Bill Martin, a political unknown in white Guilford County, could not garner enough white votes, and a white Republican was elected instead.

Eventually, after several losses, a persistent Bill Martin might well have gained enough white modernizer support in Greensboro to win one seat in a three-seat, majority-white state senate district that spanned Guilford County. But under pressure from blacks to increase the opportunities for black representation in the General Assembly, the 1982 legislature redrew the lines to create a single-seat, majority-black senate district. Martin won that election in his first try in November 1982.

Second, for blacks to win representation the Republican Party had to be weak. If the party were strong, as in Charlotte, Greensboro, and Winston-Salem, whites who did not want to support a black Democrat had a viable option in the white Republican candidate. That explains Martin's loss in 1980 even though Frye had won from the same senate district in 1978. But the metro Piedmont counties around Durham and Raleigh produced a different political story in 1980. All Republicans in Wake County (Raleigh) ran far behind the black Democrat from Raleigh, and the black candidate, newcomer Dan Blue, was elected. In Durham the Republicans failed to field a candidate. In both counties the black Democratic candidates won but by fewer votes than the successful white Democrats.

A third factor that helped blacks was single-shooting. A 1971 federal court ruling had thrown out both General Assembly laws that restricted single-shooting. But in Charlotte, Greensboro, and Winston-Salem in 1980, black political organizations urged support of the entire Democratic ticket. Therefore, when white Democrats failed to support blacks while black Democrats voted for whites, the blacks lost (Luebke and Feeney 1981).

This constellation of factors led blacks to undertake two challenges of the multimember approach. First, and most importantly, four black plaintiffs in September 1981 filed suit in federal court against the state of North Carolina on the grounds that the multimember electoral system violated the constitutional rights of all black Tar Heels. This action became known as *Gingles v. Edmisten*, named after the first black plaintiff, Ralph Gingles, and the state attorney general, Rufus Edmisten, who was formally responsible for defending the state of North Carolina. Second, in February 1982, when the Democrat-dominated General Assembly considered redistricting in accord with the 1980 census, blacks urged the creation of single-member districts both in the metro Piedmont and in the heavily black counties of the Coastal Plain. White Democrats balked at the idea, for both philosophical and practical reasons.

Philosophically, modernizer Democrats believed that the party was and should be color-blind. To build majority-black, single-member districts that usually assured the election of black representatives, in the view of white modernizers, accentuated race consciousness that might otherwise disappear gradually. Subsequently, in 1993, Robinson Everett would make precisely that argument in *Shaw v. Reno*. Traditionalist Democrats, with less sympathy for black concerns, saw no reason to allow blacks to win what appeared to them to be a guaranteed legislative seat.

White Democrats, modernizer and traditionalist alike, also opposed majority-black districts for a practical reason. In the metropolitan counties where Republicans were strong, the loss of black Democrats' votes would almost assuredly lead to some GOP legislative victories. Despite a strong argument from blacks, the General Assembly drew majority-black, single-member districts only in those counties whose election laws were subject to U.S. Justice Department approval because they fell under the provisions of the Voting Rights Act.

The redistricting decision disappointed blacks, even though they gained 4 additional seats in the house in the fall 1982 election, bringing their total to 8 of 170 seats. But blacks still believed North Carolina's redistricting plan discriminated against them in many parts of the state that were not subject to the Voting Rights Act.

The stage was set for the *Gingles* case, led by black lawyer Lani Guinier (who in 1993 became a controversial Clinton nominee as assistant attorney general for civil rights) and Leslie Winner, a white female attorney from the biracial law firm of Julius Chambers and James Ferguson in Charlotte. Chambers and Ferguson were the well-known black lawyers who had previously argued the *Swann v. Charlotte-Mecklenburg County* school desegregation case and defended the Wilmington Ten. The state nevertheless remained confident that the suit would be rejected, particularly because the 1982 election results doubled the number of black seats in the General Assembly. The state's argument was rooted in the modernizers' premise that race relations were improving gradually and the federal courts should not interfere with this political process. The state hired a Washington-based firm that specialized in voting rights cases to coordinate a defense with lawyers from the attorney general's office. The North Carolina Republican Party joined the suit in support of the black plaintiffs. Republicans correctly presumed that if the courts forced single-member districts on the state's metro Piedmont counties, some Republican legislators could be elected from majority-white suburban areas.

A three-judge federal panel in Raleigh heard the evidence in the summer of 1983 and ruled in the plaintiffs' favor in January 1984, thereby forcing seven single-member districts to be created in the state house and two in the state senate. The U.S. Supreme Court in June 1986 upheld all but one of the seats. In retrospect, it is clear that the strong 1982 revision of the 1965 Voting Rights Act provided the basis for the plaintiffs' victory. Yet when Gingles and others filed their suit in 1981, no one knew what would be the content of the new act.

The 1982 federal act focused on the "totality of circumstances" that might result in a situation where "a racial minority has less opportunity than other members of the electorate to participate in the political process and elect representatives of their choice" (Voting Rights Act of 1965, as amended June 29, 1982, quoted in Roach 1984). The Congress construed these circumstances very broadly, accepting the sociological argument that the total social forces that influence racial politics must be considered. For example, according to the law, one of the seven factors that built a plaintiff's case was whether the socioeconomic status of blacks was lower than that of whites, a condition that was virtually certain in the United States. Congress accepted the scholarly insight that a lower socioeconomic status reduces the likelihood of political participation in the United States and is, for blacks, primarily a consequence of past racial discrimination. The plaintiffs in *Gingles* could easily show socioeconomic differences in just about every institutional category in North Carolina, from the absence of indoor plumbing to the small number of blacks in professional and managerial jobs.

The plaintiffs also recounted the conscious actions of the General Assembly, from 1900 through the 1960s, to reduce black political participation and thus black political power. These included poll taxes, a literacy test, and anti-single-shot legislation. Further, they argued, the Democratic runoff primary, which began in 1915 in the one-party South as a substitute for the meaningless November election, allowed whites in the post–civil rights South to gang up against a black candidate who had led white candidates in the first primary. Former Chapel Hill mayor Howard Lee's bid for lieutenant governor in 1976 and Durham state representative Mickey Michaux's campaign for U.S. Congress in 1982 were two such examples.

Another key circumstance covered in the Voting Rights Act of 1982 dealt with the absence or presence of racial appeals. Did a white candidate draw attention to a black candidate's race in order to attract white votes? The plaintiffs in *Gingles* noted that at the turn of the century the Democratic Party used the specter of black political power to win key elections. In 1950 the U.S. Senate campaign of traditionalist Democrat Willis Smith successfully used racial appeals against Smith's opponent, former University of North Carolina President Frank Graham. In 1976 traditionalist Democrat Jimmy Green ran newspaper ads in eastern North Carolina featuring a picture of his black opponent, Howard Lee. The same advertisement said that "unless the people come out and vote on September 14, the election will be decided by a relatively small segment of the population." Such language telegraphed the importance of white votes in countering black electoral participation without actually using the words "white" and "black."

Parallel racial appeals were evident in the 1982 second congressional district runoff election between Mickey Michaux and former state legislator Tim Valentine. Michaux, who in 1972 had become the first black to represent Durham in the state house, was a blend of populist and modernizer ideologies. In the first 1982 Democratic primary he had won 42 percent of the vote, and white traditionalist Valentine, from Nash County in the Coastal Plain section of the congressional district, had shared the remaining 58 percent with another white candidate. Shortly before the runoff primary, Valentine circulated an anti-Michaux "Dear Neighbor" flyer among white voters both in the district's rural counties and in selected white traditionalist precincts within Durham County. The one-page sheet first identified the nonracial threat to traditionalist values, asking voters "whether you want to be represented in Congress by a big-government, free-spending liberal with close ties to the labor bosses." The flyer then closed with a racial appeal: "It's not easy to stop and take time to vote, but *you* must. Our polls indicate that the same well organized block [*sic*] vote which was so obvious and influential in the First Primary will turn out again on July 27. My opponent will again be *bussing his supporters* to the polling places in record number." References to a "block vote" and "bussing" communicated the information about a black candidate to white voters. And Michaux, electoral analysis indicates, received almost no white votes beyond those he had already acquired in the first primary.

A final example of racial appeals emerged shortly before the beginning of the *Gingles* trial. In the spring of 1983 the Helms campaign had run a series of newspaper and radio ads that identified Governor Jim Hunt as beholden to black voters and suggested that such white-black alliances were illegitimate.

Another circumstance identified by Congress in the 1982 bill was the electoral success rate of blacks compared with their proportion of the total population. In North Carolina in 1980, blacks constituted 5 percent of the elected officials but 22 percent of the population. Thus for each of the circumstances described above, the North Carolina evidence painted a picture of blacks handicapped by past and present discrimination.

But probably the most crucial circumstance was the level of racially polarized voting in a district. In particular, how much evidence was there that whites would support a qualified black candidate? Congress focused on whether "substantially significant" differences existed between the voting patterns of whites and blacks. In *Gingles v. Edmisten*, the plaintiffs' expert witness testified that, of the fifty-three elections that had taken place in the affected districts in recent years, strong racial polarization prevailed fifty-one times. In lay terms it meant that the preferences of black voters were undermined by most white voters who, while nominally Democrats (Black 1975), in fact refused to consider supporting a *black* Democrat.

The federal court concluded that, given the totality of circumstances, "the creation of each of the multi-member districts challenged in this action results in the black registered voters being submerged as a voting minority." Such submerging of the black vote, according to the court, was precisely what Congress had sought to prohibit under the 1982 Voting Rights Act. Consequently, the court unanimously ordered redistricting in all of the districts.

Primarily as a result of the *Gingles* decision, in November 1984 blacks won a record number of 14 seats in the General Assembly. Over time the decision's impact was felt in city councils, county commissions, and school boards across North Carolina. In most cases, after *Gingles* was upheld by the U.S. Supreme Court in 1986, local governments reached out-of-court settlements with black plaintiffs, providing for single-member districts that gave blacks an excellent chance of electoral victories in local government roughly proportional to their percentage in the population. Primarily as a result of these voting rights suits, the number of black elected officials at the municipal level jumped more than 30 percent between 1985 and 1987, from 144 to 194 seats. Prior to the *Gingles* decision, between 1980 and 1985, the number of local officials increased by just 6 percent, from 136 to 144 seats (JCPS 1980; JCPS 1985; JCPS 1987).

But white Democrats' fears of Republican victories were realized. In cities such as Charlotte and Winston-Salem, majority-white districts supported Republicans in both 1984 and 1986. To white Democratic modernizers, this showed the error of blacks' thinking, as it allowed Republicans with less sympathy for black concerns to win legislative seats. For blacks, however, two points remained salient. First, white Democrats needed to develop a political program that appealed to white voters, and they must not rely on the party loyalty of blacks to win seats in the strongly two-party sections of the state. Second, blacks believed in their right to elect candidates of their own choosing. Before the *Gingles* case, blacks could be elected in multimember districts with creditable Republican opposition only if their views were acceptable to a substantial minority of whites. Blacks supported the thrust of the revised Voting Rights Act, that the candidate need only be the choice of blacks. In the view of both Congress and most politicized blacks in North Carolina, the history of institutional racism made it likely that black and white citizens might not have the same political values and priorities.

The White Reaction against Majority-Black Districts: *Shaw v. Reno*

After the General Assembly in January 1992 finalized new majority-black congressional districts, the November 1992 elections brought the expected result. Two African Americans were among the eight Democrats elected from North Carolina's expanded membership (from eleven to twelve) in the U.S. House of Representatives. Less noticed by most white observers were the populist-leaning first-term voting records of both first district congresswoman Eva Clayton, from Warren County in the Black Belt near the Virginia line, and twelfth district congressman Mel Watt, a former state senator from Charlotte who had managed the unsuccessful U.S. Senate campaign of Harvey Gantt. Clayton and Watt usually voted along the generally economic populist lines of the Congressional Black Caucus, in contrast to the voting choices of two white congressmen representing metro Piedmont counties, David Price of Chapel Hill and Steve Neal of Winston-Salem (Luebke 1994). Price and Neal in national terms resembled the moderate positions of white southern Democrats such as U.S. Senators Chuck Robb of Virginia or Lawton Chiles of Florida. In terms of North Carolina state politics, they resembled the modernizer values of Governor Jim Hunt.

One important contrast between Watt and Clayton, on one hand, and the white Democratic congressmen elected in 1992, on the other, was their respective positions on a 1993 bill to establish a Canadian-style single-payer health insurance system (the so-called McDermott bill). Only Watt and Clayton became cosigners of the single-payer bill, while they also joined the six whites, including Price and Neal, in cosponsoring Bill Clinton's more centrist and ill-fated managed-care health reform bill (Luebke 1994).

To white modernizers offended by the gerrymandered first and twelfth districts, it was irrelevant that African American voters had two congressional representatives who more accurately reflected the district majority's left-of-center views on economic issues. This contrasted with white elected officials who generally voted more to the right than their black constituents would have preferred. For white modernizers the crucial point was that civil rights-era racial conflict was, or should be, an issue of the past. As a result, congressional districts should be drawn in a color-blind rather than a race-sensitive fashion.

Durham modernizer Robinson Everett was not alone in suing to overturn the majority-minority districts approved for the 1992 congressional elections by the U.S. Justice Department and the federal courts. In 1993 equivalent lawsuits were filed by white plaintiffs in Georgia, Louisiana, Florida, and Texas (in Texas, Hispanics also gained representation in 1992, so part of the lawsuit opposed that majority-Hispanic congressional district).

In its 1993 decision, *Shaw v. Reno*, the U.S. Supreme Court ruled on a 5-to-4 vote that the twelfth congressional district (the so-called Interstate 85 district) may have violated the equal protection clause of the U.S. Constitution and have been unconstitutional (*News and Observer* 1996b). Besides coming on a close vote, the Court's ruling was ambiguous in several ways. First, the equal protection clause was applied to white plaintiffs, who according to the ruling may have been denied their constitutional rights by the North Carolina General Assembly, because the General Assembly had included them in an acknowledgedly gerrymandered, 140-mile-long district. Was the Court saying that an African American member of Congress could not represent a white? Second, Justice Sandra Day O'Connor, author of the majority opinion, stated that a majority-minority district was automatically suspect if it "looked" strange to a federal court. Her conclusion that appearances mattered when race was a factor constituted what lawyers term "new law" (Sentelle 1996).

In its decision the Court also skirted the ultimate issue of constitutionality by remanding the *Shaw v. Reno* case back to a three-judge federal panel in Raleigh. A similar federal court had ruled in *Gingles v. Edmisten* in 1984 that the existing district plan for the General Assembly had violated the rights of African Americans by diluting their opportunity to elect candidates of their choosing (see discussion of *Gingles v. Edmisten* above). The three-judge panel in 1995 faced the question of whether race was the primary factor in the construction of the first, twelfth, and subsequent districts. Following testimony from both the state attorney general's office, in defense of the General Assembly's redistricting plan, and Robinson Everett in opposition, this panel of judges ruled that the General Assembly's action was constitutional.

Everett filed an appeal in the case, ultimately known as *Shaw v. Hunt*, to the U.S. Supreme Court. In June 1996, in accord with an earlier 1996 decision that had struck down Georgia's three majority-black congressional districts, the Supreme Court ruled in Everett's favor. Reversing the North Carolina panel's decision, the Supreme Court ruled 5 to 4 that race had been the predominant factor in the North Carolina redistricting, just as the Supreme Court found race to have (improperly) been the predominant factor in the Georgia case. Interestingly, the Supreme Court indicated in the majority opinion that factors besides race—for example, political party strength—were permissible bases for congressional redistricting; only race could not be the leading factor.

The consequence for North Carolina's congressional districts was immediate. The 1997 General Assembly, under a Supreme Court-imposed deadline, drew two black-influenced, but not majority-black, districts. Both Mel Watt in the twelfth and Eva Clayton in the first would face reelection in 1998 with greater numbers of white voters—a majority in each case—than in their previous contests.

The Future of Black Politics in North Carolina

Black Tar Heels face a political dilemma similar to that encountered by African Americans across the United States. The great majority of black voters would prefer a political program that is more egalitarian—that is, more to the left—than that advocated by modernizer-traditionalists such as Governor Hunt. But the antigovernment traditionalism of most North Carolina Republicans is even less attractive than the punitive "welfare reform" and tough-on-crime bills of Hunt and most state senate Democrats (Fitzsimon 1997a).

When white Democratic Party leaders, in both North Carolina and the rest of the South, retreated during the 1990s from their already limited populist agenda and toward both economic and social traditionalism, big corporations' domination of "legitimate" political debate in the South produced very negative consequences for the typical African American voter. The weakness in North Carolina of organized labor and other citizen organizations that could dissent from modernizer Democrats' pro-big-business agenda meant that economic-populist policy, even when introduced by a handful of populist-leaning legislators, was quickly labeled unrealistic by legislative-insider opinion-makers. For example, at the beginning of 1997, legislative insiders, following the conventional wisdom of no more tax cuts, announced to the *News and Observer* and the *Charlotte Observer* that the General Assembly would not cut the food tax during that legislative session. These two newspapers duly reported to the public in their 1997 legislative outlook reports that any cuts in the sales tax on groceries (beyond the 1 percent cut in 1996) were unlikely.

A middle-income or low-income citizen of any race might wonder why, given that state tax revenues appeared abundant, legislative insiders were so sure that a progressive tax cut was not on either Governor Hunt's, the senate Democrats' or the house Republicans' agenda. If newspapers were to be believed, citizen advocacy of such a tax cut would make no difference.

Since the median income of black Tar Heels is lower than that of whites, a food tax cut would always provide disproportionately more benefits to blacks. Yet black North Carolinians in 1997 found not a single one of the eight black Democrats in the fifty-member state senate willing to be the prime organizer of an anti–food tax bill. A rookie populist Democrat from Orange County, Ellie Kinnaird, did introduce the bill, and ten fellow Democrats, both black and white, became cosigners. Ironically for African American Tar Heels, in the state senate the initiative to cut the food tax was led by a white traditionalist Republican, Ham Horton of Winston-Salem.

The 1997 General Assembly did in fact cut the food tax by an additional 1 percent. An unholy alliance (see Chapter 3) of populist house Democrats—both white and black—and antitax traditionalist house Republicans forced the food tax cut onto the house agenda (*News and Observer* 1997c). In mid-session the house GOP leadership endorsed and easily passed the 1 percent food tax cut. In budget negotiations house Republicans held firm against senate Democratic leaders (almost exclusively modernizers and modernizer-traditionalists with no sympathy for economic populism) who opposed the food tax cut, allegedly because the state could not afford it. The 1997 budget compromise included the tax cut but, in a concession to the senate Democrats, set the implementation date for July 1998 rather than January 1998.

Significantly for a discussion of African American politics, black state senators were unable or unwilling to work as a caucus to demand of white senate leaders that the food tax cut take place in January 1998. In the case of progressive taxation issues, it appears that black representation in the state senate does not matter. Does it matter on any other issue?

The answer is yes for the spending side of the General Assembly budget. First, legislative black caucus chair Senator Bill Martin of Greensboro played a key role in 1997 in holding the line against a house Republican welfare reform program that was even more punitive than Governor

Hunt's and the senate Democrats' Work First proposals. Second, black senators such as Jeanne Lucas of Durham, a retired public school teacher, were firm advocates of increases in schoolteacher pay throughout the 1990s. In general, both African American state senators and representatives supported social spending programs whose benefits were thought to be tilted toward the low-income citizen. Further, during Dan Blue's two terms as house Speaker from 1991 until 1995, Blue and other key African American legislators, among them Toby Fitch of Wilson, sought to minimize social spending cuts (the 1991 "recession" session) and to maximize appropriations for public schools, social services, and worker health and safety (see Chapters 2 and 6 above).

But in general the narrow parameters of North Carolina's political debate (see Luebke 1981b; Luebke 1975) have led most black elected officials to avoid so-called controversial stands on economic populist issues. This avoidance of controversy by North Carolina's black legislative caucus stands in stark contrast to the Congressional Black Caucus, which over the years has developed strong positions in defense of average citizens and against tax breaks for the wealthy and big business, including opposition to the corporate welfare largesse that is integral to most Pentagon contracts with military suppliers. Veteran Democratic presidential candidate and A&T alumnus Jesse Jackson (see above) provides another contrast. Both during his 1988 presidential campaign and during the 1990s when he visited the state in support of union-organizing drives (*News and Observer* 1997k), Jackson's message focused on the centrality of economic rather than racial conflict. In Jackson's view the important conflict is between workers and the wealthy, not between white and black workers. This open discussion of economic populism was most unusual for North Carolina.

Some African American politicians who have run statewide have taken issue with Jackson's advocacy of economic populism. Two examples are Chapel Hill state senator Howard Lee and former Charlotte mayor Harvey Gantt. Lee, who in 1969 was one of the South's first black politicians to win a mayoral election in a majority-white town, Chapel Hill, ran in 1976 against white traditionalist Jimmy Green for the Democratic nomination for lieutenant governor. Lee's economic program sounded more modernizer than populist, even to the point of supporting repeal of the food tax "only if the revenue picture allows it." In 1972, when Lee ran for U.S. Congress in the heavily black second congressional district, he campaigned openly as an economic populist. Lee explained in a post-1976 interview that leading Democrats close to Jim Hunt and Terry Sanford had persuaded him to soften his economic views in preparation for the 1976 campaign (Luebke 1979).

Lee's promises about economic development were virtually indistinguishable from the campaign literature of traditionalist Jimmy Green. Not surprisingly, as noted earlier in this chapter, Green relied on racial appeals to white voters in his second primary victory over Lee. The consequence of Lee's adoption of modernizer ideology was minimal among black voters, who supported him anyway for reasons of racial solidarity. But among less-affluent whites Lee's equivocation made him just another mainstream Democratic candidate, albeit a black one.

Two decades later, while serving in the state senate, Lee was a strong supporter of education and economic development; his positions were again more modernizer than populist. Most voters in Lee's majority-white Chapel Hill-based district appeared to consider his views noncontroversial. If Lee chose to run again for statewide office, it seemed clear he would run as a modernizer.

When Harvey Gantt ran in 1990 for the U.S. Senate against incumbent senator Jesse Helms, Helms spent most of the 1990 campaign on the defensive (see Chapter 8 below). Gantt surprised Helms and most political observers with a hard-driving campaign that argued that a New South such as the growing Tar Heel state deserved a new U.S. senator. But Gantt was unwilling to undertake an economic populist attack against Helms, even though Helms was arguably vulnerable for having supported in the 1980s both the savings and loan industry bailout and a federal increase in the cigarette tax. Such a populist attack might have loosened Helms's hold on low- and middle-income whites who were inclined to view Helms as a friend of average (white) citizens.

Some African Americans dispute the notion that economic populism can help black candidates win white votes. They argue that the significance of black politicians is symbolic. It sends a message both to black and white voters that the old whites-only politics is no longer acceptable (Jones 1975, cited in Luebke 1979). This view receives backhanded support from the hostility toward blacks shown by many white North Carolinians, especially white residents of the Coastal Plain region in which blacks are a strong minority or, in some towns and counties, an absolute majority of the population. During the 1990s, for example, in most regions of North Carolina, African American U.S. Senate candidate Gantt in 1990 and 1996 received a similar or even higher percentage of the countywide vote than either of two white Democrats, Bill Clinton in 1992 and 1996 or U.S. Senator Terry Sanford in his unsuccessful reelection bid in 1992. But in the Coastal Plain region the electorate gave a smaller percentage of the vote to Gantt than to either Clinton or Sanford. Given the overwhelming tendency of blacks to vote a straight-Democrat ticket regardless of the Democratic candidate's race, it appears that Gantt's lower support was a direct consequence of Coastal Plain whites who were less willing to support a black Democrat than a white Democrat.

A second example of Coastal Plain white hostility to the demands of African Americans for racially equal treatment occurred in Enfield, a majority-black town of 3,000 located sixty miles northeast of Raleigh. In 1997 three white town commissioners refused to appropriate funds to provide sewer hookups to a low-income black section of the town, even though town commissioners eight years before, in 1989, had promised to do so. The 3-to-2 white majority avoided implementing the plan, even though the neighborhood's residents were using outhouses and children were playing around seeping raw sewage. Only a boycott of town commission meetings by the two black commissioners and the nonvoting black mayor—thus preventing the quorum needed to enact any budget for the 1997–98 fiscal year—drew any media attention to the crisis (*Washington Post* 1997; *News and Observer* 1997l).

The patent race discrimination practiced by Enfield's majority-white town board (no white neighborhood faced comparable public health hazards) in the late 1990s, coupled with the apparent unwillingness of many Tar Heel whites even to consider voting for a black candidate, stands in stark contrast to politics in the geographically close Research Triangle region. In both 1990 and 1996 the Research Triangle area gave a majority vote to Gantt over Helms, even though 75 percent of the region's voters are white. Coastal Plain blacks point to the Enfield example as clear evidence of two North Carolinas. In their North Carolina, still dominated in the late 1990s by white racial traditionalism, they believe the evidence is clear that the mere presence of a black elected official provides sufficient representation in a racially hostile sociopolitical environment. Advocates of this representation-by-color argument would also challenge the notion that middle- and low-income whites could ever sufficiently overcome their antiblack prejudice to become part of a biracial economic populist coalition.

Compared with the 1980s, North Carolina's legislative black caucus in the late 1990s provided a more diverse black membership, especially a higher percentage of African American legislators whose nonlegislative occupations require frequent interaction with whites. This contrasted with the 1980s, when black legislators, as pastors, funeral home directors, or community advocates, spent most of their work time in an all-black environment. Also, the spread of ideological preferences among black legislators became evident: from cautious modernizers close to Governor Hunt to some with strong economic populist sympathies, as well as some Coastal Plain legislators who saw themselves as representing blacks, with little or no ideology delineated. Because of the U.S. Supreme Court decision in *Shaw v. Hunt*, the required redistricting by the 2001 General Assembly would assuredly put an end to many of the black-majority districts that were established in 1992. With redistricting into more black-influenced rather than majority-black legislative districts a certainty for both the state house and the state senate, the size and policy preferences of the Tar Heel black caucus in the early twenty-first century remained unclear as 2000 approached. Put in a national context, the question remained whether the black caucus of the future would lean more toward a black modernizer, such as retired general Colin Powell, or toward an economic populist advocate of the less-affluent, such as Jesse Jackson.

8

Tar Heel Politics 1984 and 1990:
Why Helms Beat Hunt and Gantt

Jesse Helms has been unquestionably North Carolina's most controversial politician of the twentieth century. He became a household word among Tar Heels during the 1960s, when his editorials blasting black and antiwar protesters aired daily on a Raleigh television station and on statewide radio. Among those who care about national or North Carolina politics, few are neutral about Helms. To his partisans, his years in the U.S. Senate have represented a major counterattack against flawed domestic and international policies. To his detractors, Helms is an embarrassment, damaging North Carolina's long-held national reputation as the progressive pacesetter in the New South.

Both nationally and in North Carolina, no one has represented social and economic traditionalism better than Jesse Helms. But it is not his traditionalist views that make him unusual; indeed, traditionalists, especially in the Republican Party, abound in North Carolina and many other southern states. Rather, Helms makes his mark because of his forceful personality. Early in his fifth U.S. Senate term in 1997, Helms, chairman of the Senate Foreign Relations Committee, reminded the political insiders of Washington, D.C., especially Republicans, that he was not to be "messed with." He single-handedly held up the confirmation hearings for a fellow Republican, then-governor of Massachusetts, William Weld, as ambassador to Mexico. Helms insisted that Weld's antidrug credentials as a governor were too weak to make him a serious choice as ambassador to a neighboring country whose own drug-enforcement policies were in question. In September 1997 President Clinton had to back down (Cohen 1997).

Helms's actions against Weld highlighted a major characteristic of his political approach. He values ideological commitment more strongly than political party loyalty. In 1996, as Helms faced another reelection battle, he crossed party lines to work with the same Bill Clinton to enact tough international prohibitions on trade with Cuba. In his first term during the 1970s he happily worked with social traditionalist Democratic senators, mostly from the South, who shared his antipathy both toward the U.S. Supreme Court-mandated public school desegregation and toward the Court's 1973 decision that ensured a woman's right to abort a pregnancy.

Significantly, Helms won election to the Senate five times with a coalition of Republicans and Democrats, many of whom disagreed with some of his strong traditionalist beliefs. Poll data show clearly that Helms's views were not typical of those of most North Carolinians. Similar to Ronald Reagan's appeal as president, Helms's charismatic personality attracted voters who disagreed with many of his specific opinions.

Nevertheless, in national political terms Helms has stood as the leader of a successful countermovement, the New Right, that arose in response to the egalitarian movements of the 1960s (cf. Lo 1982). Within North Carolina the senator's electoral victories rarely translated into political power for other traditionalist Republicans at the state level.

Helms's Debt to the National Congressional Club

The leaders of the National Congressional Club nurtured Helms's political successes from his first U.S. Senate campaign in 1972 through his hard-fought fourth victory in 1990 against former Charlotte mayor Harvey Gantt. The club's heyday was from 1976 through 1984, as it was instrumental in key political victories of both Reagan and Helms. Helms's political confidante Tom Ellis founded the Congressional Club in 1973 to retire the

$350,000 debt that Helms had incurred during his successful 1972 race. In 1994 Helms and the leading brain truster at the club, Carter Wrenn, had a falling-out. The National Congressional Club closed its books and went out of business by 1995.

Over the years the club became one of the nation's leading fund-raisers among PACs, generating, for example, $30 million between 1980 and 1988. Even in 1987, when the club was reeling from political defeats at the hands of North Carolina mainstream Republicans, it raised $2 million (Fahy and Reid 1986; *News and Observer* 1988a). Its contributors lived across the United States, and checks commonly ranged in size from $25 to $200. At its peak the club listed 118,000 persons as members and had millions of names on its direct-mail solicitation lists (Reid 1986; Peters 1986).

The Congressional Club stood out in national and state politics for two reasons: the fervor of its political beliefs, and its technical skill at promoting those beliefs or attacking political opponents. Like Helms himself, the club had a missionary dedication to traditionalist ideology, to what its leaders called "the conservative cause." Beliefs were more important than party label, and occasionally the club even supported a Democrat. Club chairman Tom Ellis told an interviewer in 1986 that "the reason the Congressional Club exists is to do everything it can to further the conservative cause. That's what it's all about—we have to save this country" (Peters 1986, C6). Unlike many Tar Heel traditionalists who seemed resigned to the changes in American society promoted by national Democrats during the 1960s and 1970s, Ellis and Helms were determined to resist and reverse those changes. In short, the club's raison d'être was the support of ideological candidates, primarily Helms himself and Ronald Reagan.

From 1973 until Reagan's presidential election in 1980 the club's reputation grew both because its fund-raising appeals brought in millions of dollars and because the two major candidates on whom it focused, Helms and Reagan, were successful. The Congressional Club engineered a Reagan upset of Gerald Ford in North Carolina's 1976 Republican presidential primary, helped Helms in his 1978 reelection, defeated an incumbent Democratic U.S. senator in 1980, and spent $4.5 million as an independent committee for Reagan, also in 1980. The club's greatest victory occurred in 1984, when Ellis and executive director Carter Wrenn ran the multimillion-dollar advertising campaign that resulted in Helms's narrow victory over Governor Jim Hunt.

Jesse Helms's Heritage

Helms was born in 1921 in Monroe, a small county seat about forty miles southeast of Charlotte. His traditionalist values of free enterprise, racial segregation, and patriarchal family were nurtured in this small-town environment, where his father served as police chief. Fundamentalist Protestantism, in particular the Baptist denomination, provided the religious underpinnings for traditionalism in Monroe, as it did elsewhere in North Carolina and the South.

During his youth Helms's family was not particularly interested in politics. Helms enjoyed journalism and the high school band and won a state prize for his tuba playing. After graduating from high school in 1938, he enrolled in a nearby Baptist college, now known as Wingate University, only after encouragement from his high school principal, Ray House. Many years later Helms remembered House as "the greatest exponent of the free enterprise system," telling Helms that with hard work "you can make it in this country" and "you'll own your own homes and you'll have two cars and all that." Interviewed at about the same time, House recalled that in high school Helms was "a regular old boy—long-legged and bug-eyed" and always working hard on part-time jobs (quotations from Furgurson 1986, 37). When House died in 1997, Helms eulogized him as one of the most influential persons in his life.

House's mid-1980s interview with a Maryland journalist provided a good feel for the racial environment in small-town North Carolina during the 1930s from the standpoint of apolitical whites: "Segregation was a way of life. We couldn't have done anything. If we would have started a fight against it, somebody would have shot us. You had to live like that. But we didn't have malice" (Furgurson 1986, 38–39). Helms's analysis of race relations has often sounded similar to House's. The senator's public comments until the 1980s underscored his view that Jim Crow racial segregation was part of the times and that, therefore, the demands of blacks for immediate desegregation in the 1960s had been excessive (Nordhoff 1984, 12, 41, 47).

In declining to apologize for his past positions, Helms stood in marked contrast to another white southern Democrat turned Republican, South Carolina U.S. senator Strom Thurmond. Although Thurmond had been the 1948 presidential candidate of the Dixiecrat Party, which stood for racial segregation, he moderated his racial views and solicited support from South Carolina's blacks during his campaigns in the post–civil rights era

(Black and Black 1987). Similarly, Alabama's George Wallace, in his final election, a successful gubernatorial campaign in 1982, sought the vote of white and black Democrats (Carter 1995, 460–62).

In 1939, after just one year at Wingate, Helms decided to transfer to another Baptist college, Wake Forest, at the time located north of Raleigh in the town of the same name. The decision would change his life, because while attending Wake Forest he worked part time as a proofreader at the *News and Observer* in Raleigh. Owing to ideological differences with the newspaper's owners, the Daniels family, his stay at the *News and Observer* proved tumultuous. More importantly, he met his wife-to-be, Dorothy Coble, a society reporter for the *News and Observer*. After marriage in 1942, Helms developed a greater interest in politics as a result of conversations with his father-in-law (Snider 1985, 23). Jacob Coble was the first to provide specifics that fleshed out the worldview Helms brought from Monroe.

Because Helms had a hearing disability, his military service was restricted to noncombat roles. He spent most of World War II writing press releases for the navy in Elizabeth City, North Carolina. Afterward Helms decided against returning to college and worked for the *Raleigh Times* and a Roanoke Rapids radio station. Understanding the appeal of interviews in a radio newscast, he would lug a sixty-pound wire recorder to press conferences and city council meetings to speak directly with politicians. In 1948 A. J. Fletcher, founder of WRAL, then a small 250-watt radio station, offered Helms a position as news director. Fletcher, a strong advocate of traditionalist ideology, liked Helms's personality and his political beliefs. Helms later said Fletcher had been "like a second father" to him (Furgurson 1986, 45). In 1976 Helms dedicated his book of essays, *When Free Men Shall Stand*, to Fletcher and to Tom Ellis.

In May 1950 Helms made a crucial appeal on WRAL to Willis Smith supporters to gather at Smith's house in Raleigh and insist that Smith seek a runoff election against Frank Graham for the Democratic nomination to the U.S. Senate. Smith subsequently defeated Graham in a bitter runoff campaign highlighted by attacks on Graham for his alleged sympathies with communism and support of civil rights. Four decades later the extent of Helms's involvement in Smith's negative campaign remained fuzzy. Several different writers documented Helms's role as the radio-news journalist for WRAL who certainly appeared to cross the line into advocacy journalism when he broadcast an anti-Graham appeal from the Raleigh front yard of Graham's opponent, Willis Smith. Helms's radio broadcast urged anti-Graham Democrats to rally at the house to encourage Smith to call for a runoff election against Graham (Ehle 1993; Pleasants and Burns 1990; Furgurson 1986). But these accounts have failed to show conclusively what role Helms played, if any, in the development and distribution of the anonymous race-baiting attacks on Graham in the last ten days before the June 1950 runoff election. In any case, after the election Smith appointed Helms as his administrative assistant in Washington, D.C.

While in Washington, Helms served as press officer for the 1952 Democratic presidential campaign of Georgia's traditionalist U.S. senator Richard Russell. From Russell, Helms learned how to pursue unpopular political principles with shrewd parliamentary tactics on the Senate floor. Because of his strong commitment to Jim Crow segregation, Russell placed no better than third in the three-ballot Democratic convention of 1952. But he provided a role model for Helms, who remembered that Russell "would not consent to compromise, let alone be controlled by, the political manipulators" (Furgurson 1986, 59). Twenty years later Helms would make his own mark as a U.S. senator, seeking on-the-record votes on issues such as public school prayer or school busing in order to embarrass liberal Democratic colleagues who preferred to avoid such roll calls. One victim of Helms's parliamentary skill was Indiana Democratic senator Birch Bayh, whose on-the-record liberal votes provided campaign ammunition in 1980 for Bayh's youthful opponent, Dan Quayle. Quayle ended Bayh's eighteen-year Senate career in that election, won reelection to the Senate in 1986, and subsequently served from 1989 to 1993 as vice-president under George Bush.

Helms returned to North Carolina in 1953 as publicist for the North Carolina Bankers Association, where he remained for seven years. In the association's monthly, the *Tar Heel Banker*, Helms was given free rein to sound off on current political issues. He attacked the Supreme Court's school desegregation decision and criticized the *News and Observer* for its alleged antibanker mentality. In 1957 Helms blended his journalism career with electoral politics, winning the first of two two-year terms on the Raleigh City Council. As a council member Helms pursued the same anti-tax, anti-big-government themes that he would later carry to the U.S. Senate. While his city council terms helped establish his reputation as a newsmaker, his first breakthrough to a mass audience came in 1960. That year his former benefactor, A. J. Fletcher, offered him a vice-president's position at WRAL and, most importantly, a daily five-minute television editorial known as "Viewpoint." Fletcher and Helms agreed that "Viewpoint" should serve as a "voice of free enterprise." Over the next twelve years "Viewpoint" would run 2,761 times, ending only when Helms resigned to run for the 1972 Republican nomination for the U.S. Senate.

The civil rights and anti–Vietnam War movements of the 1960s as well as the related hippie counterculture provided excellent grist for Helms's editorial mill. During the dozen years beginning in 1960, a crucial period for North Carolina and the South, Helms provided ongoing commentary on religion, economics, civil rights, and foreign policy. His editorials characterized the United States as a Christian nation whose leaders ought to uphold free enterprise, family morality, and public prayer. Public welfare and other programs of Lyndon Johnson's Great Society were depicted as liberal steps on the ladder of socialism. Communism represented both a religious and an economic threat to American society. The fundamentalist Baptist base of Helms's traditionalist ideology viewed any redistribution of economic power as un-Christian and tantamount to communism. Helms wrote in his 1978 reelection campaign biography, "The loving and provident God of the Scriptures has been pushed aside in favor of a notion that the civil government is the ultimate provider and lawgiver. There is nothing to distinguish these people fundamentally from the most committed Communists who believe that evil is the consequence, not of sin, but of private property" (Helms 1976, 119).

Helms on the Campaign Trail

How has Jesse Helms won elections? That is a recurring question from many newcomers to North Carolina as well as from the national press corps, whose picture of the Tar Heel state usually consists of such forward-looking whites as Erskine Bowles, Jim Hunt, or retired University of North Carolina basketball coach Dean Smith. The simple answer is that Helms has always won more than 60 percent of the white vote in each of his five elections. Given the size of the overwhelmingly anti-Helms African American vote, Helms and indeed virtually any statewide Republican candidate can only be victorious in a November election by attaining the magic number of 60 percent of white voters. Over the years Helms has maintained his appeal to white registered Democrats, whether at the country club or at the country store.

In the opening stages of the 1984 Hunt-Helms campaign, the author sought a more complete understanding of Helms's appeal to whites by attending a Helms campaign dinner. The event was held in September 1983 at the Henderson Holiday Inn, a standard-issue Interstate 85 motel in a tobacco/textile county forty miles north of Raleigh. The Helms campaign made no profit on this $7.50 "rubber chicken and peas" affair. Nor would the campaign make any money on the dozens of other identical Saturday night dinners scheduled before the 1984 election. The dinner in Henderson was pitched to the broad middle class; the well-to-do had been invited to an earlier fund-raising reception at the local country club. It was Helms's personal political show, an amalgam of Christianity, free-enterprise economics, anticommunism, and bravado. He would be addressing primarily Jessecrats, those registered Democrats who vote in the Democratic primary in the spring and then switch to Helms and other Republicans on the statewide ticket in the November election.

Behind the podium in the Holiday Inn's banquet hall, a larger-than-life drawing of Helms spanned the wall. Next to the drawing, six-foot letters spelled out JESSE in bold red. This backdrop was the campaign's only prop; the staff carried it each weekend from town to town. As guests of honor at the head table sat the editor of the *Henderson Daily Dispatch* as well as two local ministers. Helms has never forgotten the importance of either media or religion.

Master of ceremonies for the evening was Lucius Harvin III, president of Rose's Stores, a once-thriving Henderson-based retail chain that, until the proliferation of Wal-Mart stores forced it into bankruptcy, competed with K-Mart in towns across North Carolina and much of the South. Harvin recognized that this Salute to Jesse resembled a church supper far more than a corporate board meeting. Harvin's planning committee had ensured that both strains of local Protestants—the more establishment First Congregational Church as well as the more fundamentalist Gospel Baptist Church—had places on the program. The crowd stood for the Reverend Ed Yancey's long invocation, followed by Pastor Gary Roy's rendition of the National Anthem. They remained standing for the Pledge of Allegiance.

Harvin was one of the few wealthy residents in the hall. But economic differences were not a political issue for the people gathered that night. Helms has been able to attract an economically diverse crowd of white North Carolinians on any occasion. Jessecrats respect Helms because they believe he is kindly, sincere, conservative, and Christian. They also believe he has gone to Washington, D.C., to fight for his principles, not for personal gain. Interestingly, Senate financial reports uphold that faith in

Helms. In 1988 he was among the least affluent of the 100 senators; fellow U.S. Senator Terry Sanford reported four times as much wealth (*News and Observer* 1988a). In Henderson, Helms affirmed the traditionalist belief in hard work and in the legitimacy of economic differences. He introduced the straw man of liberal Democratic handouts to great applause: "What we have to do is face up to the pressure groups who are demanding more and more handouts, and say we are going to look after the truly needy, but the truly greedy, you're way down the line" (Helms 1983b).

Helms also engaged the Henderson audience by framing the 1984 Senate election as the lonely struggle of a principled conservative against the national liberal establishment: "Every pressure group known to man is converging on North Carolina, and they're forthright in saying that their number one goal is to eliminate me from the Senate." Helms went on to name some of those groups, selecting several most likely to offend his listeners: "It's the homosexuals, labor unions, those militant feminists, all of them" versus his "talking about things I've been talking about for a long time" (Helms 1983b).

Resentment toward black aspirations for increased political power has historically fueled the voting behavior of Jessecrats. In Henderson, Helms did not miss an opportunity to slap at the most visible advocate of black political power of the 1980s, Jesse Jackson: "The big factor in this election will be whether there will be a balance to the efforts of Jesse Jackson, who came into this state earlier this year to meet with Governor Hunt and then announced that he was going to register, I-forget-what-it-was, 200- or 300-thousand blacks for the sole purpose of defeating Jesse Helms" (Helms 1983a).

But Helms offered more than serious warnings. Lightheartedly, he made cracks at the *News and Observer* and *Washington Post* reporters who were covering his speech: "Ferrel Guillory of the *News and Observer* is here from Raleigh. Ferrel and I don't agree on anything, but he's one heck of a nice guy." As the crowd warmed to his gentle media-baiting, Helms added, "Now I don't expect you reporters to be my Chamber of Commerce, but for gosh sakes get the facts straight just one time."

Helms's down-homeness was always an important part of his Tar Heel political appeal. While northern liberals remained appalled at his political victories in Washington, most white North Carolinians were undisturbed. They saw their senior senator as gentlemanly, courteous, and humorous. Style was as important as substance, and perhaps more so. On that hot September night in Henderson, Helms ended his speech with a characteristic folksy touch: "I know you're hot as the hinges of your you-know-where. But I do appreciate your coming out for so much time. You're great friends, and I love you. God bless you. Come see me in Washington."

In his closing remarks, Lucius Harvin added a line about Helms that has reassured many a Jessecrat: "You may not always agree with Jesse Helms, but you always know where he stands" (Harvin 1983). That slogan subsequently became a major theme in Helms's 1984 campaign.

In the Henderson audience were two brothers, Eddie and James Grissom. Both in their thirties, they worked in blue-collar jobs at Rose's headquarters and were using free tickets distributed at work. But the Grissoms insisted to an interviewer that they would have paid for the tickets if necessary, because they had admired Helms since they were teenagers watching his "Viewpoint" editorials on WRAL-TV. Although the brothers, both registered Democrats, had their minor beefs with Helms, they sounded as positive about him as did their company president. They agreed with Harvin that Helms should stand tough against communism, support free enterprise, and uphold personal morality. They placed political beliefs above party registration and felt that Helms's Republicanism was irrelevant. James Grissom summarized it well: "I'm with Helms on most everything. And above all he's principled" (Grissom and Grissom 1983).

Eddie and James are the "little people" on whom Jesse Helms has built his political career. To beat Jim Hunt, Helms needed people like the Grissoms to mobilize their neighbors—registered to vote but usually indifferent to politics—on Election Day 1984. A look at election returns for the Henderson area demonstrates the strength of Jessecrats. Although registered Democrats outnumbered Republicans in Vance County by 10 to 1, Helms won 57 percent of the vote in 1972, 58 percent in 1978, and 48 percent in 1984. His lack of a majority in 1984 appears to be a direct consequence of the 20 percent increase in black voter registration in Vance County between 1980 and 1984. But the Grissom brothers did their part for Helms. In an interview shortly before the 1984 election, they said that they planned to vote for Helms as well as for Jim Martin and Ronald Reagan. The Grissom brothers may not have realized it, but their decision, as registered Democrats, to vote for the entire top of the 1984 Republican ticket was a bellwether of the rise of the Republican Party appeal among native-born whites, not only in North Carolina but across the South.

The author did not hear in person another speech from Helms until nearly fourteen years later, when Helms addressed a joint session of the

1997 North Carolina General Assembly. It became clear on that day that Helms considered the 1983 Holiday Inn "stump speech" a winning presentation; his 1997 General Assembly address would include some of the identical phrases about the dangers of moral decay and threats to the free-enterprise system (Helms 1997). The difference was that in September 1983, few could have dreamed of a Republican majority in the North Carolina state house. In June 1997 Republican house Speaker Harold Brubaker sat behind Helms as Helms addressed the joint legislative session.

Just one month after Helms's Saturday evening outing at the Henderson Holiday Inn, a *Washington Post* writer was finishing off Helms's political obituary. "Barring an act of God," wrote Richard Whittle (1983), "Jesse Helms can't win." At the same time, Republicans at the White House, speaking off the record, reached a similar conclusion. Unfortunately for Jim Hunt, many members of his campaign team also believed that Hunt's victory was inevitable. After all, one statewide poll during summer 1983 showed Hunt 20 percentage points ahead of Helms. And in every previous political contest, Hunt had won comfortably. Granted that Helms represented formidable competition, Hunt and his staff felt the voters would remember his own solid, eight-year record of accomplishments as governor.

But all of them, from the *Post* to the White House to Tar Heel Democratic insiders, were wrong. With help from Ronald Reagan's coattails, Helms took 62 percent of the white vote (Reagan himself won 73 percent) (CBS News 1984). Despite an overwhelming black vote for Hunt, Helms squeezed out a 52-to-48 percent victory, a margin of 86,000 of 2.2 million votes cast. The winning formula developed by the Helms organization, including the senator's close friends Tom Ellis and Carter Wrenn at the Congressional Club, centered on a media blitz to undermine the governor's credibility and personal image.

As the 1984 campaign season began taking shape, national Democrats set their sights on North Carolina's Senate race. Although Helms was already ending his second term, Democrats believed this incumbent was vulnerable because of his controversial stands on many issues. To both white and black Democrats in Washington, D.C., Helms's relentless attacks on the food stamp program and his outspoken opposition to abortion, school busing, the Martin Luther King Jr. holiday, and gays, as well as his hard-core anticommunism, made him the worst right-wing menace since Senator Joe McCarthy.

Yet countless North Carolinians—bedrock Helms voters—had a totally different opinion of him. While 1984 Democratic National Committee chair Charles Manatt labeled Helms the Prince of Darkness, Helms supporters in North Carolina viewed him as a beacon of enlightenment, fighting for free enterprise and Christian morality. The National Organization for Women placed Helms at the top of its political enemies list. But thousands of Tar Heel families would have been honored to have Senator and Mrs. Helms come to dinner.

Even since Helms served his first term between 1973 and the November 1978 election, Tar Heel Democrats had wanted Helms's reelection bid to be framed as a referendum on Jesse Helms. In this view, Helms's negative politics undermined North Carolina's national reputation as the most progressive southern state; defeating Helms would permit the state to regain its rightful honor. But time and again Helms outwitted his opponents. In 1972 he had ridden Nixon's coattails and defended traditional values in his defeat of an incumbent U.S. congressman, Durham modernizer Nick Galifianakis (see Chapter 2).

In 1978 Claude Sitton, vigorous anti-Helms editor of the *News and Observer*, coined the phrase "Senator No" to urge his readers in the Triangle and eastern North Carolina to retire Helms and to send instead a more positive, that is, a Democratic, senator to Washington (Luebke 1984d). But Helms wore his "Senator No" label as a badge of courage, reminding voters that he was willing to stand by his principles even if he had to stand alone. In that 1978 election Helms had the good fortune to run against a Democrat, John Ingram, who himself was not known as a positive, calming force on the electorate. On the contrary, Ingram was the iconoclastic, populist-leaning insurance commissioner in whom North Carolina's modernizer business Democrats had very little confidence. If anything, Helms was seen as more sympathetic to business, albeit traditionalist business, than was Ingram. Helms maintained the upper hand through the campaign and won in November by a 54-to-46 margin.

By contrast, as the 1984 election approached, two-term incumbent governor Jim Hunt was viewed by most North Carolina and national Democrats as the perfect candidate to challenge Helms. Hunt had won reelection with 62 percent of the vote in 1980; in 1983 polls showed that three times as many North Carolinians approved as disapproved of the job Hunt was doing as governor. For Helms there was just one way to win: to transform the 1984 election into a referendum on the policies and personality of Jim Hunt. White Tar Heels in particular had to change their assessment of the governor.

Helms in Washington:
Legitimating the Traditionalist Agenda

Helms's goal in Washington has always been to stretch the parameters of political debate to the right. He wanted to reopen issues that those to his left had felt were part of a new national consensus around racial justice, reproductive rights, and détente. Helms would have no part of this consensus.

Hard work, free enterprise, patriarchal family, and Baptist morality were the core ideas that made Helms unalterably opposed to the egalitarian movements of the 1960s. The underlying theme of his ideology was that he represented normalcy; it was his opponents who were improperly trying to move America away from its God-fearing values. Helms's political core included both social and economic values. But his social traditionalism was far more controversial than his economic views.

Helms's first base of support was among North Carolina's businesses. His strong antigovernment, antitax ideology afforded him enthusiastic backing from traditionalist business as well as substantial backing from modernizers. A 1985 study of modernizer-oriented Tar Heel executives found that most had voted for Helms even though many of them disagreed with his views on race and abortion (Baker 1986). Most modernizer business people supported Helms for the Senate seat because they felt that he would be more likely than Jim Hunt to prevent new domestic spending by the federal government. The fear of national Democratic policies led these corporate modernizers to reject Hunt, even though they had previously backed him for governor in 1976 and 1980 (Luebke 1981b; Baker 1986). A preelection poll by the National Chamber of Commerce of its North Carolina members revealed that 70 percent favored Helms. Similarly in 1990, with the exception of Charlotte modernizers whom Gantt had known for years in business and political circles, few Tar Heel business leaders would support Gantt. In short, within the business community Helms held a lead over Hunt comparable to that of most incumbent Republicans running for Congress.

A second strong Helms base consisted of registered Republicans. Although the percentage of Tar Heel voters enrolled in the Republican Party has never exceeded 35 (NC Free 1997), their party loyalty has been much stronger than that of Democrats. Indeed, even with Republican and unaffiliated gains, Democrats still held a majority registration advantage. If registered Democrats were as loyal to their party on Election Day as Republicans, Democrats would never lose a statewide election.

Helms's third support base included social traditionalist whites who revered his noneconomic values. As a media commentator during the 1960s Helms had developed a strong following by attacking groups that symbolized disruption of the social order. He criticized not all blacks, but "militant Negroes," and not all students, but "beatnik students" (Nordhoff 1984, 44). When he first ran for the Senate in 1972, he opposed "forced busing" for school desegregation. The composite picture drawn by Helms was of a federal government run amok by liberals (he often called them socialists or Marxists) who sympathized with radical egalitarian movements that aimed to provide easy times for the millions (for example, blacks or college students) who preferred a handout to hard work. Despite the broad ideological attack on federal programs, Helms pragmatically held his fire regarding the federal tobacco program.

The economic ideology of Jesse Helms emphasized limited government, except for the tobacco and peanut programs that benefited Tar Heel farmers. Rhetorically, he favored a balanced budget, but he avoided any censure of President Reagan when the federal budget deficit soared in the early 1980s. In fact, his 1984 campaign speeches blamed the deficit on the Democratic liberals who had placed so many "entitlement" programs in the federal budget. Was Helms talking about cutting Social Security? When pressed, he said no. But Helms was skilled at keeping his criticism vague, winning applause from audiences who admired his antigovernment talk. He would say, for example, "I don't think anyone in any program is entitled to anything from your pockets which you worked for" (Helms 1983b). Such speechmaking confirmed the picture of a high-minded politician who was willing to stand up for "what's right" against the so-called special interests.

When the polls showed Helms trailing Jim Hunt by a huge margin in mid-1983, Helms and his Congressional Club advisers decided to promote him as a courageous, principled leader—in contrast to Hunt, whom they would portray as a pragmatic, wheeling-dealing politician with no firm beliefs. The decision to begin these early attacks on Hunt's character turned out, in retrospect, to have been crucial for Helms's uphill battle.

By contrast in 1990, Helms was slow to attack Gantt's candidacy, in part because Gantt did not win the Democratic nomination until a June runoff primary election. As noted below, Helms's attacks on Gantt came (from Helms's perspective) just in time, in the final weeks and especially the final days of the 1990 campaign.

The Helms Strategy:
Making Jim Hunt the Issue

Helms's goal was to draw public attention away from his Senate record and to the alleged liberal pragmatism of Jim Hunt. On the social side Hunt was, according to Helms, soft on abortion, blacks, and Christianity. On economic matters Helms viewed Hunt as a tax-and-spend liberal. The question was whether Helms's criticism of Hunt would stick with the voters.

The first volley that year zeroed in on race. It came via the cheapest media, radio stations and small-town newspapers, especially in eastern North Carolina. Among a series of ads highlighting Helms's virtues (protector of the tobacco program, opponent of government spending, and friend and supporter of Ronald Reagan) were attacks on Hunt as a pro-union, problack governor (Luebke 1990a, 141).

The U.S. Senate debate in September and October 1983 over the Martin Luther King Jr. holiday proved to be a windfall for Helms. National political observers thought he was foolish to attack the King holiday so stridently. But, in fact, the criticism Helms received from the national media hurt as much as a rabbit's confinement in a briar patch. To many white North Carolinians it confirmed his claim as a man who dared to stand alone for a principle. What Helms stood for, in this instance, was a traditionalist view of the United States. In a speech on the Senate floor Helms characterized King as unpatriotic and a Communist sympathizer: "King's view of American society was thus not fundamentally different from that of CPUSA (American Communist Party) or of other Marxists. While he is generally remembered today as the pioneer of civil rights for blacks and as the architect of non-violent techniques of dissent and political agitation, his hostility to and hatred for America should be made clear" (*Congressional Record*, October 3, 1983, quoted in Nordhoff 1984, 48).

Further, Helms's opposition to the King holiday proposal and the subsequent criticism of Helms in the national media tapped a strong feeling among many traditionalist Tar Heels that blacks and their white sympathizers were pushing for another giveaway, this time a paid holiday for federal employees. The King holiday issue helped Helms in the polls, particularly in areas of eastern North Carolina where black political organization could threaten white power. Coincidentally, some of these heavily black counties overlapped with the area where Helms's editorials in earlier years had been aired on WRAL-TV. Helms appeared to gain from the King controversy because he had tapped a volatile issue and because he had reached, particularly in the WRAL viewing area, thousands of voters who had long ago come to respect his political opinions.

State Republican leaders active during Helms's various Senate campaigns subsequently acknowledged "for the record" the potency of the race issue to help elect Helms and other Republican candidates, especially in the WRAL viewing area. As Frank Rouse, party chairman during Helms's 1972 campaign and subsequent policy adviser to Governor Jim Martin during the 1980s, told interviewers from the Southern Oral History Program in 1996, "Folks who live in suburbia or folks who have moved to North Carolina don't understand it, but it is an absolute fact of life. If you in 1960 were a white tobacco farmer in Eastern North Carolina, you were a Democrat. In 1996, if you are a white tobacco farmer in Eastern North Carolina, you are a Republican. Now there has been a lot of other things that have been factors, but race has been far bigger than everything else" (*News and Observer* 1997g).

The issue of the King holiday gave Helms free publicity. He accompanied this free airtime in the fall of 1983 with his first extended paid foray into Tar Heel living rooms. These 30-second TV spots had both positive and negative themes, but it was the anti-Hunt attack that reaped the most rewards. The positive ads underscored Ronald Reagan's support for the senior senator, since Reagan was more popular in North Carolina than Helms. This coattail advertising would continue until the election.

Helms's team at Jefferson Marketing, a subsidiary of the Congressional Club, developed a twofold attack on Hunt: that he was in fact a liberal, but as a deft, pragmatic politician, he sought publicly to be all things to all people. The message was simple: Helms the principled conservative faced Hunt the pragmatic liberal who sought to hide his true political colors. Helms researchers found what they identified as contradictory positions in Hunt's record on issues such as school prayer or tax increases and juxtaposed these alleged differences in the same ad. They also contrasted Helms and Hunt on symbolic issues such as the King holiday or the Panama Canal "giveaway." This latter point had been used by Republican candidate John East, with major assistance from the Congressional Club, to upset incumbent Democrat U.S. Senator Robert Morgan in the November 1980 election. Always seeking an accommodation between his core supporters, blacks and yellow-dog white Democrats, and those whites who were sympathetic both to Helms and to himself, Hunt expressed mild support for the King holiday and the Panama Canal treaty. Helms's television commercials turned Hunt's ability to forge compromises with the majority, normally considered a political asset, into a liability, while Helms's intransigence became a virtue. The tag line on these ads—"Where Do You Stand, Jim?"—could not be forgotten by friend or foe.

The Hunt Strategy:
Doing More for North Carolina

During his first two terms as governor, Jim Hunt had gained a reputation as a hard-driving, action-oriented leader who wanted to promote countless programs through the General Assembly. Along the general lines of modernizer ideology, Hunt was leaving his mark on North Carolina. The assumption of Hunt's campaign team was that he could articulate similar themes in the race against Jesse Helms. Thus, while Helms was launching his pointed negative ads against Hunt, the governor was developing his Four E's (economy, education, the elderly, and the environment), a vague set of issue areas that, like his plans for the governor's office, laid out Hunt's future goals for the U.S. Senate. Hunt chose the overall slogan "He Can Do More for North Carolina" to contrast his can-do style with the right-wing posturing of Helms.

Initially, the Hunt campaign did not recognize that the generalities of the Four E's made a weaker impression on voters, including Democrats, than the specific attacks of the Helms forces. What exactly was it that Hunt had achieved, or would achieve, for the economy or education? Was he maybe just promoting big government, wasting the taxpayers' money? Doing more for North Carolina could also be interpreted as the self-serving activities of a political machine. Even when Hunt and his associates began to acknowledge the skill of their opposition, they still thought the positive impression of the Hunt years would hold with the voters. Consequently, as the Helms campaign over the late fall and winter of 1983–84 maintained a heavy barrage of "Where Do You Stand, Jim?" ads, Hunt barely responded, believing that his advertising dollars should be saved for later. The governor's failure to launch a counterattack in the media proved costly, for by early 1984 the polls showed that Helms had caught up with Hunt. It was a remarkable comeback.

From the perspective of the 1990s, some Tar Heel Democrats recognized that Helms's hammering against Hunt for allegedly being a tax-and-spend Democrat benefiting his political machine constituted a foreshadowing of what legislative Republicans would use to take power (for example, the shocking house Republican victories in November 1994) and to try to stay in power thereafter. During the 1997 session, for example, when the house Republican majority had been shaved from a sixteen-seat margin in 1995–96 to a two-seat margin in 1997–98, house Republicans led by Representative Carolyn Russell of Goldsboro conducted lengthy hearings into an out-of-court $100,000 settlement that Governor Hunt's office had made with a disgruntled African American state employee, Algie Toomer. The melodrama of the so-called House Select Committee on Personnel Practices dominated the front pages of North Carolina's two major newspapers, the *News and Observer* and the *Charlotte Observer*, and often pushed more substantive but complicated legislative stories on taxes or health care onto the inside pages. Columnists unsympathetic to Russell's actions wondered whether Toomer's racial identity did not fuel GOP interest in the Hunt administration payout. They noted, for example, that Steve Stroud, a well-connected white Raleigh Republican who with his partner had gained $3.7 million from a right-of-way settlement far above the appraised value from the politically wired state DOT (*News and Observer* 1997a), was not called to testify before Russell's committee. Neither did the committee subpoena the state DOT officials who had approved the overpayment (Saunders 1997; Fitzsimon 1997b).

Back in the 1980s, however, North Carolina Democrats, including Hunt, were not expecting such a vigorous Republican attack. Instead of counterattacking immediately at some of Helms's vulnerable points, such as his occasional negative characterization of the Social Security system as "big government," Hunt felt defensive about the liberal charge and began laying out a variety of conservative positions. He told campaign audiences that he supported prayer in the public schools, the death penalty, aid to the far-right Nicaraguan Contras, and the Reagan military buildup. He opposed a nuclear freeze and abortion, although he did as governor favor a state abortion fund for poor women. Helms himself labeled Hunt's conservatism as "Johnny-come-lately" behavior. In the spring, during a Senate debate on organized school prayer in which Helms was a vocal advocate for a constitutional amendment, Hunt announced that he, too, supported the school prayer amendment. Helms quipped in reply, "I am glad to share my prayer book with the governor."

But Hunt's move to the right failed to have the desired impact, and perhaps even backfired. Why should Helms-leaning whites switch allegiance when Helms held the same positions and had supported them with greater fervor? Committed white and black Democrats, particularly in the metro Piedmont counties, wondered on the other hand why they should work their precincts for Hunt if he was determined to blur his differences from Helms. The effect was to engender disenchantment among Hunt's most ideological backers without winning back support from large numbers of undecided whites.

The Gantt Campaign of 1990: New South, New Senator

Precisely four decades after North Carolina's symbol of mid-century progressive politics, Frank Graham, was defeated in the 1950 race-baiting primary election in which Jesse Helms was a player for Graham's opposition, Charlotte architect and former mayor Harvey Gantt jumped into the Democratic primary of the spring of 1990. Gantt was a symbol in his own right. In 1963 he had been the first black student to attend Clemson University, a previously lily-white college in his native state of South Carolina; in the 1970s he became copartner of the first biracial architectural firm in Charlotte; and in 1983 he was elected Charlotte's first African American mayor.

For North Carolina Democrats in 1990, Gantt also symbolized a break from the white-male-dominated party of the past. For example, at that time every member of the Council of State—lieutenant governor, attorney general, state superintendent of public instruction, labor commissioner, insurance commissioner, state auditor, and agricultural commissioner, all of whom were elected at the same time as the governor—was a white man. The onus for this nondiversity lay squarely with the Democratic Party, since only one of the eight members elected in 1988 (white Republican lieutenant governor Jim Gardner) was not a Democrat. Subsequently, African American Ralph Campbell would be elected state auditor in 1992, and white woman Elaine Marshall would win the office of secretary of state in 1996.

In the 1990 primary modernizer Democrats were less than enthusiastic about Gantt's candidacy. One factor against Gantt was his Charlotte base. It remains true that, with the exception of Republican governor Jim Martin, Charlotte-area candidates for statewide office have fared poorly in both the Democratic and the Republican Parties. But the second argument against Gantt was racial and spoke to the heart of most Tar Heel white modernizers' ambivalence about the appropriate role for African Americans in the state Democratic Party. In a nutshell, Democratic establishment politicians, close to but not synonymous with then-"governor-in-exile" Jim Hunt, seemed to prefer a white modernizer to any black Democrat. Building on their awareness of Jesse Helms's racial appeals, the party insiders believed that a black Democrat, whatever the candidate's actual political beliefs, would be labeled a tax-and-spend liberal by Helms and other state Republicans. Consequently, a white candidate was preferred.

Six men ran in the May 1990 Democratic primary, and four candidates divided 97 percent of the votes. Gantt led with 37 percent, and the choice of most white modernizers, white Brunswick County prosecutor Mike Easley, ran second with 30 percent. Two nonestablishment candidates, mountain-populist Bo Thomas of Hendersonville (12 percent) and former Helms opponent in the fall of 1978 and retired state insurance commissioner John Ingram (18 percent) did not qualify for the runoff. Thinking he might win over these voters, Easley called for a June runoff with Gantt. But despite an overall drop in turnout, the 60,000-vote difference between Easley and Gantt remained the same.

Several lessons about a statewide Democratic primary and runoff elections emerged from Gantt's 1990 victory. First, like the equivalent phenomenon in North Carolina's Republican primaries, voters with stronger ideological views were more likely to cast their ballots, thus giving an advantage to Gantt, who claimed to be new and different, not moderate like Easley. Second, the six metro Piedmont counties, with significant numbers of African American voters as well as many whites who had migrated to North Carolina, bringing political values more in sympathy with northern-style national Democrats, voted 73 percent to 27 percent in favor of Gantt in the runoff election. By contrast, Gantt had only beaten Easley statewide 57 percent to 43 percent. Since the metro Piedmont counties were also among North Carolina's fastest growing, a key lesson seemed to be that the modernizer Democrat whose style and views were preferred by the Democratic old guard could not be expected to prevail in future primary battles against candidates who presented themselves as being somehow on the left. For example, partly because of population growth and partly because of the interest of urban Democrats in the Gantt candidacy, the portion of statewide votes cast by the metro Piedmont counties was 30 percent in 1990, while in the less-ideological Democratic senate primary of 1986 (Luebke 1990a, 187), metro Piedmont Democrats cast just 20 percent of the statewide vote. Arguments from inside the (Raleigh) Beltline or the equivalent argument made inside the (Washington, D.C.) Beltway, that Democratic primary voters should pragmatically nominate the candidate closest to the state's political center, especially a white centrist, were simply irrelevant to voters living outside the fascinating but narrow world of Raleigh's political insiders. Especially for the many nonsouthern Democrats who had migrated to the metro Piedmont areas, there was little interest in accommodating the social traditionalism, including the racial traditionalism (see Chapter 7 above), of North Carolina's small-town and rural white voters. The challenge for the Tar Heel Democratic Party then, just as it would become later in the 1990s for North Carolina's Republicans, was how to win a statewide general election in November with the more-ideological, not less-ideological, standard-bearer.

The Helms Counterattack: October 1990

The national press loved the prospect of a New South–Old South juxtaposition: an attractive African American who had graduated from civil rights struggles to become a successful upper middle-class professional opposing the old-fashioned white southern incumbent U.S. senator. Not only dozens of reporters from the American media, but also film crews and reporters from Europe were dogging the candidates. Until October Gantt was holding his own in the various statewide polls (Orndorff 1997), and speculation was widespread that he would retire Helms. But Gantt had two advantages that he would lose in the final weeks. First, Helms was stuck in Washington, D.C., debating President Bush's budget and thus was not crisscrossing North Carolina gaining free media exposure, especially the cost-free visuals in the short television news stories. Second, and worse for Helms, he was being asked by his Republican president to reduce the federal budget deficit by voting for a tax increase. When Helms returned to North Carolina, he distanced himself immediately from Bush's deficit-reduction plan and instead focused his on-the-stump campaigning on the alleged liberalism of Gantt.

The Helms reelection team understood that the liberalism that offended a significant percentage of white North Carolinians centered on social rather than economic issues. For example, white voters during the 1990 fall campaign were generally in favor of the educational and environmental improvements that Gantt, via his 30-second spots, promised he would advocate if he replaced Helms (Jamieson 1992, 94). Such government spending, from the perspective of a traditionalist like Helms, was surely a mistake. Yet Helms's pollsters knew that he would lose the November election if the television battleground was about education spending or environmental protection. Instead they took on the social issues that, especially in the minds of many white southerners, illustrated how liberalism had caused American society to go astray.

Beginning in early October the Helms team ran four 30-second ads focused directly on either race or other liberal social issues such as abortion rights and gays. The antigay ads linked Gantt to homosexual supporters in San Francisco and New York. A fifth ad, allegedly about Gantt's onetime support for a Charlotte-area gas tax, acoustically distorted the voice of the black man, campaign manager (and subsequent member of congress) Mel Watt, so that his on-screen comments sounded "tinny" and less credible (Jamieson 1992, 94–100). Kathleen Jamieson, a national expert on the uses and misuses of television advertising, fortuitously had a 1990 grant to study the effects of Helms's advertising on undecided white North Carolinians. Her extremely important analysis of the power of Helms's ads to awaken latent white prejudice is published in her 1992 study, *Dirty Politics*. In two focus groups of white, high-school-educated Tar Heels, all from small-town and rural areas outside the metro Piedmont counties, Jamieson documented the impact of what she termed "race-priming," in which television ads, sometimes on a nonracial topic such as abortion or gas taxes, sensitized white voters to Gantt's racial identity by manipulating his or his supporters' voice and picture (Jamieson 1992, 94–96). One such ad contained an on-screen text that criticized Gantt for being "Extremely Liberal with the FACTS" (*sic*) in his discussion of under what circumstances an abortion would be appropriate. But Jamieson noted that, using available technology, Helms admakers had caused Gantt's face to bob back and forth and had ultimately darkened his on-screen image by switching from color to black-and-white pictures. Asked to comment on the distorted image rather than the abortion text, the focus group of undecided rural whites told interviewers that Gantt's slowed voice in the TV ad evoked phrases like "stupid," "definitely black," and "the kind of really dumb black you used to see in movies" (Jamieson 1992, 96).

Helms received the most criticism after the fact for what Jamieson viewed as simply the last in a series of five racially oriented ads. The infamous "hands ad" showed white, masculine hands, with a wedding band on the third finger of the left hand, apparently reading and then crumpling a rejection letter. The voice-over stated, "You needed that job, and you were the best qualified. But they had to give it to a minority because of a racial quota. Is that really fair? Harvey Gantt says it is. Harvey Gantt supports Ted Kennedy's racial quota law that makes the color of your skin more important than your qualifications. You'll vote on this issue next Tuesday. For racial quotas: Harvey Gantt. Against racial quotas: Jesse Helms" (quoted in Jamieson 1992, 97). The text's messages were hardly subtle. "You" was meant to be members of the majority race, and "Ted Kennedy" symbolized the excesses of both economic and social liberalism. But Jamieson's careful analysis of the imagery pinpointed a black mark (the shadow of the white hand) across the letter, as well as, seconds later, the crumpling hands quickly crushing Kennedy's head and about to do the same to Gantt's (Jamieson 1992, 99). Asked by Jamieson if these aspects of the ad were intentional, Helms admaker Alex Castellanos said no. But Jamieson tentatively concluded that the five ads working together did push undecided whites with high school educations toward Helms. Gantt's pollster subsequently told Jamieson that the hands ad had also been effective in swaying college-educated white males toward Helms (Jamieson 1992, 98–99).

The lesson from Jamieson's research parallels what former state Republican chair Frank Rouse told the Southern Oral History Project: racial appeals to traditionalist whites who question blacks' right to political power are effective. A critical point, however, is that today's racial appeals are not the simple "hell, no" of the early 1960s. As analyses of the 1990 General Social Survey, a sophisticated national poll, reveal, the contemporary white, including the southern white, does not challenge African Americans' basic intelligence or their ability to be upright, patriotic citizens. Rather, the crucial insight, well understood by Helms himself and his campaign helpers, is that some whites harbor latent racial resentments against blacks for allegedly getting "government handouts" that they do not deserve (Kinder and Mendelberg, quoted in Jamieson 1992, 100).

By making white latent resentment manifest, Helms's TV ads could encourage undecided white voters to think about race, rather than beyond race to consider the value of educational or environmental programs. In that sense Gantt's narrow loss in 1990 was a more sophisticated replay of Frank Graham's similarly close defeat in 1950.

But just as some observers criticized Graham for not mounting a vigorous counterattack to the race-baiting of his segregationist opponent in June 1950 (Ehle 1993, 174–78), post-election analyses questioned whether Gantt had not let the election slip away in the last two weeks. Why, for example, did Gantt have no 30-second ad prepared in response to Helms's attack on Gantt for having been a copurchaser and then a reseller at a profit of a Charlotte television station? Helms's voice-over in his TV spot asserted that "the black community felt betrayed, but the deal made the mayor a millionaire. Harvey Gantt made government work for Harvey Gantt." But the visuals, headlines from the *Charlotte Observer*, actually mentioned only allegations and maybes about a million dollars (Jamieson 1992, 97). Rather than criticize Helms for unsubstantiated character assassination, Gantt's campaign appeared stunned and defensive. His only 30-second response was to speak sincerely but very generally about the need for voters to reject "Jesse Helms' lies." Gantt never counterattacked Helms's claims, thereby allowing Helms assertions to become "the truth" (Luebke 1990b). Such a mistake can be devastating to a campaign, since TV ads have a visual capacity to "reconfigure 'reality'" with a power that a newspaper or radio ad cannot attain (Jamieson 1992, 10).

Further, Helms's hands ad that linked Gantt to racial quotas was flatly untrue, since Gantt supported affirmative action programs for racial minorities and women but not quotas. Yet in this case as well, where a 30-second ad could have attacked Helms for distorting the facts and could have affirmed that all citizens, male and female, white and black, should be fairly considered for all jobs but not guaranteed a job, Gantt's campaign had no response (Luebke 1990b). Finally, as noted in Chapter 7, the Gantt campaign throughout had developed no special message to attract the votes of native-born white Tar Heels with lower levels of formal education. Gantt had declined to use economic populist themes to convey opposition to "the rich and special interests," two labels that just two years later Bill Clinton would heartily use against his Republican opponent (Dionne 1997, 70) and that Senate Democratic candidates such as Paul Wellstone were successfully using in the Midwest. Without the economic populist message, Gantt's support among the middle-income whites of rural North Carolina was soft. It was precisely to win over these undecided white voters that the Helms team launched the five-part ad series analyzed by Jamieson. In sum, Gantt's campaign, just like Hunt's six years before, had underestimated the abilities of the Helms opposition. A Gantt campaign that had been prepared for the worst from Helms might well have survived the nasty attacks of the last ten days.

Analyzing the Results: 1984 and 1990

In 1990 Helms won slightly more of the white vote than he had in the 1984 contest against Hunt, taking 65 percent of that vote against Gantt (VNS 1990). In an analysis of North Carolina's U.S. Senate elections in 1984, 1986, and 1990, Eamon and Elliott have argued that Helms's candidacy produces a more racially polarized election, whether his opponent is white or black (Eamon and Elliott 1994). Democratic challenger Terry Sanford's success in November 1986 against incumbent U.S. Senator Jim Broyhill seemed to illustrate their point. Broyhill won just 58 percent of the white vote and lost the seat to Sanford (CBS News 1986). But for Democrats, Helms's absence was a mixed bag, because his presence on the ticket also ensured a relatively large turnout of African Americans and white in-migrants.

When, for example, Sanford's reelection campaign in 1992 was weakened by his hospitalization, Republican challenger Lauch Faircloth, at the time not at all the political lightning rod that Helms has always been, managed to slip by Sanford with little attention to his contest. Most Tar Heels were focused on either the Clinton-Bush-Perot presidential race (narrowly won by Bush, 43 to 42 percent) or Jim Hunt's hard-fought comeback victory for governor against GOP incumbent lieutenant governor Jim Gardner. This contrasted clearly with how much the Helms-Hunt election in 1984 actually overshadowed the one-sided presidential contest that Ronald Reagan won easily over Walter Mondale.

In both 1984 and 1990, Helms's "winning share" of the white vote was almost not enough because black voters, nearly one-fifth of the electorate, cast less than 10 percent of their votes for Helms. African American turnout was high in both elections. Simultaneously, in both 1984 and 1990, the appeal of Helms to white social traditionalists mobilized through religious organizations led to a high, pro-Republican vote. This religious-right vote was particularly evident in many of the western Piedmont counties with large numbers of white working-class and Baptist-affiliated voters.

Both Hunt and Gantt sought to counteract Helms's appeal in the western Piedmont with frequent campaigning in the six metro Piedmont counties. In both campaigns the metro Piedmont vote, especially in the three Research Triangle counties, helped the Democratic candidates combat Helms's edge in the western Piedmont. Overall in the metro Piedmont, Helms received less than 50 percent of the white vote against both Hunt and Gantt. The university, state government, and research and development base of the Triangle economy attracts professionals who are more likely to prefer a candidate touting public investment in schools and the environment to an incumbent fighting the King holiday or racial quotas. This is best suggested in Orange County, home to the University of North Carolina at Chapel Hill, where both Hunt and Gantt won their highest percentage among the 100 counties (Hunt, 69 percent in 1984; Gantt, 71 percent in 1990), even though blacks constituted just 15 percent of the county's voters.

Shifting Voter Coalitions: 1984 and 1990

Exit polls from the November elections of 1984 and 1990 (CBS News 1984; VNS 1990) provide further insights into the social bases of Democrats' electoral support. From the Democrats' perspective the news is both good and bad (Luebke 1990b). The bad news is that, campaigning as they did, neither Hunt nor Gantt gained sufficient white votes to defeat Helms. While Helms's ability to win white support via racial appeals of varying levels of subtlety has been well documented (Kern 1989; Jamieson 1992), political analysts have paid less attention to how Hunt and Gantt might have appealed more effectively to white voters.

Given the extent to which their appeals to white voters were similar, it is ironic that Gantt and Hunt were engaged in intra-Democratic rivalry, in both 1990 and 1996. Both Democrats decided that Helms's lead among working-class whites was insurmountable, in the light of Helms's well-known commitment to a social traditionalist agenda such as outlawing abortion or supporting public school prayer (Luebke 1990a, 151). But surely it would have made more sense for Hunt and Gantt to attack Helms in ways that cast doubt on what he was actually accomplishing for blue-collar whites. For example, while metro Piedmont white professionals may not have minded that Helms had voted in 1982 to double the federal tax on cigarettes, both Hunt and Gantt could probably have gained white votes with an ad campaign that targeted factory workers in the western Piedmont or tobacco farmers on the Coastal Plain and reminded TV viewers of that vote. In 1984 Hunt could also have criticized Helms for doing nothing while textile imports from Asian trade allies of the United States were saturating domestic markets and North Carolina textile mills were closing, eliminating the jobs of working-class Tar Heels (Luebke 1984a; Luebke 1990a, 150–51). In 1990 Gantt might have used the plant-closing issue, although the job losses were less evident than in 1984. But Gantt could have, but did not, criticize Helms in 30-second spots for his vote to use federal dollars to rescue the scandal-ridden savings and loan industry. Combined with Helms's 1982 support of a cigarette tax increase, a vote that Democrats at the time used to label Helms and then Republican Senate colleague John East as the "tobacco tax twins," a Gantt TV attack on the savings and loan "tax giveaways" would likely have placed Helms on the defensive (Luebke 1990b). (In 1990 the term that would gain currency in mid-1990s political debate, "corporate welfare," was not part of the national or state political rhetoric.) Failure by both Hunt and Gantt to question whether white workers and farmers were well represented economically by Helms granted Helms a clear edge among such voters. After all, neither Hunt nor Gantt was ever going to be able to "out-religion" Helms on the social issues (Luebke 1990a, 151). Helms's attacks on Jesse Jackson and the King holiday in 1984 (Kern 1989, 144) or racial quotas and Gantt's television station sale in 1990 (Jamieson 1992, 97) sensitized white working-class voters to the argument that black political participation is of questionable legitimacy. "If blacks in politics worry you, vote Helms" was the blunt message of both 1984 and 1990. To be sure, the bad news about white support was worse for Gantt (who won just 35 percent) than for Hunt (38 percent).

The failure of Gantt's campaign to blunt Helms's racial appeal was especially true among older whites. The Democrats' bad news was that Gantt in 1990 won just 30 percent of the over-sixty white vote, compared with Hunt's 40 percent in the same age group (VNS 1990; CBS News 1984). Perhaps the decision of Gantt's television advertising team to deemphasize attacks on Helms's changing positions over the years on the Social Security system, in contrast to numerous anti-Helms ads on that theme by the 1984 Hunt campaign, contributed to Gantt's relatively poor showing. Exit poll data from 1984 had shown clearly that Helms was vulnerable on Social Security (Luebke 1990a, 145–46, 153–54), so Gantt's not stressing this issue in 1990 was surprising.

The 1990 exit poll also shows a strong gender gap among whites in the Gantt-Helms election, suggesting that Helms's five-part advertising campaign highlighted by Jamieson (1992, 97–100) resonated more strongly with white men than with white women. Gantt won just 31 percent of the white male vote, compared with 40 percent of the white female vote. By contrast, Hunt's 1984 campaign appealed almost equally well to white men (37 percent) and women (39 percent). The good news for Democrats in 1990 was that a campaign that strongly advocated investment in public education and environmental protection appealed to white women. Gantt's relative success hinted at a possible winning strategy for North Carolina Democrats in the twenty-first century: a campaign that explicitly targets the common concerns perceived by white women and African Americans of either gender.

In the final analysis Jesse Helms's ability to defeat both the allegedly unbeatable Jim Hunt campaign of 1984 and the demonstrably energetic and challenging Harvey Gantt campaign of 1990 made two points clear: Helms was a seemingly one-of-a-kind Republican whom any Democrat would have trouble defeating, and whether or not Helms was the unbeatable one, Tar Heel Democrats were still searching for a formula that could ensure victories for the party's statewide candidates in the 1990s and into the twenty-first century.

1996: A Replay of 1990

In 1996, when Gantt and Helms were locked in a rematch, Gantt hoped that a changed North Carolina electorate would provide him with a winning margin over Helms. But in fact Gantt's grassroots campaign was less energized than it had been in 1990. Helms kept Gantt on the defensive most of the fall by attacking Gantt's alleged sympathies for gay rights. Gantt, not Helms, ended up appearing to be the more "out-of-touch" candidate. Helms's 1996 victory margin, 53 to 46 percent, was slightly larger than it had been in 1990.

The process by which, beginning in the 1960s, white Tar Heels moved away from the Democratic Party and the related rise of the Republicans is the subject of the next chapter.

9

The Rise of the Republicans
and the Decline of the Democrats

From the early years of the twentieth century until the victories of the civil rights movement, most white southerners, including Tar Heel whites, identified with and voted for the Democratic Party. North Carolina's Republicans made their first major breakthrough in 1972, winning a U.S. Senate seat, the governor's office, and nearly one-third of the seats in the General Assembly. By 1984 any Republican candidate running statewide could expect to gain a majority of the white vote. Black voters, nearly one-fifth of the electorate, supported the Democratic ticket overwhelmingly. Democrats needed the strong black vote as well as 40 percent of the white vote to win. If Republicans won 60 percent or more of the white vote, they would be elected. In short, the swing voters in the statewide elections of the 1980s and 1990s were whites with weak partisan identification.

The rise of the Republican Party in North Carolina and across the South began as a reaction against the apparent willingness of white southern Democratic leaders to acquiesce to the demands of black southerners for racial equality. In 1964, for example, five Deep South states voted for

Republican Barry Goldwater. A libertarian Republican (Goldwater 1960), Goldwater's opposition to federal government regulation of individual states made him a hero in the eyes of many white southerners, including then-TV editorialist Jesse Helms. North Carolinians in 1964 stayed loyal to Democrat Lyndon Johnson rather than support Goldwater, as neighboring South Carolina did. But in both 1968 and 1972 Nixon won the state's electoral votes. Indeed, only once between 1968 and 1996 did a Democratic presidential candidate win a majority of Tar Heel votes. In 1976 Georgian Jimmy Carter carried the state by a comfortable margin. But Carter lost the state in 1980 to GOP challenger Ronald Reagan. In 1972 the top three places on the North Carolina ticket—president, U.S. senator, and governor—were all won by Republicans. Never before had Tar Heel Republicans had that kind of success. They won because several hundred thousand registered Democrats crossed over to vote Republican, mostly just at the top of the ticket. Until the mid-1980s, Republican success depended on this Democratic crossover vote. In 1984, for example, the state had three registered Democrats for each registered Republican (NC Free 1997). But as the Grissom brothers (see Chapter 8) suggested, being a registered Democrat did not constitute any obligation to vote Democratic.

The gradual weakening of Democratic loyalties by white southerners is known as dealignment. Dealignment means that many North Carolina whites have lost their commitment to the Democratic Party but have not yet transferred their loyalty to the Republicans. Republicans would prefer to see more whites switch their party registration to the GOP, or at least to identify with the Republican Party. This process is known as realignment (Black and Black 1987, 237). But dealignment, not realignment, characterized the white electorate until the mid-1980s.

From the mid- to late 1980s, Republicans' attempts to gain new voters or encourage longtime registered Democrats to change their official party affiliation bore fruit. For example, between Senator Helms's third (1984) and fourth (1990) reelection campaigns, the percentage of North Carolinians registered in the GOP jumped from 26 to 31, while the percentage of registered Democrats declined from 70 to 64. In the 1990s a somewhat similar pattern continued. In 1996 the percentage of Republicans rose to 34, and Democrats fell to 56. But the most important change in the 1990s was the large numbers of voters unwilling to claim membership in either political party. Between 1984 and 1990 the statewide number of unaffiliated voters had risen just slightly, from 4.4 percent to 5.5 percent. But in the next six years the unaffiliated share grew from 5.5 percent to 12.2 percent The county-by-county data suggested that the unaffiliated vote was most concentrated in the metro Piedmont areas into which there was substantial migration. One political consultant referred to the new registrants, both Republican and unaffiliated, as "cul-de-sac" voters (NC Free 1996).

The dealigned voters who held on to their Democratic registration cards were primarily native-born whites who were uncomfortable with the existence of or the pace of desegregation in North Carolina. But their political behavior was a reaction against black-induced social change. Mostly they saw little affirmative about the Republican Party.

The White Racial Reaction, 1968 and 1972

In a 1968 poll only 23 percent of white North Carolinians said they would "like to see white and Negro children go to the same school." Only 17 percent favored "letting Negroes move into white neighborhoods" (Beyle and Harkins 1975, 97). George Wallace and Jesse Helms did not need an opinion poll to know that racial equality, and especially the black power rallying cry of more militant blacks, offended most whites in North Carolina. It was a political issue waiting to be tapped. Although Wallace was much more of an economic populist than Helms (Frady 1976; Furgurson 1986; Carter 1995), their racial appeals in 1968 and 1972 were remarkably similar. Further, Helms as a TV editorialist had over the years praised Wallace's opposition to the many egalitarian movements of the 1960s. Race, especially before the 1973 Supreme Court decision establishing women's abortion rights, stood out as foremost among a constellation of issues that included the Vietnam War, long hair, and drugs.

Wallace and Helms shared a knack for capturing the resentments of whites in well-turned phrases and paragraphs. As Helms editorialized in 1965 about Martin Luther King Jr.'s nonviolent movement, "It is about as nonviolent as the Marines landing on Iwo Jima, and it is a 'movement' only in the sense that mob action is moving and spreading throughout the land" (Nordhoff 1984, 53). Voting for Wallace or Helms could, in Wallace's phrase, "send them a message." "Them" was the national Democratic Party and the political and cultural protesters of the 1960s. In short, the target was liberalism, real and imagined (cf. Bartley and Graham 1975, 132).

The Wallace vote in 1968, when voters could choose among three major candidates, correlates strongly with the level of black political participation in the state's 100 counties. The higher the proportion of registered blacks in a county, the more likely that county's voters gave Wallace a majority.

Wallace did not win a single county where blacks made up less than 10 percent of the electorate (37 counties). By contrast, excluding the 6 counties of the metro Piedmont (won by Hubert Humphrey in Durham and Orange, and by Richard Nixon in Forsyth, Guilford, Mecklenburg, and Wake), Wallace won 64 percent of the 28 counties with a black voter registration of 10 to 25 percent, and carried 79 percent of the counties where blacks constituted more than 25 percent of the electorate. In short, racial resentment fueled the 1968 Wallace campaign.

A comparison of Wallace's 1968 vote and Helms's 1972 totals indicates that Helms's statewide base was wider than Wallace's. In 1972 in the metro Piedmont, the western Piedmont, and the Mountains, Helms picked up straight-Republican voters who were supporting Richard Nixon's reelection and in 1968 had supported Nixon instead of Wallace.

But Helms's support was especially strong on the Coastal Plain and in the eastern Piedmont, particularly in counties where people could have watched "Viewpoint" live on channel 5. His fame in those parts of eastern North Carolina led him to an absolute majority (54 percent), and most of this margin of difference came from dealigned whites who were registered Democrats. These registered Democrats who switched to Helms became known as Jessecrats. Although by the 1980s Jessecrats would increasingly vote as "Repubo-crats," that is, they would support other Republicans as well, especially in statewide races, the 1972 election showed that down east, GOP candidates besides Helms had not taken root. Successful gubernatorial candidate Holshouser, for example, won 10 percent fewer votes than did Helms, just 44 percent in the Coastal Plain counties.

The Emerging Republican Appeal, 1972 to 1980

Wallace's support in 1968 and 1972 and Helms's victory in 1972 were clear examples of white dealignment from the Democrats. But because both politicians had strong personal appeal in those elections, their vote tallies were an incomplete indication of voters' willingness to jettison the Democrats in favor of the Republican Party. By contrast, two uncharismatic politicians, Jim Holshouser, a mainstream Republican state legislator from Boone who unexpectedly won the 1972 governor's race, and John East, a traditionalist college professor from Greenville who upset the incumbent U.S. senator in November 1980, provided a clearer picture of the growing Republican appeal.

In the June 1972 Republican runoff primary, Holshouser defeated Jim

Gardner, a former congressman (1967–68) and former gubernatorial candidate (1968). It was a victory of a Republican modernizer over a Republican traditionalist. Holshouser's support of economic diversification and improved race relations—hallmarks of modernizer ideology—were hardly distinguishable from the views of his Democratic opponent, Greensboro businessman Skipper Bowles. Holshouser publicly urged black voters to split their ticket by supporting him for governor (Black 1975, 76). In marked contrast to Holshouser's modernizer politics, John East was a right-wing ideologue handpicked by the Congressional Club to run a long-shot candidacy against incumbent U.S. Senator Robert Morgan. Morgan appeared unbeatable because of his decades-long involvement in the state Democratic Party and political ties to all stripes of Tar Heel Democrats, but especially to traditionalists (he had, for example, managed I. Beverly Lake's campaign against Terry Sanford in 1960) (Spence 1968, 15).

Despite ideological differences between Holshouser and East, their patterns of voter support were remarkably similar. Statewide, Holshouser won 51 percent of the vote in 1972, and East eked out slightly more than 50 percent in 1980. The sources of their support, which differed from Helms's statewide bases, suggested a more stable indication of GOP strength. They also provided a picture of Republican voting when popular presidential candidates (Nixon in 1972 and Reagan in 1980 and 1984) led the ticket. First, many loyal GOP voters live in the rural, small-town areas of the Mountains and western Piedmont. This is historical Republicanism, rooted in the antiplanter feelings of nineteenth-century small farmers who had nothing to gain from a slave economy. Holshouser won 57 percent of the Mountains and western Piedmont vote in 1972, and East took 56 percent in 1980.

Second, in the Piedmont's growing metropolitan areas around Charlotte and the Triad, the steady influx of northern business-oriented voters since World War II enabled Republicans to expand grassroots party organizations. In 1952 the Charlotte-area congressional district supported Dwight Eisenhower (the state went for Adlai Stevenson) and, more importantly, elected North Carolina's first Republican congressman since the turn of the century (Bartley and Graham 1975, 90). Since 1980 this business in-migration had increased markedly, especially in Charlotte. During the 1980s and 1990s in both Charlotte and the Triad cities of Winston-Salem, Greensboro, and High Point, Republicans defeated Democrats regularly in contests for the county commission and the state legislature. The Republican trend was far less pronounced in Raleigh, where state government employees had historically favored the Democrats. However, business-oriented voters moving to the Research Triangle Park added to GOP strength in Wake County (Raleigh). In Durham and Orange Counties the in-migration had a university flavor, and these two counties retained their Democratic strength. Holshouser's vote totals in 1972 reflected this varying GOP strength in the metro Piedmont: 55 percent in Mecklenburg, Forsyth, and Guilford; 53 percent in Wake; and 45 percent in Durham and Orange. In a similar pattern East won 52 percent in Mecklenburg and the Triad, 47 percent in Wake, and 40 percent in Durham and Orange. Overall in the metro Piedmont, Holshouser captured 53 percent of the vote, while East was held to 49 percent. East's lower level of support probably reflected urban voters' preference for mainstream rather than Congressional Club Republicans.

The third area of Republican strength after 1972 was in the small towns and rural areas of eastern North Carolina. As a rule, in most of these eastern counties Republicans did not even file for county and legislative offices. Although ideologically similar to Helms, East's vote in eastern North Carolina resembled Holshouser's. Holshouser won 43 percent in the Coastal Plain and eastern Piedmont in 1972, while East was held to 44 percent in 1980. By contrast, in these same counties Helms received 54 percent in 1972 and 53 percent in 1978.

The parallel totals in eastern, western, and small-town Piedmont North Carolina for Holshouser and East contrasted with East's poorer showing in the metro Piedmont. This suggested that the Congressional Club's heavily ideological, traditionalist campaign against Morgan in 1980, especially in 30-second TV spots, may have been a case of overkill. The anti-Morgan advertising (for example, attacking Morgan for the alleged giveaway of the Panama Canal), for all the publicity it afforded the Congressional Club (Greenhaw 1982, 167), appears to have cost John East votes in the metro Piedmont, where voters were least sympathetic to traditionalist campaign themes. At the same time, Holshouser's modernizer brand of Republicanism in 1972 seems to have won him as many votes in the non-metro Piedmont as did East's Congressional Club traditionalism in 1980. In short, a slight majority of voters was prepared to support a Tar Heel Republican for statewide office by 1980, regardless of candidate ideology.

The Ascendant Republicans, 1984–1996

Tar Heel Republicans were euphoric after the November 1984 election. They had swept the presidential, gubernatorial, and U.S. Senate races, won five of the eleven congressional seats, and sent more legislators to Raleigh than at any time since the 1972 Nixon-Holshouser-Helms sweep. But the real evidence that North Carolina had become a two-party state emerged in November 1986. For North Carolina Republicans, the 1986 election was important because, except for losing the U.S. Senate seat to Democratic icon Terry Sanford and two congressional seats (the fourth in the Research Triangle and the eleventh in the Mountains) that had narrowly gone to the GOP in 1984, the party held its own despite the absence of a Republican presidential candidate to motivate Tar Heel whites to go to the polls. Republicans did have an effective incumbent governor, Jim Martin, who stumped for his party's candidates. Significantly, the GOP did not lose ground in the General Assembly and even gained seats at the county commission level. In almost all of the state west of Raleigh, including most of the large cities, Republicans provided stiff challenges to Democrats. Statewide in 1986, Republican judges won about 45 percent of the vote, totals similar to those of Republican Council of State candidates (from lieutenant governor to insurance commissioner and auditor) in 1984. Thousands of Democrats crossed over to support Reagan, Martin, and Helms in 1984 and Broyhill in 1986.

In 1988 Democrats hoped that their gubernatorial candidate, incumbent Lieutenant Governor Bob Jordan, would unseat Governor Martin. In fact, Republicans whipped the Democrats in North Carolina for several reasons. The most important is that the GOP coupled a strong incumbent governor's personality with a "let's keep a good thing going" nonissue message that conveyed normalcy and prosperity to voters. The Democrats sought to counter the Jim Martin pitch with the claim that he had been an ineffective and even absent governor (Democratic television spots pointed out that, while the General Assembly was meeting in Raleigh, Martin was out of town watching the Kentucky Derby or sailing in the Caribbean on a family vacation). The Jordan campaign expected that the voters would prefer a hard-working Democrat to an incumbent Republican who was, because Democrats controlled the legislature, necessarily less involved in legislative policymaking than Democrats. To their surprise on Election Day, Jordan and other modernizer Democrats learned that Martin's simple message of "reelect me" was compelling. It appears that many white voters, especially in affluent white precincts of the metro Piedmont, reacted negatively to incumbent Democratic power brokers such as Bob Jordan, house Speaker Liston Ramsey, and state senator Tony Rand, the candidate for lieutenant governor. The typical white Tar Heel in 1988 seemed to give the

Democratic majority little recognition for passing educational, environmental, and highway programs in the General Assembly. Rather, white voters seemed to agree with Martin's assertions that he was, or at least should be, setting North Carolina's political agenda.

In the November election Martin defeated Jordan 56 to 44 percent, an improvement over his 54-to-46 percent victory over Rufus Edmisten four years earlier. Exit polls indicate that Martin received about two-thirds of the white vote, and he needed only 60 percent to win. As expected, more than 90 percent of blacks supported Jordan, even though Martin had advertised on black radio stations across North Carolina in hopes of taking black votes away from Jordan.

Martin ran an effective two-pronged campaign for the white vote. First, his overall theme of normalcy and prosperity permeated his television advertising, primarily emphasizing the goals of his administration and its record of achievement. This television campaign highlighted Martin the modernizer politician, willing to use government to provide schools, highways, and environmental protection. His ads showed white and black children in classrooms together, as well as shots of the Cape Hatteras lighthouse. An outsider watching the TV spots would have been hard pressed to know whether this sincere-sounding man in his dark suit and red tie was a New South democrat or a New South Republican.

Tar Heel Republican strategists recognized by the summer of 1988 that, unlike in 1984, when incumbent President Ronald Reagan was significantly more popular than the relatively unknown candidate Jim Martin, the coattails of Martin would be virtually as long as Bush's. Recognizing Martin's popularity and his wide lead over Jordan in the preelection polls, the Martin team scheduled tandem campaigning by Martin and Jim Gardner, candidate for lieutenant governor, during the week before Election Day. They focused on the state's Republican heartland, the western Piedmont, and adjoining metro Piedmont cities such as Charlotte and Greensboro. Martin specifically asked his campaign audiences to be sure to support Gardner as well as himself.

The strongest region for both Martin and Gardner was the western Piedmont, where Martin took 62 percent and Gardner won 58 percent of the vote. Martin's second best region was the metro Piedmont; he won between 55 and 64 percent of the vote in Guilford, Forsyth, Wake, and Mecklenburg Counties. The only metro Piedmont counties to deny Martin a majority were the two Democratic strongholds, Orange and Durham. Gardner won Forsyth, Wake, and Mecklenburg, but by substantially smaller margins.

Tar Heel Republican leaders after November 1988 were jubilant about their local and statewide success. Two months later, at the General Assembly, forty-five house Republicans added insult to injury by coalescing with twenty Democrats to topple four-term incumbent Democrat Liston Ramsey by electing instead maverick Democrat Joe Mavretic to the Speaker's chair (*Charlotte Observer* 1989a). The 1989–90 session would symbolize both Republican power and Democratic disunity.

In fact, some Republican analysts at the time were aware that the GOP ascendancy was more fragile than it looked at first glance. Most importantly, by 1988 the vein of Jessecrat voters had been tapped out. This did not mean that the whites who were disaffected by the growing biracial character of the state Democratic Party were no longer supporting Helms and even other Republican candidates at the state and local levels. Rather, in the sixteen years since Helms had first won election, many of his diehard fans from his WRAL-TV editorial days had died.

Younger generations of white voters, even those in the Coastal Plain, would never as a group hold firmly to the racial segregationist views that many of their grandparents supported. So a candidate who ran with the hard edge of a Jesse Helms, except perhaps Helms himself because of his extraordinary campaigning skill, would not prosper as well among younger native-born white Tar Heels.

The transplant vote was also problematic for Republicans. Although many of the well-educated in-migrants either to the metro Piedmont counties or to the retirement counties continued to register Republican, these new voters, especially if they were not from other southern states, were distrustful of traditionalist Republicans who campaigned on a religious-right agenda. The statewide Republican candidate who ran without strong elements of modernizer ideology—commitment to public education and at least some support for environmental protection—was in fact vulnerable to defeat by a Democrat who did espouse modernizer views.

This potential GOP weakness was visible in both the 1990 and the 1992 general elections, even though it was obscured by two U.S. Senate election victories: Helms's come-from-behind reelection bid over Harvey Gantt in 1990 and Democrat-turned-Republican Lauch Faircloth's retirement of his onetime friend Terry Sanford in 1992. GOP vulnerability was most clearly seen in the 1992 loss of stalwart Republican candidate Jim Gardner, who had first won a seat in the U.S. Congress in 1966 by upsetting a longtime Democratic incumbent. Gardner generally hewed to a traditionalist agenda. As the GOP candidate for governor in 1968, for example, he had openly supported third-party candidate George Wallace (Black 1976, 111). But in 1988, running for lieutenant governor on the same ticket as incumbent Governor Martin, Gardner played down his traditionalism and sounded more like mainstreamer Martin, a blend of modernizer and traditionalist (see Chapter 2; Luebke 1990a, 183–84). As noted above, Gardner as Martin's ticketmate won a narrow statewide election, 51 percent to 49 percent, over Fayetteville modernizer Tony Rand. In the six metro Piedmont counties Gardner nearly won a majority, 49 percent, against Rand (in the same counties in the same election Martin won 58 percent against Bob Jordan), while winning comfortably, 55 percent to 45 percent, in the Mountain region (Martin took 58 percent of the Mountain vote).

When Gardner in 1992 took on Democratic comeback gubernatorial candidate Jim Hunt, he sought to paint Hunt as a liberal; Gardner himself ran, Helms-like, as a traditionalist. The results were unsettling to any Republican who had believed that *any* Republican could beat any Democrat. Two factors beyond Gardner's traditionalist ideology, to be sure, were working in the Democrats' favor: veteran Democrat Hunt campaigned in 1992 more vigorously than had Rand in 1988, and the Clinton 1992 campaign in North Carolina was also more enthusiastic than the Dukakis campaign had been in 1988. Nevertheless, it seems clear that traditionalist Gardner was a weaker GOP candidate than mainstreamer Gardner. In the metro Piedmont, Gardner's vote dropped from 49 percent in 1988 to 39 percent in 1992, and in the Mountains it fell from 55 percent to 49 percent.

Another indication of post-1988 voter doubts about traditionalism is suggested by a review of the Helms-Gantt 1990 totals in the U.S. Senate race. Although Helms defeated Gantt thanks to a strong finish (see Chapter 8), the six counties of the metro Piedmont, by far North Carolina's fastest-growing region, voted 43 to 57 percent against Helms. This contrasted with the 49 percent metro Piedmont support for mainstreamer Gardner in 1988. In accord with the view that Helms's TV advertising based on racial appeal in the campaign's closing days was crucial for his victory, Helms in the other regions of the state (where native-born white Tar Heels are more prevalent) garnered 57 percent of the vote, allowing him to win statewide with 53 percent. The lesson here was that social traditionalism, particularly if linked to racial images of the Old South, appeared to hurt a statewide Republican in the fast-growing regions of the state.

The 1990 election also helped house Democratic candidates more than house Republicans. Democrats won seven additional seats, bringing their

1991 margin to 81-39 over the Republicans. With restored seats and a sense of unity, Democrats buried the Mavretic Speakership coalition. In January 1991 Democrats made history by electing Dan Blue as Speaker, the first African American to chair a southern state house since the 1870s (cf. Franklin 1947).

When Lauch Faircloth defeated Sanford in November 1992, most observers noted that outcome as emblematic of the continuing Republican gains in North Carolina. But although it had an impact in Washington, D.C., because it shifted one U.S. Senate seat into the Republican column, its meaning for long-term Republican prospects was less certain. Faircloth, who in 1984 had run unsuccessfully (he placed third with 16 percent of the vote) for the Democratic nomination for governor as a modernizer (Luebke 1990a, 172), was guided by the Congressional Club in 1992 to run a Helms-like traditionalist campaign. But unlike the 1992 Gardner-Hunt campaign, in which the candidates' opposing views and mutual antipathy were clear, Sanford's heart-valve operation and lengthy rehabilitation meant that Faircloth was running against an almost invisible candidate.

It is noteworthy that unlike the 1990 Gantt-Helms or the 1992 Gardner-Hunt races, the Democratic candidate opposing a traditionalist Republican did not run well in the metro Piedmont region. While Hunt was beating Gardner by 18 percent in the metro Piedmont, Sanford's lead was just 4 percentage points. This suggests strongly that Sanford's health prevented him from presenting himself as he truly was: one of North Carolina's most important architects of antitraditionalist politics. A healthy Sanford heralding his modernizer views would surely have run more strongly in the metro Piedmont counties. Indeed, a strong 1992 Sanford effort statewide similar to his successful 1986 Senate campaign (Luebke 1990a, 199–200; Luebke 1987c) might have defeated Faircloth.

The Republicans' winning 1994 campaign for the state house and their near-win in the state senate solidified the notion of a two-party North Carolina. Significantly, a combination of traditionalist and at least modernizer-leaning Republicans defeated modernizer Democrats in a host of urban districts. As a rejoinder to the notion that modernizer voters were rejecting Republican candidates, GOP leaders were pleased that voters in Greensboro, Asheville, Raleigh, and Wilmington had elected an ideologically diverse group of Republicans to seats in the General Assembly.

In 1996 Republicans' power was reduced in Raleigh, and both Republican congressmen who had won in 1994, Funderburk in the second district and Heinemann in the fourth, were replaced by Democrats. But the good news for Republicans was also evident. Helms defeated Gantt again, this time easily; the house Republicans retained a narrow 61-to-59 margin but were able to reelect Harold Brubaker as Speaker; the twelve congressional seats were divided equally between the two parties; and Republicans held 42 percent of all county commission seats in North Carolina, an all-time high.

Further, in the 1996 state treasurer's race, in which the GOP ran a modernizer white woman against an older, traditionalist-leaning white Democratic male, the Republican candidate, Ann Duncan, won 48 percent of the vote. This contrasted with just 43 percent statewide for the traditionalist GOP gubernatorial candidate, Robin Hayes. Most importantly, in the metro Piedmont Duncan, a former state legislator from Winston-Salem, won 47 percent of the vote (versus Hayes's 39 percent). In Durham and Orange Counties, the state's Democratic stronghold, Duncan took 42 percent, compared with 27 percent for Hayes. The relative standing of the female statewide Republican candidate—all the other unsuccessful GOP candidates for Council of State offices were white males—in the metro Piedmont in 1996 raised important positive possibilities for Tar Heel Republicans in 2000 and 2004.

The Erosion of Democratic Traditionalism

The attempt of the Democratic Party in the 1980s to respond to some of the political demands of labor, women's, and environmentalist organizations constituted an important shift in North Carolina politics since the early 1970s. Gone from the Democratic Party was the statewide candidate who unabashedly opposed the goals of blacks or environmentalists. The defeat of a once-powerful Democratic state senator, Harold Hardison, as he sought higher office typified the decline of the party's traditionalist appeal. Further, the early retirement in 1995 of Secretary of State Rufus Edmisten signaled that a good-old-boy cultural style had lost most of its appeal in North Carolina Democratic circles.

The 1988 candidacy of state senator Harold Hardison for the Democratic lieutenant governor's nomination illustrated how traditionalist politicians became convinced by the late 1980s that their power-brokering legislative record on behalf of traditionalist business interests was no longer enough to win a statewide Democratic primary. But despite adopting a modernizer veneer, Hardison, a veteran traditionalist senator from Lenoir County, seventy-five miles east of Raleigh, lost decisively in the May 1988 primary.

In the 1970s and 1980s Hardison had worked openly against efforts by environmentalists to strengthen antipollution regulations. He secured passage in early 1973 of the so-called Hardison amendments, which stipulated that no North Carolina air or water quality or hazardous-waste standards could be more exacting than those of the federal government. Beginning in 1981 the Reagan administration weakened environmental standards. When Tar Heel environmentalists in response attempted to maintain strict state standards despite the president's action, the Hardison amendments stood in the way. Hardison opposed the environmentalists at this point, leading the fight to keep his earlier amendments on the books.

As a state senator, Hardison consistently favored the insurance industry in its unsuccessful effort to restrict corporate liability in damage suits (the so-called tort reform bills). He also voted against the Equal Rights Amendment and the state abortion fund. Consequently, Hardison won the support of many corporate interests, including some modernizers, as well as backing from antiabortion activists. Nevertheless, Hardison's campaign tried hard to change his image as an economic and social traditionalist. Despite the Hardison amendments, his supporters defined him as "moderate and reasonable" on environmental issues (O'Connor 1987a). He added a well-known advocate of the Equal Rights Amendment to his campaign staff and touted the names of black Democrats who had endorsed his candidacy.

Several years after the 1988 primary, a journalist's investigation revealed that a number of Coastal Plain businessmen had violated campaign finance law by secretly funding Hardison's campaign beyond the legal limit. Among those who apparently approved of Hardison's deep-felt opposition to environmental regulation was Hardison's former legislative colleague and major Coastal Plain pork producer Wendell Murphy. But the statute of limitations made any discussion of prosecution moot (*News and Observer* 1993).

The funding debacle made it clear after the fact that Hardison had not changed his political values but had merely camouflaged them. Hardison had recognized that many of the Jessecrats were no longer participating in Democratic primaries. Further, as elsewhere in the South, blacks were becoming an increasingly significant part of the Democratic electorate, especially in primaries. Segregation and even coded antiblack messages were no longer acceptable in the party (Black and Black 1987, 292–96). Further, as the Democratic Party became more aligned with the environmentalist and women's issues promoted by many party activists, any candidate who sought to win a statewide primary election found it necessary to pay at least lip service to these issues. Because of greater population growth, especially in-migration in many of the state's urban centers, a traditionalist image became a liability for Democrats such as Hardison who sought statewide office.

But Hardison's attempts to posture himself as a moderate between traditionalism and modernism failed. Fayetteville state senator Tony Rand defeated Hardison 43 to 26 percent in a three-person race. Hardison disappeared from state politics after 1988; his defeat signaled the shift in the Democrats' primary voting base that made it impossible any longer for a strong traditionalist to win a statewide Democratic primary.

The case of Edmisten was more complicated. Edmisten effectively used his position as counsel to U.S. Senator Sam Ervin during the 1973 nationally televised Watergate hearings to gain a statewide reputation. A year later the Democratic State Executive Committee appointed him attorney general to replace Robert Morgan, who had resigned to run for the U.S. Senate. Edmisten subsequently won three elections for attorney general (1974, 1976, and 1980) by comfortable margins. A native of Watauga County in the Mountains, he prided himself on his folksy ways. They brought him favor with many small-town and rural white Democrats across the state. Edmisten played the banjo and sang country and gospel tunes at political rallies, and he developed close political ties with most of the state's 100 sheriffs.

When Edmisten ran for the Democratic nomination for governor in 1984, his platform revealed that his country style was just that. He was neither an economic populist who would campaign for repeal of the food tax nor a social traditionalist who opposed abortion rights for women. In fact, Rufus, as he liked to be called, held to modernizer values barely different from those of Jim Hunt or Terry Sanford. Yet his style harkened back to a rural economic traditionalism, in which, as a "country boy," he promised to serve the people well.

Edmisten lost badly to former college professor Jim Martin in 1984, and cultural style made a difference. In the metro Piedmont counties, for example, Edmisten won just 43 percent of the vote against Martin. Meanwhile, Jim Hunt, who shared many political values with Edmisten but had a far more serious, probusiness demeanor, won 53 percent in those same counties in his unsuccessful race against Jesse Helms. Edmisten's country style probably alienated him from upper middle-class voters who preferred Martin's professional tone. In several university precincts in metro Piedmont counties, Edmisten won 20 percent fewer votes against Martin than Hunt had against Helms.

Edmisten later won two terms as secretary of state beginning in 1988, but he would be pressured into resigning in 1995. A newspaper investigation and subsequent state audit showed he had improperly instructed office employees to help him with personal projects on state time. By the 1990s Edmisten was a throwback to an earlier time in North Carolina, when being a good old boy was a good enough reason to be elected. Many urban modernizer Democrats were delighted that his arguably illegal actions as secretary of state appeared to end his political career.

Ironically, North Carolina Republicans recruited their world-famous local elected official, NASCAR champion Richard Petty, to run for secretary of state against Edmisten in 1996, forcing a fascinating battle between country boys. By the time Edmisten resigned, Petty, a veteran county commissioner from Randolph County near Greensboro, had already committed to run on the 1996 Republican ticket. When North Carolina voters in November 1996 had a choice between Petty and Elaine Marshall, a "citified" lawyer and former state senator, they rejected Petty. Just as Edmisten had encountered in 1984, the greatest resistance to Petty came from the metro Piedmont counties (Petty won just 38 percent of the vote in the metro Piedmont compared with 48 percent in the rest of North Carolina).

Confusion in the Democratic Elite, 1988 to 1996

North Carolina Democrats in the 1990s faced an undeniable fact: the percentage of Tar Heels registered as Democrats had declined steadily since Republican Jim Martin was first elected governor in 1984 until 1996, from 70 to 56. At first glance the data seemed to make no sense, since a Republican won the governor's race in 1984, when registered Democrats were more prevalent, and the Republican lost in 1996, when the percentage of registered Democrats was at its lowest level ever. But examining party success and failure at lower levels, such as in the General Assembly or on county commissions, presented a clear picture of Democrats in decline. After the 1984 elections, for example, Democrats held three-fourths of the 120 state house seats and 80 percent of all county commission seats. After 1996 Democrats held not quite one-half of the state house seats and just 58 percent of county commission seats.

The defeat of Harold Hardison in the 1988 primary affirmed the ascendancy of modernizers in statewide primary elections. Modernization themes became especially clear in Jordan's 1988 race against incumbent Governor Jim Martin. His gubernatorial campaign emphasized three issues: education, economic development, and the environment. Both Tony Rand and Parks Helms, a former state legislator from Charlotte who was the third major candidate in the 1988 Democratic primary for the lieutenant governor nomination, shared Jordan's political values.

Education and economic development were classic modernizer issues. Both Terry Sanford in the 1960s and Jim Hunt in the 1970s had placed these themes at the center of their campaigns. In their and Jordan's view, the state should play a major role in expanding jobs and people's qualifications for those jobs.

Martin's convincing win over Jordan in 1988 indicated, as suggested above, that simply promising education, economic development, and environmental protection was not a sufficient basis to win an election. Democrats in the spring 1990 primaries opted for a shift in emphasis. By a decisive margin the more energetic and original modernizer candidate, African American architect Harvey Gantt, defeated the "safer" modernizer, white district attorney Mike Easley, in the June 1990 runoff primary. While Gantt's vigorous campaign in support of education and the environment raised the fascinating possibility of a November 1990 upset of Senator Helms, in the end, of course, Helms prevailed.

With Jim Hunt's return to the governor's race in 1992, Democrats opted for another experienced modernizer. But the 1992 ticket in North Carolina was led by a fellow southerner, Bill Clinton, whose campaign had a sharper economic populist edge than Jim Hunt's. Presidential candidate Clinton invoked class imagery to express sympathy for average citizens "working harder for less" while corporate executives earned "outrageous salaries" (Dionne 1997, 70). It is unclear whether Clinton's overall themes as well as the Clinton-Gore decision to campaign in person to try to carry the state's electoral votes (George Bush in fact won narrowly) had any impact on Democratic success. But evidence at the lower ends of the lengthy ballot suggested that Clinton's message did matter. At the county commission level, for instance, 1992 was the only election year between 1984 and 1996 in which Democrats increased their percentage of county commission seats (North Carolina Association of County Commissioners 1996). The party also lost only a handful of seats in the General Assembly.

Between 1992 and 1994 state Democrats held power in Raleigh but atrophied at the grassroots level. As a result of election board "purges" of non-voters in all parties after 1992 and the Democrats' failure to undertake voter registration campaigns, Democrats actually suffered a net loss in registered voters between the two elections: 31,000 fewer Democrats were registered, compared with an increase of 124,000 registered Republicans and of 106,000 who registered as unaffiliated (NC Free 1997). The disillusionment among Tar Heel Democrats was twofold. At the national level Clinton's missteps regarding the roles of gays in the military (cf. Luebke 1995) and the subsequent failure of his health care reform plan (cf. Johnson and Broder 1996) sowed seeds of doubt in Democratic circles. Second, within North Carolina, under-the-surface dissension between many traditionalist-leaning (usually white) Democrats, among them Governor Hunt, and populist-leaning (mostly black) Democrats, among them Speaker Blue, over solutions to the crime issue (see Chapter 7) left Tar Heel Democrats divided and unprepared for the November 1994 election. This contrasted with the enthusiasm of state Republicans, who papered over their ideological differences and even convinced state house and senate candidates to pledge support to a North Carolina version of Newt Gingrich's Contract for America (cf. *News and Record* 1995).

Democrats' directionless and minimal campaigning during the fall of 1994 had a high cost. Not only on Election Day did General Assembly seats shift heavily into the Republicans' column, but the GOP also added fifty-six county commissioners to their ranks statewide, the largest one-time gain in the state's history. In 1996 Democrats in the General Assembly won seats back that they had lost in 1994. However, the number of Democratic county commissioners continued to drop to an all-time low.

For Democrats in decline, a major problem was that, unlike Republicans, no clear ideology or ideologies were visible to help structure internal party debate. Although Tar Heel Republicans by contrast experienced continual public conflict between the social traditionalist wing, heavily influenced by the religious right, and advocates of a pro-big-business economic agenda, the GOP had the advantage of offering party members clear lines of disagreement. Analysis of the Democrats' political divisions suggested ideological differences did exist. On one hand, many urban, especially metro Piedmont, Democrats supported environmental protection and a strong agenda to help women and children and showed some sympathies for economic populism and a related fight against continuing racial inequality. On the other hand, both many small-town and urban Democrats with stronger commitments to big business were skeptical of any big-government spending programs. They opposed populist economics and believed that African American issues were already too visible in the North Carolina Democratic agenda.

Not surprisingly, most black Democrats were more inclined to support the metro Piedmont agenda. But significantly, the Democrats' ideological conflict was not a public issue. The state's press corps apparently did not see the Democrats' conflict as real, even though the conflict was similar to the much-publicized Republican debate. Seemingly not aware themselves of what the intraparty issues were, the state's Democratic elected officials and activists did not appear poised to lead the party into the twenty-first century.

10 The Future of North Carolina Politics

Since the first Republican sweep in 1972, the style of North Carolina politics changed. Gone from the General Assembly leadership were the rural style and views of traditionalist Democrats. Further, for one term, 1995–96, traditionalist Republicans dominated house politics. But the November 1996 election almost cost Speaker Brubaker his Republican majority. In 1997–98 house Republicans did rule, but they ruled by adopting modernizer policies: a big-spending state budget only marginally different from that of senate Democrats. To the dismay of a small minority of house Republicans, Brubaker's second term appeared to be a victory for a mainstream Republicanism much closer to the ideology of former governor Jim Martin than to that of 1996 gubernatorial candidate Robin Hayes.

Three dimensions of Tar Heel politics seemed likely to shape party prospects in the first decade of the twenty-first century. First, African American participation was a permanent force in the electorate and among elected officials. The percentage of black North Carolina voters—about 19—had not changed between the mid-1980s and mid-1990s. But the number of black elected officials did rise during that period. For example, 16 percent of all Tar Heel county commissioners in 1997 were black, compared with just 8 percent of all commissioners a decade earlier (North Carolina Association of County Commissioners 1996). This rise was attributable to black plaintiffs' successful voting-rights challenges of district boundaries; some increase in white support for black candidates in general elections, especially in the metro Piedmont; and greater African American influence within Democratic primary elections, so that blacks increasingly were the party nominees on the November ballot. (This last point was an unintended consequence of the greater propensity of whites, but not blacks, to register Republican or unaffiliated in the 1980s and 1990s.)

Second, North Carolina had become a two-party state. Although many Tar Heel whites retain their Democratic registration, they have joined new and long-standing Republicans to establish a competitive two-party system in statewide elections. The Republican Party has appealed to voters' antitax and anti-big-government sentiments and openly argues that what is good for business is good for North Carolina voters. Especially since 1984, the Democratic Party has been on the defensive, searching for a formula that will appeal to both white and black Tar Heels. Because of its core support from blacks—by far the Democrats' most loyal constituency—as well as from environmentalists, public school teachers, feminists, and organized labor, Democrats felt compelled to promote some programs that would not necessarily sit well with big business. Teacher salary increases, Jim Hunt's Smart Start program to enhance early childhood education, less-punitive unemployment compensation, and food tax cuts were among the issues that General Assembly Democrats advocated during the 1990s.

The third major change during the 1990s was one of the least noticed. Trapped in their own past experiences, many politicians as well as newspaper reporters and editors continued to think about North Carolina society as it was in the 1970s and early 1980s. They failed to see how the state had changed economically and where population increases and related voter growth were occurring. Such opinion leaders could have recalled, for example, the days when tobacco farmers in Johnston County on the western edge of the Coastal Plain or semiskilled textile workers in Gaston County, a blue-collar, western Piedmont county near Charlotte, constituted a fixed percentage of the Tar Heel electorate. But in fact, by the mid-1990s Johnston County had fewer farmers raising tobacco, more factory workers, and more spill-over suburbanites from Raleigh than a decade before. Illustrating suburbanization's impact in Johnston County between

1984 and 1996, the number of voters increased by 37 percent. Statewide, the number of voters increased 15 percent in the same years. Gaston County also changed in those dozen years, but in a different way from Johnston. Gaston's voter increase (6 percent) was far below the state average but close to the western Piedmont regional increase of 9 percent.

In Gaston County the kinds of manufacturing jobs available constituted the major shift. Numerous low-wage and nonunion textile and apparel factories closed; the most prominent newcomer in the 1980s was Freightliner, a heavy-truck manufacturer that Mercedes-Benz would come to own. Significantly for the county, site of the famed unsuccessful Gastonia textile strike of 1929 (cf. Pope 1942; Salmond 1995), the UAW won a vigorously contested election in 1991 and signed a contract with Freightliner. Not only did the Freightliner jobs bring more money into the area economy, but it was possible that the UAW members would help to reshape the content of local politics.

Most of all, politicians and journalists tended to overlook the population and voter growth that was occurring in those North Carolina counties that relatively well-educated in-migrants considered attractive. While the statewide increase in the vote between 1984 and 1996 was 14 percent, it was 31 percent in the six metro Piedmont counties. In the southernmost part of coastal North Carolina, attractive to tourists, retirees, and the film industry, New Hanover County, including Wilmington, showed a 47 percent increase in that twelve-year period, and neighboring Brunswick County increased its vote by 37 percent. The two western Piedmont counties located southeast (Union) and northeast (Cabarrus) of Charlotte, both growing primarily as a consequence of suburbanization, increased voter turnout between 1984 and 1996 by 40 percent and 28 percent, respectively.

Stated differently, the six metro Piedmont counties; the neighboring suburbanizing counties such as Johnston, Union, and Cabarrus; and coastal counties such as New Hanover accounted for almost all of North Carolina's population growth between the mid-1980s and the mid-1990s. The metro Piedmont region, for example, constituted 26 percent of the statewide vote in November 1984; twelve years later that same region made up 32 percent of the statewide vote. In simplest terms, how state policy affects tobacco farmers in 2000 or 2004 will not carry the same electoral impact it had in 1972. The size of the Tar Heel electorate in support of the national political consensus against cigarette consumption continues to grow; the number of North Carolinians who can affix to their cars a favorite bumper sticker on the Coastal Plain (Tobacco Pays My Bills) continues to decline.

The state's economic transition toward more high-tech and well-paying research-and-development jobs; higher-paying, more capital-intensive manufacturing employment; and an expanding, if low-paying, tourism and retirement sector has also led to a shift in the relative political importance of cultural values. For example, in almost every legislative election that took place in North Carolina's growing counties in November 1996, the winners in both parties were those candidates who avoided a strong commitment to the social traditionalist ideology of the religious right.

The Shifting Fortunes of Mainstream Republicanism

During the 1980s mainstream Republicans felt they had found a winning model to guarantee the party's future. Their recipe was simple: blend modernizer programs, such as public school or highway construction, that big business considered necessary infrastructure investments in North Carolina's future with a commitment to social traditionalism, especially anti-crime and antiabortion themes. Serving up Jim Martin as gubernatorial candidate in 1984 and as incumbent seeking reelection in 1988, mainstream Republicans, including Martin himself, liked what they had wrought. In both 1984 and 1988 nearly two-thirds of white North Carolinians supported Martin. His dominant message was that he represented an alternative to the tax-and-spend policies of the Democrats. A poll conducted for Democratic Party leaders after the election suggests reasons why Martin's economic message played well. More than 50 percent of white Tar Heels, in every region of the state, believed that the Republicans were doing a better job than the Democrats of "working for a fair tax system." Similar majorities thought the Republicans were more capable of balancing the federal budget. This perception of Republican fiscal expertise persisted despite record deficits rolled up in the first term of the Reagan administration. Even white Democrats did not feel the Democrats were fiscally more responsible. Republicans had won the symbolic battle as the better keeper of the purse strings.

This strategy of managerial competence worked for Martin in 1984 and 1988, as he captured a majority in some affluent university precincts in the Durham–Chapel Hill area. Voters there apparently did not know of Martin's antiabortion and anti-King holiday positions. As they approached the 1990s, mainstream Republicans believed they also had evidence of traditionalist GOP strategies that did not work. For example, in the fall of 1986, first-term Republican congressman Bill Cobey, representing Chapel Hill and Raleigh (the fourth congressional district) demonstrated the dangers of public identification with fundamentalist Christians (cf. Wyman 1987). Elected to Congress as part of the 1984 GOP sweep, Cobey during his reelection campaign sent a strongly worded letter to religious-right voters in which he identified himself as an "Ambassador for Christ." As a consequence, it seems that many affluent Republicans in North Raleigh and Cary stuck with U.S. Senate candidate Jim Broyhill but, unhappy with Cobey's New Right image, switched to his challenger, modernizer Democrat David Price. Price easily defeated Cobey.

The 1988 mainstream GOP goal supposedly was a strong statewide ticket for all Council of State positions. Never in the twentieth century had a Republican won any of these seats. Would there be a coattail effect? Would the appeal of George Bush and Jim Martin lead to sufficient straight-ticket voting by dealigned Democrats for the GOP Council of State candidates to win office? The intended strategy was to present the Republican candidates as fiscal conservatives, committed to economic development and improved public schools and highways. In contrast to their Democratic opponents, they could not be labeled big spenders or, to use Republicans' favorite catch-all slogan, liberals.

But after the Republican primaries in May, only one member of the GOP Council of State ticket, candidate for lieutenant governor Jim Gardner, enjoyed any statewide reputation. This illustrated once again how talent-thin were Tar Heel Republicans. Gardner campaigned in 1988 as a mainstream Republican, in accord with Martin's blend of modernizer and traditionalist ideology. In retrospect, the mainstream GOP position was simply a temporary move for Gardner, who in his early political life had been widely viewed as a "militant segregationist" (Black 1976, 111). He was first elected to Congress at age thirty-four, upsetting an incumbent Democrat in 1966 from the congressional district around Gardner's Rocky Mount home. When he ran as the Republican gubernatorial candidate in 1968, Gardner openly endorsed George Wallace, despite the fact that Richard Nixon was the Republican candidate. Asked during 1968 why a Republican would support Wallace, Gardner replied, "I've never heard [Wallace] say anything I disagree with" (Black 1976, 111). Reflecting on that campaign in a 1988 interview, Gardner said he was "an early Jesse Helms" (Sitton 1988). In the highly polarized 1968 election year Gardner won 47 percent of the vote, garnering some support from both Wallace and Nixon voters. His Democratic opponent, Bob Scott, won—thanks to a biracial coalition that foreshadowed Democratic strategies of the 1980s and 1990s.

A majority of whites voted for Gardner, but Scott captured the black vote overwhelmingly and enough of the white vote to win the race.

In 1988 Gardner put racial issues on the sideline. A changed North Carolina seemed to suggest that, except for Jesse Helms, no Republican had a chance to win statewide by openly criticizing the growing power of the black electorate. For the GOP mainstream the question was whether the party would build on the expanded power base that had begun with legislative victories and Martin's election in 1984 and reelection in 1988.

But just as national analyses of Republican Party differences have shown (Hodgson 1996), not all Tar Heel Republicans were willing to concede to Governor Martin's team that the mainstream approach was the correct one. From the early 1970s, when Governor Holshouser and Senator Helms symbolized the two perspectives (Luebke 1990a, 133), until the 1990s, when Charlotte mayor Richard Vinroot lost to state house majority whip Robin Hayes in the May 1996 Republican gubernatorial primary, the intra-party conflict has revolved around the relative importance of economic and noneconomic issues. Mainstream Republicans are so named because they are rooted in the historic economic ideology of the national Republican Party. While critical of an activist state that promoted economic reform such as Franklin Roosevelt's New Deal, national Republicans supported a less-egalitarian activist state that promoted business prosperity. From the 1950s to the 1980s this was the Republicanism of Dwight Eisenhower, Gerald Ford, or Robert Dole.

The GOP antimainstream forces were initially identified as Helms Republicans or, in recognition of the organization that promoted both Helms and his ideology, Congressional Club Republicans. Club Republicans centered their party organizing on noneconomic aspects of traditionalist ideology. Examples of these were prayer in the public schools or an active antiabortion position. Mainstream Republicans typically agreed with these points of view, but they rarely promoted such issues as the basis for their political involvement. Martin, for instance, sent a mailing with little fanfare to religious-right Christians across the state during the spring of 1988 reminding them that he, unlike his Democratic challenger, opposed the state abortion fund for low-income women.

Congressional Club Republicans usually turned their antitax ideology and social traditionalism into a broadside attack on the alleged liberalism of political foes. With club support Helms successfully ran four such campaigns for the U.S. Senate against Democratic opponents. But when the club took sides in subsequent Republican primaries between 1986 and

1988, it was defeated decisively. U.S. Senate candidate David Funderburk could not convince GOP voters in the May 1986 primary that his mainstream opponent, Jim Broyhill, was a "closet liberal." As the club's television spots pointed out, Broyhill had voted for a congressional budget also supported by Speaker of the House Tip O'Neill, a Massachusetts liberal and favorite whipping boy of New Right Republicans. Republican primary voters found this insufficient evidence to reject Broyhill. After twenty-two years as a congressman from western North Carolina, Broyhill enjoyed a reputation as dean of the state's Republicans; Funderburk's GOP credentials paled by comparison. Perhaps illustrating the relative strength of the two factions, Broyhill defeated Funderburk by a margin of 67 to 30 percent (Ku Klux Klan leader Glenn Miller received 3 percent of the vote).

In 1987 the Congressional Club also promoted a challenge to Jack Hawke, Martin's choice for party chair. It selected Barry McCarty, then a professor at Elizabeth City Bible College, who promised to promote a more traditionalist agenda than the alleged pragmatism of Hawke. Open factional fighting erupted at numerous county conventions, but at the state convention Hawke held many more delegates than McCarty, a parallel to Broyhill's easy victory. As a face-saving device for the club, in the interest of party unity during the upcoming 1988 election year, Hawke was declared the victor by acclamation.

Hawke remained as Republican Party chair through the 1994 elections and is usually credited for developing the successful low-tech attacks (radio ads and direct mail) on Democratic incumbents that led to the Republican takeover of the house in the November election. Nevertheless, social traditionalists never acceded to the ideology of a mainstream Republican like Hawke. The departure of the Congressional Club from intraparty activities in North Carolina in the late 1980s merely left an opportunity for another group. The club's successor was the Christian Coalition, founded nationally in 1988 by religious broadcaster Pat Robertson after his failed campaign for the Republican presidential nomination.

The Christian Coalition was more successful than the Congressional Club had been in mobilizing social traditionalist whites to active involvement inside the Tar Heel Republican Party. Three factors appeared to make the difference. The Christian Coalition, first of all, had a name that, to the politically uninitiated in North Carolina, sounded like the natural home for any fundamentalist Protestant who was concerned about restoring "family values" by fighting the alleged decline of morality in American society. Second, the organization's national presence and patented voter guides, which skirted campaign finance laws by supposedly providing balanced pros and cons on various issues, ensured free television news coverage from the national networks, which reinforced local organizing efforts at fundamentalist churches. Third, the Congressional Club had always been less concerned about building local parties and most focused on Election Day outcomes, particularly in the years between 1976 and 1990, when the club's political wizards, Tom Ellis and Carter Wrenn, were working for Ronald Reagan and Jesse Helms (Luebke 1990a, 126; Wrenn 1987).

In the early 1990s more county Republican parties fell under the control of the Christian Coalition. Indeed, its continued strength at the local level encouraged the GOP 1992 gubernatorial candidate, incumbent lieutenant governor Jim Gardner, to run a traditionalist-style campaign against the Democrats' comeback candidate, former governor Jim Hunt. This contrasted with the winning mainstream Republican campaign that Gardner had run in 1988 as part of the Jim Martin team. As noted above, Gardner lost badly in 1992. In the same election, however, social traditionalist Republicans did make headway in some legislative races. Among the winners was Robin Hayes, a born-again Christian from Cabarrus County, northeast of Charlotte.

When Hawke encouraged Republicans to field candidates in districts where Democrats had always dominated, he could not limit the candidate selection to the mainstream Republicans whose blended ideology he preferred. In fact, religious-right volunteers were at least as likely as mainstreamers to come forward. As part of the November 1994 rising Republican tide, surprise state house winners included social traditionalists such as Alamance County's Dennis Reynolds, a fundamentalist Christian private-school teacher, and Pitt County's Henry Aldridge, a retired dentist from the Coastal Plain who made a national name for himself in 1995 by asserting that a woman could not get pregnant from rape ("the juices won't flow" was the much-cited quote). The risks inherent in placing unknown, untested candidates on the ballot—who then win because of factors such as a statewide sweep—became even more evident with two other 1994 GOP winners. Alamance County's Ken Miller, a strident antigovernment economic traditionalist, was censured by the state house in 1996 for his acknowledged sexual harassment of a teenage page during the 1995 session. Buncombe County attorney Larry Linney, a rare African American Republican and traditionalist, who believed that big-government programs were hamstringing poor blacks' efforts at self-sufficiency, was in trouble with state or federal courts at various points during his single 1995–96 term. A state court convicted Linney in 1996 of misappropriating funds from a client's account. Neither Miller nor Linney served beyond his initial term.

Infamous personalities aside, the GOP problem was that the religious-right wing of the party would not stop its battle for control. After initially selecting Jim Hastings, a Mountain Republican with close ties to the mainstream wing, state Republicans in 1996 elected Sam Currin, a former Helms backer and federal prosecutor. Currin replaced Hastings because Hastings was indicted on federal income tax evasion charges. (In 1997 Currin easily turned back mainstreamers' attempts to replace him.) The continuing internal battles led to state legislator Hayes's challenge of and upset victory over the mainstream Republican choice (and odds-on favorite), Charlotte mayor Richard Vinroot. Vinroot ran a weak campaign, unable, for example, to convince Republican voters or a skeptical press corps that he actually was against abortion (a key litmus test in contemporary North Carolina and southern Republican politics). Christian Coalition activists turned out heavily for the May 1996 primary, while other Republicans viewed both candidates unenthusiastically. Incumbent Democrat Jim Hunt must have been smiling all the way; the Republican religious right, by supporting a hard-core social traditionalist, had helped the party pick a far weaker candidate to run as the Republican standard-bearer in the November election.

Speaker Brubaker and other house Republicans also learned during the 1996 short session of the legislature that their 1994 majority victory was *not* a mandate to shut down government. In an event eerily similar to what had occurred just months before on congressional Speaker Newt Gingrich's watch—a federal government shutdown in November 1995 because of a Republican-Democrat impasse over the budget (Dionne 1997, 323)—Brubaker declared in June 1996 that 1994 North Carolina voters had given the GOP a mandate to spend less and, if necessary to meet that goal, to adjourn the General Assembly without a 1996–97 budget. But house Republicans were holding up, among other issues, schoolteacher salary increases, a billion-dollar-plus statewide school construction bond proposal, and any possible action against the water pollution caused by the Coastal Plain's booming industrial hog operations. Antigovernment traditionalism was not, in fact, what North Carolina voters thought they had been supporting when they elected a Republican house majority in November 1994.

Governor Hunt milked the North Carolina government shutdown every bit as effectively as President Clinton had worked over the Gingrich Republicans. After traveling around the state visiting places that were allegedly harmed by the Republican budget shutdown, Hunt in July 1996 convened the General Assembly in a special session. The renegotiated budget passed both houses later that month. The November 1996 elections seemed to send legislative Republicans a message about economic traditionalism: it's okay to campaign against government spending, but don't cut my programs and, more notably, do something about education and the environment (cf. Luebke 1996). The Democratic fall 1996 campaign was simple, a promise that the governor as well as senate and house Democrats would not cut government spending the way the Republicans appeared to be willing to do. The result was a net gain of six seats for senate Democrats (30 to 20 in the 1997–98 session), seven seats for house Democrats (59 to 61 in the 1997–98 session), and a comfortable reelection victory for Jim Hunt of 56 to 43 percent.

Tar Heel Democrats on the Defensive

The North Carolina Democratic Party was built in the early to mid-twentieth century on the twin foundations of economic development (progress) and racial segregation. In the 1990s it faced the challenge of how to build a winning political platform for the future. As part of the modernization process, by the 1970s Tar Heel Democrats, like other southern Democrats, had abandoned their identification with old-fashioned racism. Since then the party continued its commitment to an activist state by promoting and subsidizing private economic investment. Similar to their support in principle of racial equality, the Democrats also promised allegiance to women's equality. In short, the dominant position in the 1980s Democratic Party was moderate and supportive on social issues such as race and gender. But on economic issues the party maintained a distinct probusiness, modernizer flavor. For example, despite clear majorities in both houses of the General Assembly, no populist initiatives to reduce the food tax received any serious consideration in Democratic leadership circles.

The 1980s platform that heeded big business's agenda on most economic issues and yielded to African Americans and women of both races on social issues presented several problems for Democrats. First, the Democrats' historic identification with Tar Heel economic development became endangered as Republicans increasingly claimed responsibility for economic prosperity. At the top of the ticket, presidential candidates such as Ronald Reagan, especially in 1984, conveyed a convincing image of Republicans as the anti-big-government and progrowth party. Further, in both 1984 and 1988 a skilled Republican governor such as Jim Martin developed an economic program and rhetoric that blurred policy differences between him and modernizer Democrats such as Jim Hunt and Terry Sanford. Yet Martin retained a strong traditionalist identification with tax repeal. The Democrats were forced to defend existing taxes as necessary to fund North Carolina's major government programs, while Martin claimed an equal commitment to these programs but insisted that the state's economy could prosper even more if certain taxes affecting business were eliminated. Not surprisingly, North Carolina businesses during the 1980s increasingly identified with the state GOP, just as they had begun to do so years before in presidential elections. In particular, white male businessmen came to prefer strongly the mainstream Republicans such as Jim Martin rather than modernizer Democrats who were saddled with a political debt to organized black and feminist constituencies.

The Democrats' second problem was that their positions on race and gender issues hurt them among white voters who were suspicious of equality, whereas blacks and women, especially the former, questioned whether the support for equality was more than just window dressing. In the 1980s, for example, black Democrats believed that abolition of the runoff primary, not support of the King holiday, was the true test of white modernizers' commitment to racial equality (Oleck 1988). Similarly, in the 1980s, Democrat-leaning women were upset that white male party leaders were slow to act on concerns such as wage discrimination in comparable job classifications in state government (the so-called comparable worth issue) or the financial well-being of women in property distribution and child support related to divorce. Further, despite Hunt in the governor's office and legislative majorities, Hunt and other party leaders could not win passage of the Equal Rights Amendment in 1982. In short, Democratic leaders had not delivered on issues that would make either African American or feminist constituencies excited to work for the party on Election Day (cf. Luebke 1990a, 187).

A third problem for Democrats in the 1980s was that the tilt of most candidates toward big business meant that, conversely, the party lacked a commitment to a populist economic program that might stir less-affluent voters, especially whites who did not have an overriding interest in either racial or gender issues. Leading Democrats were unwilling, in populist fashion, to shift the burden of taxation to big business and the affluent by closing any of the numerous loopholes that permeated the state tax code. On the contrary, as a result of Democrats' legislation in the 1980s, North Carolina became more dependent on regressive sales taxes. Republicans improved their standing among middle-income and low-income whites by labeling Democrats the tax-and-spend party.

Despite these three major issues, all of which Jim Martin exploited to win the governorship in 1984 and 1988, North Carolina Democrats, like most of their fellow southern Democrats, failed to seize the initiative to rethink the party's direction. Indeed, in North Carolina established Democratic Party leaders in early 1989, right after Martin's reelection, selected Lawrence Davis, a corporate Democrat who opposed abortion rights, as Democratic state executive director. For the Democratic women's and black constituencies who were paying attention, this was hardly a positive message (Yeoman 1989).

The unarticulated question was whether the women and African Americans who were increasingly the core of the North Carolina Democratic Party should not play a larger role in the development of a more equity-oriented, economic populist Democratic program. One major reason the issue did not come to the fore is that the party establishment co-opted potential opponents. A number of white and black women as well as black men accepted figurehead positions in the state party. Meanwhile the Democrats' political program remained locked into the big-business-oriented modernizer model of the past. As if to symbolize the party's commitment to the past, Democrats in 1992 overwhelmingly nominated Jim Hunt to a third term. It was not that Hunt's opponent, Attorney General Lacy Thornburg, represented a coherent set of more populist ideas than Hunt, although he was more critical of big business than Hunt was. The irony was, rather, that in response to the departure of white male businessmen to the Republicans, Hunt in 1992 actually ran on a campaign that appealed less, not more, to the less-affluent women and blacks who were becoming perforce the party's natural base. Wanting to keep their decades-long Republican nemesis, Lieutenant Governor Jim Gardner, from winning the governor's office, most populist-oriented Democrats avoided a public disagreement with Hunt's political shift to the right. All brands of Democrats unified in 1992 to help Hunt beat Gardner and to help Clinton come close to defeating Bush in North Carolina. But a serious debate about the Tar Heel Democrats' future was once again avoided.

Why the Plutocracy Fights Campaign Finance Reform

The Excellent Schools Act, Governor Hunt's lead issue in 1997, was in southern regional perspective nothing exceptional. Many of the bill's features had been previously developed by Kentucky and Tennessee, and the pay increase primarily prevented young teachers from abandoning teaching in North Carolina's public schools because of the relatively low income compared with jobs in the private sector (cf. *News and Record* 1997c). The 1997 environmental package that restricted industrial hog production made headlines because it deviated from the normal pattern of state politics; major business interests—the plutocracy in Key's term (1949)—were *not* able to defeat the reform efforts.

The growing cost of legislative and statewide political campaigns, coupled with the willingness of wealthy individuals and business PACs to ante up the dollars, provided an excellent illustration of plutocratic rule. Significantly, the house Republicans' success in 1994 had the effect not of ending the corporate domination of state government policy but, rather, of providing big-business interests with two parties to which to distribute their largesse (*News and Observer* 1997f). The reaction of North Carolina's three leading politicians to citizen efforts during the 1997 General Assembly to provide more information about campaign contributors was telling.

Governor Hunt was silent. A twenty-year veteran of the money-brings-political-influence game, Hunt said nothing about the citizen efforts, mostly led by grassroots Democrats in the Durham–Chapel Hill area, to reform campaign finance. Like the Clinton-Gore reelection efforts (but with no evidence that he stretched the meaning of the statutes as far as his Washington counterparts did), Hunt's fund-raising in 1996 relied on major donors, a number of whom were rewarded for their donations and their bundling of others' donations by appointments to the perennially politicized state Board of Transportation. The state DOT's status as the nexus of the money-and-politics game was illustrated by Hunt's DOT secretary Sam Hunt, a Burlington businessman and former legislator (and no blood kin), who served at DOT from 1993 to 1995 and then left state government formally to become chief fund-raiser for the governor's 1996 campaign.

Among the 1996 DOT actions defended by Jim Hunt were a $3 million overpayment to Steve Stroud and Carleton Midyette, well-connected Raleigh realtors who would later work with the governor to bring a National Hockey League franchise to an expanded new basketball arena for North Carolina State (*News and Observer* 1997a). In 1997 Hunt supported a $1 million avenue, the so-called Ram Road, requested by Greensboro donor and DOT board member Doug Galyon (he and his family gave $10,000 to Hunt in 1996). The road allowed major sports donors at the University of North Carolina in Chapel Hill to have an exclusive, quick exit after viewing basketball games at the Dean Smith arena. Ram Road was placed on the state's construction list without a single consultation with the Chapel Hill Town Council, despite the avenue's location within town limits (*Charlotte Observer* 1997d).

This initial pattern of top DOT officials helping wealthy, well-connected citizens was subsequently chronicled in a series of investigative stories, primarily by the *Charlotte Observer* and the *News and Observer*, between September 1997 and January 1998. Two DOT board members, Carroll Edwards of Union County (he and his family gave Hunt $35,500 in 1996) and Odell Williamson of Brunswick County ($23,000 to Hunt in 1996), resigned their seats after newspapers reported that DOT construction was benefiting them personally (*Charlotte Observer* 1997c; *News and Observer* 1997n). James Cartrette, a Columbus County donor to Hunt, told the *Wilmington Star-News* that he and his son had been promised a DOT board seat and a Wildlife Commission slot in exchange for donations (*Sunday Star-News* 1997). Although Cartrette later recanted his charge, the growing DOT controversy led the *Charlotte Observer*, the *Greensboro News and Record*, the *Winston-Salem Journal*, and the *News and Observer* to call for reform.

The Hunt administration was initially unmoved. The reason probably lay in the data reported in 1997 by Democracy South, a Chapel Hill-based campaign finance watchdog group. Hunt's appointees to the DOT board gave, directly and through their families, $652,000 to his 1992 and 1996 reelection efforts (*News and Observer* 1997p).

But when political connections were found to govern the use of highway safety funds (*News and Observer* 1997q), and ethical and legal questions continued about other DOT board members' conduct and that of top DOT administrators (cf. *Charlotte Observer* 1997g), Jim Hunt felt compelled to act. A crowning blow was the revelation that Governor Hunt himself had asked state highway administrator Larry Goode to reconsider an engineer's recommendation against a Wilson County bridge that would have helped Hunt's neighborhood (Williams 1998).

When Hunt in January 1998 named a new secretary at DOT, reduced the powers of the state highway administrator, and called for more input from average citizens into DOT decision making, he was acknowledging the possible negative effects of big money on state politics. It was a significant change from the Jim Hunt who had refused to discuss campaign finance reform during the 1997 session.

Speaker Brubaker took an active stand against campaign finance reform during the 1997 session. He openly rejected calls for public financing of campaigns and in particular objected to a bill passed by the state senate that would have prohibited "soft money"—unlimited dollars from individuals or corporations to assist so-called political party building. Brubaker seemed to be aware of a new reality in Tar Heel politics, one well established in national politics (cf. Clawson, Neustadtl, and Scott 1992): Republicans far more than Democrats benefit from soft money. In 1996, for example, state Republicans received five times as much money as state Democrats.

Brubaker and house Republicans also supported a big-business request not to list the occupation of contributors donating more than $100 to a statewide or legislative campaign. But on the last day of the 1997 session, worried that an awakened public might view them negatively as the major obstacle to any campaign finance reform legislation, house Republicans conceded the point about donor occupation to the senate Democrats, and a compromise bill became law. On the key point, similar to the U.S. Senate Republicans' success in killing the McCain-Feinstein campaign finance reform bill, state house Republicans prevailed in 1997 in maintaining the legality of soft money.

Just after the 1997 session Brubaker also added a bipartisan flavor to the money-and-politics DOT connection by appointing the twenty-seven-year-old son of Charlotte businessman Charlie Shelton, who had given $100,000 to Republican candidates and committees during 1996, to a newly created legislative seat on the DOT board. The Sheltons epitomized efforts by some wealthy Tar Heels to be serious players in state politics. While Charlie funded Republicans, his brother and fellow businessman, Ed Shelton, provided funds to state Democrats. In particular, Ed was a major donor to the 1992 and 1996 Hunt campaigns.

Senate Democratic leader Marc Basnight took a more supportive approach to campaign finance reform than Hunt or Brubaker, although he refused to allow passage of fellow senate Democrat Wib Gulley's public financing bill. Observers differed on whether Basnight supported campaign finance reform pragmatically because of the Republican advantage in soft-money fund-raising or because of a principled opposition to high-priced campaigns. Whatever his reason, Basnight's support of any campaign finance reform in the 1997 General Assembly (he symbolically assigned the bill the number Senate Bill 1) was the reason any reform measures became law.

Modernizers' Move to the Right

Modernizer ideology endorses an activist state government to facilitate economic development. Nevertheless, particularly after the house Republican majority took power in 1995, modernizers were more willing than ever to adopt an antitax perspective that is at the heart of economic traditionalism. In 1995, for example, it was the modernizer-oriented senate Democrats who first advocated repeal of the tax on intangible wealth (Senate Bill 8), a tax paid in sizable amounts only by corporations and the top 5 percent of North Carolinians. The house Republicans' income tax reduction plan (House Bill 2) distributed greater tax benefits to average families than did the senate tax-cut bill (North Carolina Budget and Tax Center 1995). Its shortcoming, however, was that the 400,000 low-income Tar Heels who already owed no income tax received no benefits from the Republican bill. In short, North Carolina's working poor were short-changed by both parties in 1995. Combining the intangibles tax repeal and the income tax reductions, tax burdens were disproportionately cut on North Carolina's most affluent citizens.

Meanwhile, the modernizer impulse to spend was not focused on the less-affluent majority. Indeed, even without the pressure from traditionalists to cut spending, modernizer policy in North Carolina demonstrated a spending bias away from the needs of poor and working-class Tar Heels. For example, in 1995 the state's per capita spending on primary and secondary public education was thirty-ninth among the fifty states, and about average in the South (*News and Record* 1997c). But expenditures for higher education, programs from which the children of North Carolina's affluent citizens were more likely to benefit, ranked eighteenth among the fifty states.

In 1989 modernizers and traditionalists alike under house Speaker Mavretic and senate Democratic leader Henson Barnes passed a regressive gasoline and diesel fuel tax increase as well as many other vehicle fee increases in order to pay for the massive HTF program (see Chapter 3). Even with marginal increases between 1989 and 1997 to help fund city bus systems, the state DOT's public transportation budget for bus and rail— the one most likely to help carless, that is, low-income Tar Heels—was just 3 percent of the highway budget (Luebke 1990a, 52–53, 189). Efforts in the 1990s to increase funding for public transit by reducing expenditures for highways (including sprawl-encouraging suburban loops in the metro Piedmont) were opposed by the DOT and Governor Hunt. Hunt's Transit

2001 initiative to help rural and urban public transit was primarily funded by additional regressive taxes and fees, not by tapping the existing, already relatively high state fuel tax.

This fuel tax directed toward construction of roads on the HTF list provided clear benefits to the highway construction industry and land developers. It allowed legislators to take credit for new highways in their districts. But in a startling example of poor planning, DOT acknowledged in early 1998 that road maintenance was lagging. Maintenance funds for highways and bridges, especially in western North Carolina, were insufficient. If the lengthy HTF list were ever finished, maintenance needs would be even greater (*News and Observer* 1998b). The highway-building legislation, ignoring transit and maintenance, appeared to be a modernizer program run amok.

While modernizers and most traditionalists were passing and defending the tax and fee increases to build highways, the General Assembly passed numerous special tax breaks, primarily for big business. Many of these tax benefits were discussed by only a limited group of legislators and lobbyists. In some cases the tax breaks became law without even being mentioned in the press. During 1987, for example, a state senator won passage of a short item ensuring that North Carolina banks could continue a multimillion-dollar tax break that the 1986 federal tax reform legislation had ended at the federal level and that normally would have been ended at the state level as well. When in 1995 veteran Democrat John Gamble, a retired physician from Lincolnton, sought to end the banks' tax break, Speaker Brubaker sent the bill to end the tax loophole to the House Financial Institutions Committee, a majority of whose members had received campaign funding from banks and/or were bankers or served on bank boards (*Charlotte Observer* 1995). All but four banking committee members voted in April 1995 to kill Gamble's bill.

Another tax loophole, worth about $60 million annually to the multinational corporations that advocated the bill, passed in 1988. At the urging of R. J. Reynolds/Nabisco, which had announced plans to build a new cookie factory east of Raleigh, the General Assembly unanimously passed a revised corporate taxation formula that would give large corporations a multimillion-dollar annual tax break. Hardly a legislator questioned whether the new formula could hurt smaller corporations by raising their tax bills. Nor did legislators debate whether North Carolina's pressing educational and health needs should have precluded such a tax benefit to big business. Reynolds and other corporate lobbyists, as well as modernizer Democrats in both houses who supported the bill, claimed that this tax expenditure would encourage out-of-state corporations to locate their factories in North Carolina (Guillory 1988). But such statements were based on faith rather than evidence. Meanwhile, the 1988 General Assembly postponed funding on a health care program for indigent North Carolinians (Yeoman 1988b).

In 1997, despite a thriving economy that brought in record state revenues, senate Democratic leaders refused to fund a pilot needle-exchange program to prevent the spread of AIDS and postponed a one-cent cut in the food tax by six months. But they passed with little debate a $2 million cut in the inheritance tax (benefiting only individuals inheriting an estate in excess of $600,000) and a new $3 million break for multinational corporations based outside North Carolina. For its part, the traditionalist-oriented house Republican majority would have refused to pass the needle-exchange program and would have reduced the inheritance tax by even more than the senate had. Pressured by populist house Democrats, the house Republicans were far more enthusiastic cutters of the food tax. But while demanding some food tax cut in the 1997 budget negotiations with the senate Democrats, house Republicans acquiesced in a delay until July 1, 1998, to reduce the tax to 4 percent. These various steps by the two controlling parties suggest a consensus on social issues to avoid making policy that would enrage the religious right. For example, even though many persons contracted AIDS from drug use, a public health measure was denied because of the association of AIDS with homosexuality. Further, on tax policy most traditionalist and modernizer politicians addressed first the economic needs of corporations and the well-to-do. The less-affluent majority benefited only if their needs coincided with the political agenda of big business and wealthier citizens.

The General Assembly's Unholy Alliance

The modernizer shaping of Tar Heel politics in the post–civil rights movement period led to an activist state government that ensured a level of infrastructure investment in schools, transportation, and water and sewer lines so that business could prosper. But modernizers sought to fund these programs disproportionately from sales and other regressive taxes, so that the tax burden on big business and the wealthy could be kept at a minimum.

Two modernizer actions, one beginning in the 1960s and the other in the mid-1990s, were strong indicators of modernizer politicians' proclivity to work hand in glove with business interests. The notion that "if it's good for business, then it's good for North Carolina" also meant that the primary goal of modernizers has not been to lower taxes on or to provide direct benefits to average-income consumers. Arguably the most controversial modernizer tax move was the 1961 decision of Governor Terry Sanford, supported by Democrats in subsequent years, to convince the General Assembly to reimpose the 3 percent sales tax on groceries. Over the next thirty years Democrats raised the food tax gradually, along with the general sales tax, until it reached 6 percent in 1991.

In 1996 Governor Jim Hunt advocated a series of corporate subsidies to encourage economic investment in North Carolina, especially from national and even international firms. Known as the William S. Lee Act in honor of the late former chairman of Duke Power Company, the legislation extended state corporate subsidies, albeit on a sliding scale, to all 100 North Carolina counties (Manuel 1997). The governor and his legislative allies, including modernizer Republicans, argued that the tax credits were necessary even in boom areas such as the Research Triangle or metropolitan Charlotte because North Carolina would otherwise be at a competitive disadvantage with other states (see Chapter 5). Advocates of the Lee bill similarly argued that further direct benefits to corporations, such as generous no-cost-to-business customized job training at community colleges, were necessary. In the view of the state Department of Commerce, which took its cues from Governor Hunt, the many subsidies to would-be corporate investors in North Carolina were justified in order to keep the state competitive in industrial or administrative-office recruitment with other, especially southern, states.

The food tax and corporate subsidies had in common the spawning of an unusual political alliance in the General Assembly. Populist Democrats joined traditionalist Republicans in opposing the modernizer policy that disproportionately helped big business. Populists were part of this unholy alliance because they opposed government benefits directed excessively toward the economically powerful; traditionalists joined because they opposed on principle a big-taxing, big-spending state government. In coming together to oppose the food tax, the alliance members focused on a regressive tax that hurt the majority. In opposing the economic development subsidies that both populists and traditionalists termed corporate welfare (cf. Paget 1997, 192–93), the unholy alliance was affirming its opposition to government providing direct benefits to big corporations that, according to the alliance, these corporations certainly did not need. In this view the Lee Act was merely giving in to corporate blackmail of taxpayers in the competing states; it was a race to the bottom, to see which state would most deplete its treasury in trying to entice a company to locate within its boundaries. For populist opponents, every dollar granted to relocating industry was a dollar that could not be used to improve education programs (CED 1994; *News and Record* 1997c).

The unholy alliance was most successful in the state house in cutting the food tax by a total of two cents during the 1996 and 1997 sessions. Modernizers and modernizer-traditionalists in the state senate actively opposed cutting the food tax. In the senate view, tax cuts for the wealthy, such as the 1995 intangibles tax repeal, that also helped the less-affluent middle- to upper middle-class voters who owned some stock, were good public policy. But tax cuts that helped the poor and middle class disproportionately, such as a food tax cut, were not "affordable." Senate leader Basnight and Governor Hunt both held to this position in 1996 and 1997. Senate Democrats actually tried to show that the public did not want a food tax cut by manipulating the phrasing of questions on a statewide poll ("Should the General Assembly cut the food tax or help public education?"). Populist house Democrats responded that Democratic senate leaders had steadfastly refused to consider public opinion data on the 1995 intangibles tax cut (all statewide polls showed a majority *opposed* such a tax cut) before introducing Senate Bill 8.

In both sessions led by Speaker Brubaker, the Republican-controlled state house provided a political debate starkly different from that in the state senate. Populist house Democrats in 1995 introduced bills that would repeal entirely, or at least cut in part, the 6 percent sales tax on groceries and advocated this position among fellow members, including antitax traditionalist Republicans. When the two groups built a majority coalition to remove a food tax bill from committee and onto the house floor for debate, Speaker Brubaker forced GOP traditionalists to rescind their support. But this step and others by Brubaker to prevent a food tax cut during the 1995 session (house Republican leaders argued that the income tax cut already helped less-affluent citizens enough) gave an important political advantage to house Democrats. Recognizing this, house Democrats placed a food tax cut on their 1996 election-year agenda.

To the Democrats' surprise, house majority whip Robin Hayes, as part of his successful campaign to win the Republican gubernatorial nomination in May 1996, switched from an opponent to a proponent of a food tax cut. During the spring 1996 GOP primary race, Hayes linked the food tax cut to another favorite issue of economic traditionalist Republicans, an elimination of alleged surplus state government workers. Hayes brought his "Four No More" agenda to the 1996 General Assembly short session that began just days after his upset primary victory. His slogan was designed to appeal both to food tax opponents and to Tar Heel voters tired of Jim Hunt's attempt to win another (fourth) term as governor.

House Democrats and Republicans sparred, of course, over which political party deserved credit for the food tax cut. But only as a result of the unholy alliance, with a house Republican in the Speaker's chair, did a food tax cut pass. In earlier sessions, both in the early 1990s and in the mid-1970s, modernizer Democratic leaders in the senate and the house had blocked attempts to cut the food tax by either traditionalist Republicans or populist-leaning fellow Democrats. (Greensboro state senator McNeill Smith had led an unsuccessful effort in the 1975 and 1977 sessions.) In May 1996, once the house bill passed overwhelmingly, 107-3, senate Democrats and Governor Hunt joined in support of the election-year measure.

In 1997 the opening efforts of the anti–food tax cut coalition were identical to those in 1995–96. House Republican leaders tried early in the 1997 session to block consideration of a bill initiated by Democrats to cut the food tax. But when several Republican traditionalists supported house Democrats in a successful surprise move to debate a bill to cut the food tax despite the attempt by house GOP leaders to kill the bill, Brubaker recognized that house Republicans were once again on the political defensive (*News and Observer* 1997c). When state tax revenue collections were higher than expected, house Republican leaders seized the political opportunity. House majority leader Leo Daughtry, an acknowledged candidate for the 2000 gubernatorial election, took public credit as the Republican sponsor of the cut. But in 1997, with no election on the horizon, both senate Democratic leaders and Governor Hunt this time saw no reason to pass the bill. Consistent with their longtime modernizer blind-spot (see Chapter 2) as to the merit of both tax cuts and spending programs (for example, public schools or Smart Start early childhood education) for average Tar Heels, Basnight and Hunt allowed Daughtry and the Republicans to take credit for insisting on legislation to cut the food tax. As if to punctuate their opposition to a tax break for the middle- and low-income majority, senate Democrats insisted that the food tax cut be delayed for six months (*News and Observer* 1997m). Both house and senate Republicans were privately overjoyed about their public-relations coup.

The unholy alliance also attempted to block the growing subsidies for large corporations embodied in the 1996 Lee Act as well as in the refined

1997 version of the bill. In this, however, most amendments to reduce the amount of subsidy failed because modernizer house Democrats supported the subsidies, as did many house Republicans who followed Speaker Brubaker's lead. Brubaker's desire to maintain a close working (read: campaign contributions) relationship with Tar Heel big business overcame any traditionalist opposition to free-spending government subsidies (*News and Observer* 1997f). But attempts by big business to achieve its goals in the state house were not always successful. For example, when North Carolina-chartered banks in 1995 and 1996 sought the right to raise interest rates and fees, noting that the state's big-three banks (NationsBank, First Union, and Wachovia) were already circumventing the law by issuing their bank cards from Delaware or other states friendly to bank profits, their bill sailed through the state senate. In the house, however, traditionalist Republican Julia Howard rallied a dozen of her colleagues against the bill on behalf of "the little guy and gal." The banks' bill died when these Republicans were joined by most of the house Democrats, including modernizers such as Mountain Democrat Bob Hunter, who were troubled that banks would make bigger profits at the expense of their middle- and low-income constituents.

One example of the victorious unholy alliance actually predated the house Republican majority. Populist-leaning Democrats, among them 1991–94 house Speaker Dan Blue, opposed the lottery as another regressive, if voluntary, tax, because low- and middle-income persons are so much more likely than the wealthy to spend dollars on the lottery. Traditionalist Republicans rooted their opposition in fundamentalist Protestantism: the lottery as a form of gambling is immoral. Throughout the 1980s and 1990s this unholy alliance thwarted the efforts of prolottery legislators, mostly modernizers of both parties, and the lobbying corporations that profit from state lotteries. The usual pattern was for a lottery referendum bill to pass the state senate but to languish in the state house.

Citizen Advocates as Outgroups: The Right and the Left Compared

One consequence of the new two-party legislature was the increase in income opportunities for lobbyists. Corporations that once relied on a single lobbyist or two to communicate with the Democratic majority in both houses found, beginning in 1995, that twice as many lobbyists were necessary, because house Republicans in particular wanted to be lobbied on issues by a Republican. For example, former Martin administration official and Gardner staffer Don Beason found himself in great demand. Longtime powerful Democratic lobbyists such as Zeb Alley were compelled to hire Republican associates; the University of North Carolina system added a Republican to its lobbying team; and during the 1997 session, former Democratic and Republican modernizer governors Sanford and Holshouser lent their names to a bipartisan lobbying-oriented law firm.

Citizen advocates, for the most part, could not afford enough lobbyists to speak for them in Raleigh. Although religious-right Republicans were represented on some issues by the Family Policy Council, and the mostly Democratic environmentalists had representation via the Sierra Club and Conservation Council, both out-groups' lobbyists could only be effective if they were strengthened by numbers. Citizens had to attend hearings at the General Assembly, or at least send letters, postcards, and e-mail.

The social traditionalism of the religious right lacked the big-dollar contributions that were associated with big-business agenda items (for example, contributions from Blue Cross–Blue Shield to create a political climate friendly to their goals [*News and Observer* 1997f]). But since the house Republican sweep in November 1994, the religious-right agenda, often with political cues coming from former Christian Coalition director Ralph Reed in Washington, D.C., had strong advocates, especially in the state house. Besides the successful anti-sex-education legislation of Robin Hayes, social traditionalist Republicans pushed antiabortion bills in both 1995–96 and 1997–98 and passed an antievolution bill through the state house in 1997. Despite strong opposition from most metro Piedmont Democrats, two bills, one a ban on the so-called partial-birth abortion (an issue imported from national political debates) and the other requiring women to wait twenty-four hours before proceeding with an abortion, also passed the state house in 1997 by comfortable margins. But signaling a reluctance to support the entire religious-right agenda (in contrast to agreeing to kill the needle-exchange bill), the state senate in 1997 refused to consider any of the three bills passed by the house.

At the same time, leading Democratic senators in both 1995 and 1997 reversed their previous support (1991–94) for a state abortion fund for poor women, indicating to advocates of abortion rights that they were not willing to stand up for such an expenditure when legislative Republicans were focusing their campaigns on the issue. Such a move indicated that the social traditionalist grassroots advocacy was scaring modernizer Democrats into abandoning longtime allies on the left. But this impact of the religious right was unreported in the press and thus invisible to most citizens, because the senate Democrats never put the issue to a vote on the senate floor. Bachrach and Baratz (1963) termed such legislator decisions that take place off the record and behind closed doors "non-decisions."

Left-leaning advocacy groups besides women's rights organizations also encountered non-decisions in the General Assembly. Throughout the 1990s several groups sought to increase spending for children's health care, including regulation of day care standards and protection from abuse by negligent parents or guardians. The typical response from even modernizer Democrats was that "the money isn't available" to fund this cause. When, however, an investigative newspaper series or a tragic death of children with attendant headlines and TV news stories occurred on this issue, then North Carolina state government "in crisis" was willing to act (cf. *Salisbury Post* 1997). A similar reluctance by General Assembly modernizers to invest in child-centered activity took place in K–12 school budgets. North Carolina's state and local school funding remained so low in the 1990s that individual school Parent-Teacher Associations were forced to continue fund-raising for certain school activities. For example, in Forsyth, an affluent metro Piedmont county, the school board expected school-based volunteer organizations to purchase all playground equipment. One obvious consequence was that schools with higher percentages of low-income parents had less funding available. Public school teachers in North Carolina also noted that they have been expected to buy many of their own school supplies and to provide their own or parents' funds and volunteer time to "spruce up" their classrooms. This contrasted to other states, especially in the Northeast and Midwest, where school districts budgeted such funds.

Environmentalists were the most successful outgroups on the left in the 1990s. The metro-Piedmont-dominated Sierra Club was joined by more low-income-based citizen groups from the Coastal Plain such as the Friends of Tillery (a Halifax County farm community) to fight the expansion of corporate hog production. But it remains unclear whether the environmentalists' success was not linked to public health disasters of the mid-1990s, such as fish kills in the Neuse River linked to the pfiesteria organism and massive spills of hog waste due to unexpectedly high levels of rain. These "natural" events, coupled with Representative Morgan's ire toward the hog industry that had dared to seek to expand in his retiree-heavy legislative district (see Chapter 3), may have had more impact than did the power of average citizens in increasing government regulation and oversight of economic activity in the Coastal Plain.

Finally, outgroups on the right and the left were helped beginning in the mid-1990s by tax-exempt educational foundations that challenged the dominant ideology's hold over public policy. Beginning in 1994 the libertarian-oriented John Locke Foundation, funded primarily by the family of former Raleigh GOP state representative Art Pope, became a much-quoted source of antispending economic traditionalism. Seeking before his 1996 reelection campaign to affirm his partial evolution toward traditionalist ideology, Governor Hunt made a point of participating in Locke Foundation activities. While the foundation reveled in its new status as a must-visit stop for many would-be statewide candidates, it surprised many Raleigh insiders in early 1997 with its scathing attacks on house Republican leaders for their 1996 pork-barrel spending that had initially evaded public scrutiny. Since the Locke Foundation was funded by Republicans, its willingness to criticize both Democrats and Republicans increased its credibility as a critic of big-spending state government (*News and Observer* 1997a).

In response to the Locke Foundation's success as an economic traditionalist voice, populist Democrats in 1995 established a countervoice, the Common Sense Foundation. Although lacking the funding and thus the larger staff and more extensive activities of Locke, Common Sense nonetheless provided an intellectual challenge to modernizer and modernizer-traditionalist Democrats. It criticized the Hunt administration and senate Democrats just as vigorously as the actions of social traditionalist or mainstream Republicans. On occasion Common Sense and Locke held joint press conferences to oppose, from right and left, the efforts of big business and powerful legislators of either party to promote corporate welfare (cf. Glasberg and Skidmore 1997). Another populist-leaning research group, the Raleigh-based Budget and Tax Center, also published regular reports on the fiscal impact on low-income citizens of the various General Assembly budget and tax policy choices. On occasion this center also collaborated with the Locke Foundation. For example, a jointly authored op-ed article criticized a little-debated issue: the willingness of house and senate leaders to raise revenue by allowing local general sales tax increases (Gerlach and Hood 1997).

The Class Bias in Electoral Participation and the Democrats' Future

Conventional wisdom in North Carolina politics holds that lower-income citizens participate less in politics because they are satisfied with the status quo. In particular, working-class whites are said to support corporate domination of state politics. Modernizer Democrats, in particular, offer this explanation to account for their cordial relations with corporate lobbyists. By this account, General Assembly politics can legitimately be a battle for the allegiance of North Carolina businesses and wealthy individuals, given the choice of many middle- and low-income citizens not to vote, especially in nonpresidential years. But an alternate explanation strikes at the basic relationship between social class and politics in a democracy: the less-affluent citizens are inactive because they are less likely to believe they can affect public policy (Botsch 1981).

In fact, numerous statewide polls show that less-affluent Tar Heels would spend more on education and care less about tax cuts than does the affluent minority. Each statewide poll, from a massive 10,000-interview study commissioned by Democrats after the 1984 election losses (Hamilton 1984; Luebke 1990a, 194) to smaller samples undertaken for dailies such as the *Charlotte Observer* or the *News and Observer*, revealed that most North Carolinians, white or black, favored economic-populist policies that lowered taxes on themselves (for example, repeal of the food tax) and opposed reducing either the corporate income tax or the property tax on stocks and bonds. While such preferences were not surprising to any student of public opinion polling, such findings were studiously ignored by Democrats such as Governor Jim Hunt or state house and state senate leaders of both parties.

The lowered electoral participation was not unique to North Carolina. But evidence existed, in both North Carolina and other states, that the less-affluent citizens would increase their voting levels only if they perceived that their political involvement made a difference. In the 1984 race for the U.S. Senate, the Helms campaign convinced disproportionate numbers of working-class whites, especially in the western Piedmont, that it was in their self-interest to help reelect their senior senator. In a parallel fashion in 1988, Jesse Jackson persuaded working-class blacks, many of whom had never cared about politics, to register to vote so that they could support him in North Carolina's Democratic presidential primary. President Clinton is generally credited with increasing participation in his 1992 campaign by stressing a "People First" theme and helping to depress turnout to a record low percentage in 1996 by making far fewer appeals to the political discontent of the average citizen. In North Carolina, for example, the number of 1996 voters was four percent *lower* than in 1992.

Precisely this issue, whether to encourage more participation or to try to win with the existing electorate, faced Tar Heel Democrats as they approached the 2000 campaign. It was especially difficult as Democrats both to the left (populists) and to the right (modernizer-traditionalists) found that the Christian Coalition and related social traditionalist organizations had persuaded many working-class whites in the 1996 election to reject any Democrat out-of-hand. A certain percentage of less-affluent whites with fundamentalist-Protestant religious ties were in a sociopolitical cocoon. In 1996 U.S. Senate candidate Harvey Gantt ran numerous TV ads appealing to their economic concerns. But these religious-right-influenced, blue-collar voters in western Piedmont industrial counties, for example, appeared, on the basis of county results, to be preoccupied with a social morality agenda. For example, a 1996 Christian Coalition "nonpartisan" voter guide distributed in the western Piedmont showed pictures of Gantt (so dark as to obliterate any facial detail) and Helms, with Gantt listed as saying "yes" to homosexual rights while Helms's column showed a "no."

What should North Carolina Democrats do if a percentage of less-affluent whites appear firmly inside the religious-right cocoon? One answer came from national observers of the Democrats' dilemma. Sociologist Paul Starr and political journalist E. J. Dionne both argued in 1997 essays that Democrats needed to move to the left with a promise to address average citizens' economic securities with a "more appropriate government" that would meet people's needs for affordable health care and a public education system that worked for their children (Dionne 1997, 336–37). Starr advocated in particular that Democrats abandon the antigovernment rhetoric of balanced budgets that was rooted in Reaganism. Democrats should stand for public investment that allowed average families to improve their living standards; they should not be preoccupied with big business's goal to keep inflation down by raising interest rates (Starr 1997).

Applying this reasoning to North Carolina politics, Democrats should increase their party recruitment of less-affluent citizens, especially women of all races and all racial and ethnic minorities. They should reject the Locke Foundation mantra that cutting government spending is the goal. Populist and modernizer Democrats should affirm, for example, that the state's investment in K–12 and community college education is *not* excessive. Why should the tenth largest state, and overall one of America's fastest-growing states, rank thirty-ninth in public school spending? If this hypothesis is accurate, then a more passionate Democratic Party, tied to a state government more focused on health care, education, and environmental protection, should attract enough voters to win both legislative majorities and statewide elections in the twenty-first century.

This new Democratic Party would give voice to average voters' belief that state government should not serve primarily the economic needs of big business. It would recognize that the public was dissatisfied with unresponsive large-scale institutions, both big government and big business (Luebke and Zipp 1983). The new Democrats would stop ignoring less-affluent citizens' unease with the power of big business (cf. Zipp, Landerman, and Luebke 1982), and they would recognize that the less-affluent preferred a political party that would explicitly address the economic needs of a middle-income majority (cf. Edsall 1984). At the same time, the modernizer- and populist-based Democrats would welcome, as Franklin Roosevelt had six decades before, support from business interests sharing the view that less social inequality, not more, made for a better North Carolina and a better America. To win with this strategy, Tar Heel Democrats would need to end, by their own vigorous get-out-the-vote efforts, the turnout bias that favored the Republican-leaning upper middle- and upper-class voters.

The defeat of Virginia Democrats in November 1997 provided Tar Heels with a stark negative example. Failing to include any economic populist themes in their statewide campaigns, Virginia Democrats lost all three statewide races and control of the legislature. Exit polls from 1997 revealed that the core Democratic constituency—the high-school-educated citizens—were three times less likely than college-educated professionals to vote. The upper middle class voted disproportionately and clearly favored Virginia's Republicans (*Richmond Times-Dispatch* 1997b).

The Advantage for Pragmatic Republicans

Senate Democrats and a Democratic governor such as Jim Hunt, sitting comfortably in a position of power, might initially question why they should welcome a more populist Democratic Party. But the growing ability of Tar Heel Republicans to campaign as pragmatists without the sharp edge of antigovernment and social-morality traditionalism should provide Democrats good reason to fear the future.

Case studies one and two were the successful campaigns of Republican mayors of North Carolina's two largest cities. As Charlotte mayor in the mid-1990s, Richard Vinroot lobbied the General Assembly to regulate billboards. His successor, Pat McCrory, won passage at the 1997 General Assembly of a referendum bill to raise the Charlotte sales tax in order to fund transit. Neither government regulation nor a tax increase was usually associated with southern Republicans. But this pragmatism was so successful that no Democrat raised a serious candidacy against either Vinroot's or McCrory's reelection campaigns in the 1990s. Similarly, Raleigh mayor Tom Fetzer, although he played the more conventional GOP tune of lowering property taxes and opposing some city spending, intimidated experienced Democrats from trying to defeat him when he ran successfully in 1997 for his third two-year term.

Even North Carolina's two U.S. senators, Jesse Helms and Lauch Faircloth, both of whom prided themselves on their traditionalist ideology, made a point periodically to show pragmatically what they had accomplished for "the folks back home." In late summer during his 1996 reelection race against Harvey Gantt, Helms ran a series of ads in different North Carolina media markets explaining what he had done for Charlotte, how he had saved that program in Winston-Salem, and how he had helped the Research Triangle. Such messages softened Helms's image sufficiently so that in 1996 he won more native-white Tar Heel support than he had in his 1990 contest against Gantt.

As if taking his cue from Helms, Faircloth, toward the end of his first term in 1996–97, very publicly helped to appropriate money for parklands in western North Carolina and supported new construction for federal buildings in the Research Triangle Park. Further, Faircloth astounded environmentalists when, in September 1997 on the day of federal oversight hearings on the deadly organism pfiesteria, which had killed millions of Neuse River fish, he introduced an appropriations bill for anti-pfiesteria research. It seemed particularly ironic since Faircloth owned a Sampson County cattle farm where a waste spill in 1996 had killed thousands of fish in the nearby Black River.

The lesson for the twenty-first century for Tar Heel Republicans was clear. The growing population in the metro Piedmont and in the many retirement counties was composed primarily of voters who opposed a hard traditionalist agenda. As long as the party could avoid candidates such as Jim Gardner (1992 would-be governor), Robin Hayes (1996 would-be governor), and NASCAR champion and former county commissioner Richard Petty (1996 would-be secretary of state), Republicans would have an excellent chance of winning statewide elections as well as majority control of both the state house and the state senate.

The Consequences of In-Migration for
Tar Heel Politics

The late 1980s and 1990s brought a spate of writing on the eventual Republican domination of the changed and growing southern states (cf. Black and Black 1987; Applebome 1996; Katznelson 1997). But the relative growth in North Carolina in certain counties, primarily via the migration of many nonsoutherners, and the population stagnation or near-stagnation in most other counties, has led to a somewhat different picture for North Carolina's foreseeable future. In short, the Tar Heel state will probably continue to look more like its southern neighbor to the north, Virginia, and its larger cousin very far south, Florida, which some doubt is southern at all.

The evolution of once-solid-Democrat southern states into firmly Republican ones will continue to occur in some parts of the South, primarily in Deep South Alabama, Mississippi, and South Carolina. Perhaps Georgia (although the growth in metropolitan Atlanta mostly militates against strong social and economic traditionalism) will also join the newly solid Republican South. But North Carolina has too many antitraditionalist migrants to become solidly Republican. Note, for example, that in both the 1990 and the 1996 U.S. Senate elections a majority of Tar Heel whites who had lived in the state less than ten years supported a black man, Harvey Gantt. While native-born North Carolinians gave only about one-third of their votes to Gantt, their relative size in the statewide electorate was declining.

North Carolina's political future will likely be closely contested between Republicans and Democrats into the twenty-first century. Republicans will try to demonize the Democrats as tax-and-spend liberals; Democrats will seek to stereotype Republicans as heartless Newt Gingriches who would deny social programs to the needy young and old people of the Tar Heel state. But most importantly, who wins in the twenty-first century will heavily depend on how Republicans and Democrats solve the strong intraparty conflicts that, in the late 1990s, showed no immediate signs of easy resolution.

Bibliography

Abrams, Douglas Carl. 1978. "A Progressive-Conservative Duel: The 1920 Democratic Gubernatorial Primaries in North Carolina." *North Carolina Historical Review* 55:421–41.

Adams, Jerry. 1981. "That Freakish Thing: A Memo Dooms the Labor Center." In Eric B. Herzik and Sallye Branch Teater, comps., *North Carolina Focus*. Raleigh.

AFL-CIO Legislative Report. 1987. Raleigh.

———. 1997. Raleigh.

Anderson, Eric. 1981. *Race and Politics in North Carolina: The Black Second*. Baton Rouge.

Applebome, Peter. 1996. *Dixie Rising: How the South Is Shaping American Values, Politics, and Culture*. New York.

Ashby, Warren. 1980. *Frank Porter Graham: A Southern Liberal*. Winston-Salem.

Bachrach, Peter, and Morton Baratz. 1963. "Decisions and Nondecisions: An Analytical Framework." *American Political Science Review* 57:632–42.

Baker, Frances. 1986. "North Carolina Elite Attitudes toward Women, Blacks, and Labor." Paper presented at annual meeting of Southern Sociological Society, New Orleans, April.

Bartley, Numan V., and Hugh D. Graham. 1975. *Southern Politics and the Second Reconstruction*. Baltimore.

Bass, Jack, and Walter DeVries. 1976. *The Transformation of Southern Politics*. New York.

Bell, John L., Jr. 1982. *Hard Times: The Beginning of the Great Depression in North Carolina, 1929–1933*. Raleigh.

Betts, Jack. 1985. "Rendering unto Caesar: A Taxing Problem for the 1985 Legislature." *North Carolina Insight* 7:2–7.

Beyle, Thad. 1981. "How Powerful Is the North Carolina Governor?" *N.C. Insight* 3:3–11.

———. 1997. "Cost of Congressional Campaigns in North Carolina." *NC DataNet* 15 (June): 12–14.

Beyle, Thad, and Merle Black, eds. 1975. *Politics and Policy in North Carolina*. New York.

Beyle, Thad, Merle Black, and Arlon Kempel. 1975. "Sanford vs. Wallace: Presidential Primary Politics in North Carolina." In Thad Beyle and Merle Black, eds., *Politics and Policy in North Carolina*. New York.

Beyle, Thad, and Peter Harkins. 1975. "The 1968 Elections in North Carolina." In Thad Beyle and Merle Black, eds., *Politics and Policy in North Carolina*. New York.

Billings, Dwight B., Jr. 1979. *Planters and the Making of a "New South": Class, Politics, and Development in North Carolina, 1865–1900*. Chapel Hill.

Black, Earl. 1975. "North Carolina Governors and Racial Segregation." In Thad Beyle and Merle Black, eds., *Politics and Policy in North Carolina*. New York.

———. 1976. *Southern Governors and Civil Rights*. Cambridge, Mass.

Black, Earl, and Merle Black. 1987. *Politics and Society in the South*. Cambridge, Mass.

———. 1992. *The Vital South: How Presidents Are Elected*. Cambridge, Mass.

Botsch, Robert Emil. 1981. *We Shall Not Overcome: Populism and Southern Blue-Collar Workers*. Chapel Hill.

Brummett, John. 1994. *Highwire*. New York.

Budget. 1959. *Summary Budget of the State of North Carolina*. Raleigh.

Calhoun, Craig. 1988. *North Carolina Today: Contrasting Conditions and Common Concerns*. Raleigh.

Carter, Dan T. 1995. *The Politics of Rage: George Wallace, the Origins of the New Conservatism, and the Transformation of American Politics*. New York.

CBS News. 1984. *CBS Election Day Election Poll (North Carolina)*. New York.

———. 1986. *CBS Election Day Election Poll (North Carolina)*. New York.

CED (Corporation for Enterprise Development). 1987. *Making the Grade: The 1987 Development Report Card for the States*. Washington, D.C.

———. 1994. *Bidding for Business: Are Cities and States Selling Themselves Short?* Washington, D.C.

Chafe, William. 1981. *Civilities and Civil Rights*. Reprint. New York.

Charlotte Observer. 1987. "Why Myrick Beat Gantt: 2 Local Political Experts Examine the Mayoral Election." November 8.

———. 1988. "Martin Holds Steady; Jordan Slips in New Poll." October 16.

———. 1989a. "Ramsey Ousted as House Speaker." January 12.

———. 1989b. "Revolt Was 10 Weeks in Making." January 12.

———. 1991a. "N.C. Inspection Program Ranks Last in U.S." September 5.

———. 1991b. "In Hamlet Fire, Government Safety Nets Gave Way." September 22.

———. 1995. "Donors Write N.C. Laws Their Way." June 25.

———. 1997a. "Shinn: Uptown Out." March 27.

———. 1997b. "Arts Council Money Cut." April 2.

——. 1997c. "Edwards Quits N.C. Road Board." October 25.

——. 1997d. "UNC Students to Protest Building of Ram Road." November 14.

——. 1997e. "Road Board Is Dominated by Campaign Leaders, Donors." November 16.

——. 1997f. "Transportation Department Trips." December 8.

——. 1997g. "Road Deal Made Costly Turnaround." December 13.

——. 1997h. "Union Lays Its Cards on Pillowtex's Table." December 18.

——. 1998. "Hunt Put the Brakes on Bridge." January 10.

Clark, Daniel J. 1997. *Like Night and Day: Unionization in a Southern Mill Town*. Chapel Hill.

Clawson, Dan, Alan Neustadtl, and Denise Scott. 1992. *Money Talks: Corporate PACs and Political Influence*. New York.

Clean Water Fund. 1988. *Clean Water Update*. Vol. 2. Raleigh. June.

Clinton, William Jefferson. 1997. Address before the General Assembly of North Carolina. March 13.

Clotfelter, James, and William R. Hamilton. 1972. "Beyond Race Politics: Electing Southern Populists in the 1970s." In H. Brandt Ayers and Thomas H. Naylor, eds., *You Can't Eat Magnolias*. New York.

Cobb, James. 1984. *Industrialization and Southern Society, 1877–1984*. Lexington, Ky.

Cohen, Richard. 1997. "A Debate We Never Had." *Washington Post*. September 18.

Conway, Mimi. 1979. *Rise Gonna Rise: A Portrait of Southern Textile Workers*. New York.

Crow, Jeffrey J. 1984. "Cracking the Solid South: Populism and the Fusionist Interlude." In Lindley S. Butler and Alan D. Watson, eds., *The North Carolina Experience: An Interpretive and Documentary History*. Chapel Hill.

CTJ (Citizens for Tax Justice). 1987. *The Sorry State of State Taxes*. Washington, D.C.

——. 1996. *State Taxes*. Washington, D.C.

Davidson, Osha Gray. 1996. *Broken Heartland: An Expanded Edition*. Iowa City.

Dionne, E. J., Jr. 1997. *They Only Look Dead: Why Progressives Will Dominate the Next Political Era*. New York.

Dittmer, John. 1994. *Local People: The Struggle for Civil Rights in Mississippi*. Urbana, Ill.

Domhoff, William. 1972. *Fat Cats and Democrats: The Role of the Big Rich in the Party of the Common Man*. Englewood Cliffs, N.J.

Doty, Mercer, and Doris Mahaffey. 1979. "Which Way Now?" In Eric B. Herzik and Sallye Branch Teater, comps., *North Carolina Focus*. Raleigh.

Dowd, Edward. 1976. "Respondent to 'Earnings, Profits, and Productivity in North Carolina.'" In Jane A. Begoli, ed., *Proceedings, Employment-Management Relations: Issues in the South*. University of North Carolina, Charlotte. November.

Durden, Robert F. 1984. "North Carolina in the New South." In Lindley S. Butler and Alan D. Watson, eds., *The North Carolina Experience: An Interpretive and Documentary History*. Chapel Hill.

Durham Morning Herald. 1987a. "Cities-Highways Bill Gets House Approval." July 1.

——. 1987b. "Senate Approves Bill on School Spankings." July 1.

——. 1988. "U.S. Labor Groups Lost 62,000 Members in 1987." January 24.

Eamon, Thomas, and David Elliott. 1994. "Modernization versus Traditionalism in North Carolina Senate Races." *Social Science Quarterly* 75 (June): 354–67.

Earle, John R., Dean D. Knudsen, and Donald W. Shriver Jr. 1976. *Spindles and Spires: A Re-Study of Religion and Social Change in Gastonia*. Atlanta.

Edmonds, Helen G. 1951. *The Negro and Fusion Politics in North Carolina, 1894–1901*. Chapel Hill.

Edsall, Thomas. 1984. *The New Politics of Inequality*. New York.

Effron, Seth. 1987. "Breaking New Ground in Economic Development Subsidies." *News and Record*. Greensboro. August 2.

Ehle, John. 1993. *Dr. Frank: Life with Frank Porter Graham*. Chapel Hill.

Ehringhaus, J. C. B. 1934. "The Sales Tax Has Its Virtues." In Lindley S. Butler and Alan D. Watson, eds., *The North Carolina Experience: An Interpretive and Documentary History*. Chapel Hill. 1984.

Elazar, Daniel. 1972. *American Federalism*. New York.

Employment Security Commission. 1987. "Employment and Wages in North Carolina, Second Quarter 1987." Raleigh.

———. 1990. "Employment and Wages in North Carolina, 1990." Raleigh.

Escott, Paul D. 1985. *Many Excellent People: Power and Privilege in North Carolina, 1850–1900*. Chapel Hill.

Fahy, Joe, and Ford Reid. 1986. "Money Machine Rakes It In, Spends Little on Candidates." *Virginian-Pilot*. Norfolk. May 11.

Feeney, Patrick. 1983. "At-Large Elections, Black Political Representation, and Social Change: A North Carolina Case Study." M.A. thesis. University of North Carolina, Greensboro.

Ferguson, James S. 1981. "Progressivism in Decline." In Eric B. Herzik and Sallye Branch Teater, comps., *North Carolina Focus*. Raleigh.

Finger, Bill. 1981. "Forces of Paradox." In Eric B. Herzik and Sallye Branch Teater, comps., *North Carolina Focus*. Raleigh.

Fitzsimon, Chris. 1997a. "Inside the Beltline." *Journal of Common Sense* 3, no. 3 (September): 3, 15.

———. 1997b. "Left Legislative Update." On-line. August 29.

Fleer, Jack D. 1994. *North Carolina Government and Politics*. Lincoln, Nebr.

Fox, Rosemary K. 1982. "Social Action against Injustice: Impact of the United Church of Christ Movement in Support of the Wilmington Ten." Unpublished paper. Department of Sociology, University of North Carolina, Greensboro.

Frady, Marshall. 1976. *Wallace*. New York.

Frankel, Linda Jean. 1986. "Women, Paternalism, and Protest in a Southern Textile Community: Henderson, N.C., 1900–1960." Ph.D. dissertation. Harvard University.

Franklin, John Hope. 1947. *From Slavery to Freedom: A History of American Negroes*. New York.

———. 1994. "Growing Economic Inequality." *Trumpet of Conscience* 10 (Fall): 1–2.

———. 1997. Address before the General Assembly of North Carolina. July 22.

Friedlein, Ken. 1986. "Selling Industry on North Carolina." *North Carolina Insight* 8:43–49.

Furgurson, Earnest. 1986. *Hard Right: The Rise of Jesse Helms*. New York.

Galifianakis, Nick. 1987. Interview with author. Durham, May 9.

Gerlach, Dan, and John Hood. 1997. "N.C. Legislators Show Troubling Trend toward Sales Tax." *Charlotte Observer*. September 20.

Glasberg, Davita Silfen, and Dan Skidmore. 1997. *Corporate Welfare Policy and the Welfare State*. Hawthorne, N.Y.

Goldman, Robert, and Paul Luebke. 1985. "Corporate Capital Moves South: Competing Class Interests and Labor Relations in North Carolina's 'New' Political Economy." *Journal of Political and Military Sociology* 13:17–32.

Goldwater, Barry M. 1960. *The Conscience of a Conservative*. Shepherdsville, Ky.

Goodman, Vanessa, and Jack Betts. 1987. *The Growth of a Two-Party System in North Carolina: A Special Report* (North Carolina Center for Public Policy Research). Raleigh. December.

Goodwyn, Lawrence. 1976. *The Populist Movement*. New York.

Greenhaw, Wayne. 1982. *Elephants in the Cotton Fields: Ronald Reagan and the New Republican South*. New York.

Greensboro Daily News. 1978. "Winston Policemen Eye Union Affiliation." September 20.

———. 1980. "Ward Choice Up to Voters for Fourth Time." May 4, May 7.

———. 1982. "Council Adopts District Rule in Greensboro." June 24, November 16, December 17.

Greensboro Record. 1977. "This Time, ERA Fight May Be More Gentlewomanly." January 19.

———. 1979. "Study Sees More Union Support in South." June 13.

Greider, William B. 1992. *Who Will Tell the People: The Betrayal of American Democracy*. New York.

Grissom, Eddie, and James Grissom. 1983. Interview with author. Henderson, N.C., September 17.

Guillory, Ferrel. 1988. "Lawmakers Give Green Light to Tax Giveaways." *News and Observer*. Raleigh. July 8.

Hall, Bob. 1985a. "Jesse Helms: The Meaning of His Money." *Southern Exposure*. Durham. February.

———. 1985b. "The 1984 North Carolina Voter Registration and Turnout." Unpublished memorandum. Institute for Southern Studies, Durham.

———. 1997. "Who Are Those Mystery Men?" *News and Record*. Greensboro. September 14.

———, ed. 1988. *Environmental Politics: Lessons from the Grassroots*. Durham.

Hall, Jacquelyn Dowd, James Leloudis, Robert Korstad, Mary Murphy, Lu Ann Jones, and Christopher B. Daly. 1987. *Like a Family: The Making of a Southern Cotton Mill World*. Chapel Hill.

Hamilton, Richard. 1972. *Class and Politics in the United States*. New York.

Hamilton, William. 1984. "The Political Views of North Carolinians: A Report to North Carolina Democratic Candidates." Unpublished report. Washington, D.C.

Hammer and Company Associates. 1961. *The Economy of Western North Carolina*. Atlanta.

Harvin, Lucius, III. 1983. Remarks at Helms-for-Senate dinner, Henderson, N.C., September 17.

Hellman, Mark. 1988. "Durham's Progressive Coalition." In Bob Hall, ed., *Environmental Politics: Lessons from the Grassroots*. Durham.

Helms, Jesse. 1976. *When Free Men Shall Stand: A Sobering Look at the Supertaxing, Superspending Superbureaucracy in Washington*. Grand Rapids.

———. 1983a. Interview with author. Henderson, N.C., September 17.

———. 1983b. Speech at Helms-for-Senate dinner, Henderson, N.C., September 17.

———. 1997. Address before the General Assembly of North Carolina. May 27.

Herald-Sun. 1995. "N.C. House Democrats Break Ranks." Durham. July 23.

Hightower, Jim. 1997. *There's Nothing in the Middle of the Road but Yellow Stripes and Dead Armadillos*. New York.

Hobbs, Samuel Huntington, Jr. 1930. *North Carolina: Economic and Social*. Chapel Hill.

Hodges, Luther H. 1962. *Businessman in the Statehouse: Six Years as Governor of North Carolina*. Chapel Hill.

Hodgson, Godfrey. 1996. *The World Turned Right Side Up: A History of the Conservative Ascendancy in America*. New York.

Houghton, Jonathan. 1993. "The North Carolina Republican Party from Reconstruction to the Radical Right." Ph.D. dissertation. University of North Carolina, Chapel Hill.

Hughes, Joseph T., Jr. 1982. "Targeting Desirable Industries." *N.C. Insight* 5:27–35.

Hunt, James Baxter, Jr. 1981. "Microelectronics: The Key to the Future." *N.C. Insight* 4:17.

———. 1982. *Addresses and Public Papers of James Baxter Hunt, Jr., Governor of North Carolina*. Vol. 1, *1977–1981*. Raleigh.

Institute of Government. 1997. *North Carolina Legislation, 1997*. Chapel Hill.

Jamieson, Kathleen Hall. 1992. *Dirty Politics: Deception, Distraction, and Democracy*. New York.

JCPS (Joint Center for Political Studies). 1973, 1980, 1985, 1987. *Black Elected Officials: A National Roster*. Washington, D.C.

Johnson, Haynes, and David S. Broder. 1996. *The System: The American Way of Politics at the Breaking Point*. Boston.

Judkins, Bennett M. 1986. *We Offer Ourselves as Evidence: Toward Workers' Control of Occupational Health*. Westport, Conn.

Katznelson, Ira. 1997. "Reversing Southern Republicanism." In Stanley B. Greenberg and Theda Skocpol, eds., *The New Majority*. New Haven.

Kern, Montague. 1989. *Thirty-Second Politics: Political Advertising in the Eighties*. New York.

Key, V. O., Jr. 1949. *Southern Politics in State and Nation*. New York.

King, David D. 1988. Interview with author. Raleigh, September 7.

King, Wayne. 1978. "North Carolina's Leaders Worried by Blemishes on State's Image." *New York Times*. February 22.

Kozol, Jonathan. 1991. *Savage Inequalities: Children in America's Schools*. New York.

Lamis, Alexander P. 1984. *The Two-Party South*. New York.

Lavelle, J. M. 1981. "We Were All Bigots: Election '81 Decided by City-Wide White Backlash." *North State Reader* 1.

Lefler, Hugh Talmage, and Albert Ray Newsome. 1973. *North Carolina: The History of a Southern State*. 3d ed. Chapel Hill.

Leiter, Jeffrey. 1986. "Reactions to Subordination: Attitudes of Southern Textile Workers." *Social Forces* 64:948–74.

Lineberry, Danny. 1996. "The 1995 Legislature in Retrospect: Republican Lawmakers Work to Deliver Their Contract." *North Carolina Insight* 16, no. 3: 102–18.

Liner, Charles D. 1979. "The Origins and Development of the North Carolina System of Taxation." *Popular Government* 45:41–49.

———. 1981. "State and Local Government Finance over the Past Fifty Years." *Popular Government* 46:32–36.

———. 1982. "Government Spending and Taxation: Where Does North Carolina Stand?" *Popular Government* 48:30–41.

———. 1991. "Changes in North Carolina's Tax System: The Last Decade." *Popular Government* 57:2–9.

———. 1997. "Comments on the Center's Article on the Business Tax Burden in North Carolina." *North Carolina Insight* 17, no. 2–3: 80.

Lo, Clarence. 1982. "Counter-movements and Conservative Movements in the Contemporary U.S." *Annual Review of Sociology* 8:107–34.

Lubell, Samuel. 1964. *The Future of American Politics*. New York.

Luebke, Paul. 1975. "Political Attitudes in a West German Factory: A Political-Sociological Analysis of Chemical Workers." Ph.D. dissertation. Columbia University.

———. 1979. "The Social and Political Bases of a Black Candidate's Coalition: Race, Class, and Ideology in the 1976 North Carolina Primary Election." *Politics and Society* 9:239–61.

———. 1980. "Repeal Food Tax; Raise Taxes on Liquor, Corporations." *Charlotte Observer*. May 11.

———. 1981a. "Activists and Asphalt: A Successful Anti-expressway Movement in a 'New South City.' " *Human Organization* 40:256–63.

———. 1981b. "Corporate Conservatism and Government Moderation in North Carolina." In Merle Black and John S. Reed, eds., *Perspectives on the American South*, vol. 1. New York.

———. 1981c. "Neighborhood Groups vs. Business Developers in Durham: Expressway Politics in the Scarce Energy Age." *Carolina Planning* 7:42–48.

———. 1984a. "Carolina Democrats after the Deluge." *The Sun*. Baltimore. December 5. Reprint. *News and Record*. Greensboro. January 22, 1985.

———. 1984b. "Dear Senator Helms; Dear Governor Hunt." *North Carolina Independent*. Durham. August 31.

———. 1984c. "The Helms-Hunt Race in North Carolina." *St. Petersburg Times*. August 12.

———. 1984d. "State of Competition: North Carolina's Senate Race and the Newspapers' Battle to Cover It." *Washington Journalism Review* 6:21–23.

———. 1985. "North Carolina: Still in the Progressive Mold?" *News and Observer, 400th Anniversary of North Carolina Special Edition*. Raleigh. July.

———. 1985–86. "Grass-roots Organizing: The Hidden Side of the 1984 Helms Campaign." *Election Politics* 3:30–33.

———. 1987a. "The Food Tax Epitomizes Tar Heel Tax Inequality." *News and Record*. Greensboro. April 19.

———. 1987b. "Newspaper Coverage of the 1986 Senate Race—Reporting the Issues or the Horse Race?" *North Carolina Insight* 9:92–95.

———. 1987c. "Style, Substance, and Symbolism: The Sanford-Broyhill Race of 1986." *Election Politics* 4:11–14.

———. 1987d. "Take to the Stump; Hit Issues Hard; That's Sanford's Lesson to Democrats." *Atlanta Constitution*. January 28.

———. 1990a. *Tar Heel Politics: Myths and Realities*. Chapel Hill.

———. 1990b. "Why Helms Won: Answer Isn't Purely Black and White." *News and Record*. Greensboro. November 11.

———. 1991. "Southern Politics: Past and Future." In Joseph Himes, ed., *The South Moves into Its Future: Studies in the Analysis and Prediction of Social Change*. Tuscaloosa.

———. 1994. "In Defense of Majority-Black Congressional Districts." *News and Record*. Greensboro. September 25.

———. 1995. "The Trouble with Bill." *News and Observer*. Raleigh. February 10.

———. 1996. "State Legislature at Critical Juncture." *Trumpet of Conscience* 12 (Summer): 1, 7.

Luebke, Paul, and Ruth Easterling. 1997. "Stop the Fat Cat Express." *Charlotte Observer*. April 14.

Luebke, Paul, and Patrick Feeney. 1981. "Sophisticated Gerrymandering? At-Large Districting and Black Political Representation in the North Carolina General Assembly." Paper presented at the annual meeting of the Southern Sociological Society, Louisville, Ky., April.

Luebke, Paul, Bob McMahon, and Jeff Risberg. 1979. "Selective Industrial Recruiting in North Carolina." *Working Papers for a New Society* 6:17–20.

Luebke, Paul, Steven Peters, and John Wilson. 1986. "The Political Economy of Microelectronics." In Dale Whittington, ed., *High Hopes for High Tech: Microelectronics Policy in North Carolina*. Chapel Hill.

Luebke, Paul, and Jeff Risberg. 1983. "Jesse Helms: Leader of the Countermovement Pack." Paper presented at the annual meeting of the American Sociological Association, Detroit, September.

Luebke, Paul, and Joseph Schneider. 1987. "Economic and Racial Ideology in the North Carolina Elite." In James C. Cobb, ed., *Perspectives on the American South*, vol. 5. New York.

Luebke, Paul, and Barry Yeoman. 1988. "Democrats Ignore Pro-Choice Vote." *News and Record*. Greensboro. November 27.

Luebke, Paul, and John Zipp. 1983. "Social Class and Attitudes toward Big Business in the United States." *Journal of Military and Political Sociology* 11:251–64.

Luger, Michael. 1986. "The States and Industrial Development: Program Mix and Policy Effectiveness." In J. Quigley, ed., *Perspectives on Public Finance and Policy*. New York.

McLaughlin, Mike. 1997. "Cabarrus Creates a Ripple in the Economic Development Pond with Its Incentive Grant Program." *North Carolina Insight* 17, no. 2–3: 31–33.

McLaughlin, Mike, and Bud Skinner. 1997. "Can We Brighten the Future for Rural North Carolina?" *North Carolina Insight* 17, no. 2–3: 100–120.

Mahaffey, Doris, and Mercer Doty. 1979. *Which Way Now? Economic Development and Industrialization in N.C.: A Report by the North Carolina Center for Public Policy Research*. Raleigh.

———. 1981. "Which Way Now? Economic Development and Industrialization in North Carolina." In Eric B. Herzik and Sallye Branch Teater, comps., *North Carolina Focus*. Raleigh.

Malizia, Emil, Robert E. Crow, et al. 1975. *The Earnings of North Carolinians*. North Carolina Office of State Planning. Raleigh.

Manuel, John. 1997. "North Carolina Economic Development Incentives: A Necessary Tool or Messing with the Market?" *North Carolina Insight* 17, no. 2–3: 23–49.

Marshall, F. Ray. 1967. *Labor in the South*. Cambridge, Mass.

MCNC (Microelectronics Center of North Carolina). 1985. *Annual Report*.

MDC. 1986. *Three Views of Rural Economic Development in North Carolina*. Chapel Hill. Minority report to the 1988 Democratic platform, Democratic National Convention, Atlanta.

Molotch, Harvey. 1976. "The City as a Growth Machine: Toward a Political Economy of Place." *American Journal of Sociology* 82:309–32.

Moore, Barrington. 1966. *Social Origins of Dictatorship and Democracy*. New York.

Morse, Lawrence. 1978. "Wages in North Carolina: An Evaluation of the Potthoff Report." *North Carolina Review of Business and Economics* 4:3–9.

Mullins, Terry, and Paul Luebke. 1982. "Symbolic Victory and Political Reality in the Southern Textile Industry: The Meaning of the J. P. Stevens Union Contract." *Journal of Labor Research* 3:81–88.

———. 1984. "The Corporate Campaign against J. P. Stevens: The Impact on Labor Relations in the 1980s." *North Carolina Review of Business and Economics* 8:23–27.

Myerson, Michael. 1978. *Nothing Could Be Finer*. New York.

National Education Association Datasearch. 1987. *Rankings of the States, 1987*. Washington, D.C.

NCDOA (North Carolina Department of Agriculture). 1986. *Agricultural Statistics*. Raleigh.

———. 1990. *Agricultural Statistics*. Raleigh.

———. 1997. *Agricultural Statistics*. Raleigh.

NDDOC (North Carolina Department of Commerce). 1986. *Blueprint on Economic Development*. Raleigh.

———. 1986–87. *Business in North Carolina*. Raleigh.

———. 1988. *North Carolina Economic Development Report, 1987*. Raleigh.

NCDOT (North Carolina Department of Transportation). 1988. *Transportation Improvement Programs, 1988–1996*. Raleigh. December.

NC Free. 1996. "Special Report: Voter Registration Trends." July 27.

———. 1997. "Special Report: Election and Voter Trends, Part 1." July 22.

News and Observer. 1977a. "Person Industry Hunters Quit." Raleigh. August 10.

———. 1977b. "Hunt Cites Industrial Growth." Raleigh. December 23.

———. 1977c. "Citizens Fight 'Power Structure' to Lure Philip Morris into Area." Raleigh. December 25.

———. 1978a. "Hunt Defends '10' Decisions as Correct." Raleigh. February 12.

———. 1978b. "PPG Employees Will Vote on Union." Raleigh. July 6.

———. 1981a. "UAW Fights for a Place in the Sun (Belt)." Raleigh. April 12.

———. 1981b. "Trio Tied to Congressional Club to Fight Tax Hike." Raleigh. May 12.

———. 1981c. "Motor Fuels Tax Supporters, Opponents Continue Attacks." Raleigh. May 30.

———. 1981d. "Ads Attack 'Cronyism' among Hunt Supporters." Raleigh. June 4.

———. 1981e. "Voting Rights: Is U.S. Law Still Needed?" Raleigh. August 23.

———. 1983. "Helms, Falwell Begin North Carolina Voter Registration Drive." Raleigh. July 6.

———. 1986. "Broyhill, Sanford, Top Spenders." Raleigh. November 4.

———. 1988a. "Sanford Reports Assets of $2 Million; Helms Declares $325,000." Raleigh. June 5.

———. 1988b. "Nomination Blocked as Helms Battles State Department." Raleigh. June 26.

———. 1992. "Many On-Job Deaths Not Investigated." Raleigh. February 16.

———. 1993. "Donations to Hardison Called Illegal." Raleigh. May 8.

———. 1995a. "Boss Hog: North Carolina's Pork Revolution." Raleigh. February 19–26.

———. 1995b. "State Discloses Another Big Spill of Hog Farm Waste." Raleigh. July 1.

———. 1996a. "Irked Valentine Wants Hog Panel to Get to Work." Raleigh. January 19.

———. 1996b. "Minority Districts Rejected." Raleigh. June 14.

———. 1996c. "Labor Unions Test Case." Raleigh. November 30.

———. 1997a. "Lawmakers Bring Home the Bacon." Raleigh. February 14.

———. 1997b. "Dome: Goode Subject for Discussion." Raleigh. February 19.

———. 1997c. "Dome: Luebke Tries Quiet Approach." Raleigh. April 15.

———. 1997d. "Quietly, Blacks and Latinos Seek Common Ground." Raleigh. May 4.

———. 1997e. "Anatomy of a Deal." Raleigh. May 11.

———. 1997f. "Much Campaign Money Tied to Special Interests." Raleigh. May 28.

———. 1997g. "Frank Rouse: Building the New Republican Party." Raleigh. July 6.

———. 1997h. "Ozone Breaks Bad-Air Limit." Raleigh. July 16.

———. 1997i. "Education Basic Right, Court Rules." Raleigh. July 25.

———. 1997j. "Towns Embroiled in Mixed Blessings of Immigration." Raleigh. August 3.

———. 1997k. "Jackson Returns to His People." Raleigh. August 15.

———. 1997l. "Impasse in Enfield." Raleigh. August 19.

———. 1997m. "The Long Session." Raleigh. August 29.

———. 1997n. "Williamson Resigns Seat on DOT Panel." Raleigh. November 8.

———. 1997o. "A Rift in the Movement." Raleigh. November 24.

———. 1997p. "DOT Board Members Give Loads of Campaign Cash." Raleigh. November 25.

———. 1997q. "DOT Uses Millions in Safety Money for Political Projects." Raleigh. December 16.

——. 1998a. "Reluctant Warrior from the Heart of Hog Country." Raleigh. January 18.

——. 1998b. "The Road to Ruin." Raleigh. January 18.

News and Record. 1984. "Knox Won't Back Edmisten in Race." Greensboro. June 29.

——. 1985a. "Martin Restates Proposals for Some Tax Elimination." Greensboro. January 23.

——. 1985b. "State Ranks 8th in Survey on Business Climates." Greensboro. June 8.

——. 1987a. "Assembly Isn't Cross Section." Greensboro. February 8.

——. 1987b. "Job Recruiter Incentive a Switch." Greensboro. August 3.

——. 1993. "Board: Koury Deserves Assistance." Greensboro. October 3.

——. 1995. "State Republicans Begin New Era." Greensboro. January 22.

——. 1996a. "Symbol of the Old South Is Dividing the New South." Greensboro. January 28.

——. 1996b. "Voter-Drive Efforts Come under Fire." Greensboro. October 30.

——. 1996c. "Who Will Stand Up for the Bus Riders?" Greensboro. December 7.

——. 1996d. "Confederate Battle Flag Drawing New Divisions." Greensboro. December 28.

——. 1997a. "A New County, a New Life." Greensboro. May 4.

——. 1997b. "Residents Differ on Greensboro's Growth." Greensboro. September 7.

——. 1997c. "Southern Growth May Stall." Greensboro. September 25.

——. 1997d. "Some Schools Face Language Crisis." Greensboro. November 15.

New York Times. 1997. "With Iron Gavel, Helms Rejects Vote on Weld." September 13.

Noland, Terrance. 1998. "Powers of Concentration." *Business North Carolina* 18, no. 2 (February): 46–56.

Nordhoff, Grace, ed. 1984. *"A Lot of Human Beings Have Been Born Bums": Twenty Years of the Words of Jesse Helms.* Durham.

North Carolina Association of County Commissioners. 1996. *County Lines.* November 26.

North Carolina Budget and Tax Center. 1995. "An Analysis of the 1995–96 House Base General Fund Budget." May.

——. 1997. "Tax Policy Changes in the 1990s: What Are Their Effects?" *BTC Reports* 3, no. 15 (October): 1–6.

North Carolina Center for Public Policy Research. 1986, 1988, 1996. *Rankings of the Lobbyists.* Raleigh.

North Carolina Magazine. 1993. "What Will Hunt Do?" 51, no. 1 (January): 42–50.

O'Connor, Paul. 1987a. "Hardison's Pro-Business Record May Block His Nomination." *Durham Sun.* May 5.

——. 1987b. "When It Comes to Economic Development, Jim Martin and Bob Jordan Have Big Plans." *North Carolina Insight* 9:40–43.

Oleck, Joan. 1988. "Runoff: To Its Foes, It's a Primary Concern." *Virginian-Pilot.* Norfolk. May 29.

OPR (Office of Population Research). 1997. *Estimates of North Carolina Population.* Raleigh.

Orndorff, Jason. 1997. "2nd District: Ethridge Regains Traditional Democratic Seat." *NC DataNet* 15 (June): 3–4.

Orth, John V. 1982. "Separation of Powers: An Old Doctrine Triggers a New Crisis." *N.C. Insight* 5:36–47.

OSBM (Office of State Budget and Management). 1986. "State Rankings 1986." 1st ed.

——. 1987a. *Population Counts for North Carolina Counties*. Raleigh.

——. 1987b. *Revised Estimates of North Carolina Population*. Raleigh.

——. 1988. *Revised Estimates of North Carolina Population*. Raleigh.

——. 1997. *Revised Estimates of North Carolina Population*. Raleigh.

Osborne, David E. 1992. *Reinventing Government: How the Entrepreneurial Spirit Is Transforming the Public Sector*. New York.

Paget, Karen M. 1997. "The Battle for the States." In Stanley B. Greenberg and Theda Skocpol, eds., *The New Majority*. New Haven.

Parramore, Thomas C. 1983. *Express Lanes and Country Roads: The Way We Lived in North Carolina, 1920–1970*. Chapel Hill.

Payton, Boyd. 1970. *Scapegoat: Prejudice-Politics-Prison*. Philadelphia.

Peters, Mason. 1986. "New Right Crusaders Hunt Liberal Prey in Sen. Helms' National Political Holy War." *Virginian-Pilot*. Norfolk. May 11.

Peterson, Bill. 1984. "Jesse Helms' Lessons for Washington: Big Bucks, Street Fighter Skills, Racist Appeals, and Charisma Still Work." *Washington Post*. November 18.

Pinsky, Mark. 1977. "Wilmington 10: The Trial They Never Had." *Nation*, no. 224, 754–56.

Pleasants, Julian M., and Augustus M. Burns III. 1990. *Frank Porter Graham and the 1950 Senate Race in North Carolina*. Chapel Hill.

Pope, Liston. 1942. *Millhands and Preachers*. New Haven.

Reed, John S. 1990. *Whistling Dixie: Dispatches from the South*. Columbia, Mo.

Reid, Ford. 1986. "Fundraising." *Virginian-Pilot*. Norfolk. May 11.

Richmond Times-Dispatch. 1997a. "Honoring Henry Howell." July 12.

——. 1997b. "Rich, Educated Go to Polls; Analysts: Democrats Must Mobilize Downscale Voter." November 16.

Risberg, Jeffrey Earl. 1981. "Social Class, Race, Education, and Liberalism-Conservatism in the South: An Analysis of North Carolina Survey Data." M.A. thesis. University of North Carolina, Greensboro.

Roach, Janet H. 1984. "The Voting Rights Act: Dilution of Block Voting Power." *Campbell Law Observer*. February 24.

Robinson, W. S. 1950. "Ecological Correlations and the Behavior of Individuals." *American Sociological Review* 15:351–57.

Rosenfeld, Stuart. 1983. *After the Factories*. Southern Growth Policies Board, Research Triangle Park, N.C.

Roy, Donald. 1975. "Fear Stuff, Sweet Stuff, and Evil Stuff: Management's Defenses against Unionization in the South." Unpublished manuscript. Durham.

Salisbury Post. 1997. "Newsmakers of the Year: Deaths of Four Children in 97 Caused Tremors from Rowan to Raleigh." December 31.

Salmond, John A. 1995. *Gastonia 1929: The Story of the Loray Mill Strike*. Chapel Hill.

Salter, John R., Jr. 1979. *Jackson, Mississippi: An American Chronicle of Struggle and Schism*. Hicksville, N.Y.

Sampson, Gregory. 1986. "Employment and Earnings in the Semiconductor Electronics Industry: Implications for North Carolina." In Dale Whittington, ed., *High Hopes for High Tech: Microelectronics Policy in North Carolina*. Chapel Hill.

Saunders, Barry. 1997. "Speaking of Great Deals." *News and Observer*. Raleigh. June 9.

Schneider, Joseph. 1985. "Preachers and Politics: New Christian Right Ideology among North Carolina Fundamentalist Ministers." M.A. thesis. University of North Carolina, Greensboro.

Sentelle, David B. 1996. "Racial Gerrymandering." *Catholic University Law Review* 45 (Summer): 1249–57.

Sitterson, J. Carlyle. 1957. "Business Leaders in Post–Civil War North Carolina, 1865–1900." In J. Carlyle Sitterson, ed., *Studies in Southern History*. Chapel Hill.

Sitton, Claude. 1988. "It's Too Soon to Say This Is a New Jim Gardner." *News and Observer*. Raleigh. May 15.

Smar, Larry. 1997. "4th District Races in 1994 and 1996." *NC DataNet* 15 (June): 4–6.

Smith, Bob. 1965. *They Closed Their Schools: Prince Edward County, Virginia, 1951–1964*. Chapel Hill.

Snider, William D. 1984. "What Did the 'Mecklenburg Thing' Mean?" *News and Record*. Greensboro. June 17.

———. 1985. *Helms and Hunt: The North Carolina Senate Race, 1984*. Chapel Hill.

Solomon, Norman, and Jeff Cohen. 1997. *Wizards of Media Oz: Behind the Curtain of Mainstream News*. Monroe, Maine.

Spence, James R. 1968. *The Making of a Governor: The Moore-Preyer-Lake Primaries of 1964*. Winston-Salem.

Starr, Paul. 1997. "An Emerging Democratic Majority." In Stanley B. Greenberg and Theda Skocpol, eds., *The New Majority*. New Haven.

Sternlicht, Ann, and Bill Finger. 1986. "Who Makes State Economic Development Policy?" *North Carolina Insight* 8:22–35.

Stevenson, David E. 1975. "Gubernatorial Transition in a Two Party Setting: The Holshouser Administration." In Thad Beyle and Merle Black, eds., *Politics and Policy in North Carolina*. New York.

Stoesen, Alexander R. 1984. "From Ordeal to New Deal: North Carolina in the Great Depression." In Lindley S. Butler and Alan D. Watson, eds., *The North Carolina Experience: An Interpretive and Documentary History*. Chapel Hill.

Stuart, Brad. 1981. "Making North Carolina Prosper." In Eric B. Herzik and Sallye Branch Teater, comps., *North Carolina Focus*. Raleigh.

Sunday Star-News. 1997. "Road to Nowhere." Wilmington, N.C. September 21.

Thu, Kendall, and E. Paul Durrenberger. 1994. "North Carolina's Hog Industry: The Rest of the Story." *Culture and Agriculture* 49:20–23.

Tilley, Nannie M. 1985. *The R. J. Reynolds Tobacco Company*. Chapel Hill.

Tolbert, Charles, Patrick Horan, and E. M. Beck. 1980. "The Structure of Economic Segmentation: A Dual Economy Approach." *American Journal of Sociology* 85:1095–1116.

Tomaskovic-Devey, Donald, and Vincent J. Roscigno. 1996. "Racial Economic Subordination and White Gain in the U.S. South." *American Sociological Review* 61:565–89.

Troy, Leon, and Neil Shaeflin. 1985. *U.S. Union Sourcebook*. West Orange, N.J.

U.S. Department of Commerce. 1986. *Major Shippers Report*. Washington, D.C.

U.S. Department of Labor. 1970. *Employment and Wages, 1970*. Washington, D.C.

——. 1987. *Employment and Wages, 1987*. Washington, D.C.

——. 1990. *Employment and Wages, 1990*. Washington, D.C.

VNS. 1990. Voter News Service, North Carolina Exit Poll.

Vogel, Ezra F., and Andrea Larson. 1985. "North Carolina's Research Triangle: State Modernization." In Ezra F. Vogel, *Comeback, Case by Case: Building the Resurgence of American Business*. New York.

Washington Post. 1997. "Old Foes, New Tensions in North Carolina Town." August 14.

Wheaton, Elizabeth. 1987. *Codename GREENKILL: The 1979 Greensboro Killings*. Athens, Ga.

Whitman, Mebane Rash. 1997. "The Business Tax Burden: How Big a Touch on North Carolina Companies?" *North Carolina Insight* 17, no. 2–3: 50–79.

Whittington, Dale. 1986. "Microelectronics Policy in North Carolina: An Introduction." In Dale Whittington, ed., *High Hopes for High Tech: Microelectronics Policy in North Carolina*. Chapel Hill.

Whittle, Richard. 1983. "Jesse Helms Has a Problem: He's Destined to Lose in '84." *Washington Post*. October 23.

Williams, Ed. 1998. "Governor Hunt's Bridge." *Charlotte Observer*. January 11.

Wolff, Miles. 1970. *How It All Began: The Greensboro Sit-ins*. New York.

Wood, Phillip J. 1986. *Southern Capitalism: The Political Economy of North Carolina, 1880–1980*. Durham.

Worrell, Mark W. 1995. "4th: The 'Price' of Low Voter Turnout." *NC DataNet* 7 (March): 6–7.

Wrenn, Carter. 1987. Interview with author. Raleigh, March 27.

Wyman, Hastings, Jr. 1987. "Yes, but Then Again, No: Social Issues and Southern Politics." *Election Politics* 4:15–18.

Yeoman, Barry. 1988a. "More Dreams than Dollars." *North Carolina Independent*. Durham. June 30.

——. 1988b. "The Convention TV Didn't Cover." *North Carolina Independent*. Durham. July 28.

——. 1989. "Lawrence Davis' Right Turn." *Independent Weekly*. Durham. March 23.

Yeoman, Barry, et al. 1992. "Paving under the Influence" (5-part series). *Independent Weekly*. Durham. May 20–June 17.

Zingraff, Rhonda, and Michael Schulman. 1984. "The Social Bases of Class Consciousness: A Study of Southern Textile Workers with a Comparison by Race." *Social Forces* 6:98–116.

Zipin, Paul. 1982. "North Carolina's Individual Income Tax." *Popular Government* 48:24–29.

Zipp, John F., Richard Landerman, and Paul Luebke. 1982. "Political Parties and Political Participation: A Reexamination of the Standard Socioeconomic Model." *Social Forces* 60:1140–53.

Index

American Tobacco Company, 84
Amnesty International, 145
Antiwar movement, 28, 161, 167, 191
Apparel industry: traditionalism of, 20, 30, 98–99, 112, 117; wages in, 23, 30, 81, 83, 84, 89, 93, 98–99, 117; opposition of to high-tech industry, 30, 36; and Martin, 36; place of in North Carolina's manufacturing sector, 81, 82, 83–84, 93; regional distribution of, 88, 89; campaign contributions to Helms from, 98–99; problems facing, 98–99, 209; labor relations in, 112–13, 117
Archer, Bill, 19
Armey, Dick, 19
Asheboro, 132
Asheville, 85, 90, 199
Asian Americans, 80, 132–33
Atlanta, Ga., 21, 24, 78, 101, 236
Atlantic Committee for Research in Education (ACRE), 65
Aycock, Charles B., 7, 8, 22, 25

Balance Agriculture with Industry (BAWI) plan (Miss.), 93
Ballenger, Cass, 117
Banking and finance industry, 2, 26, 34, 36, 46, 79, 82, 85, 113, 223, 228
Baptist Church, 20, 21, 122, 164, 167, 173, 185
Barnes, Henson, 222
Barnett, Ross, 141
Basic Education Plan (BEP), 38, 64, 65–66
Basnight, Marc, 56, 62, 74, 127, 221, 226, 227
Bayh, Birch, 166
Beasley, David, 23
Beason, Don, 229
Bell South, 14
Bennett, Bert, 33
Berry, Harriet Morehead, 9
Bickett, Thomas, 14

Big business. *See* Business community
Blacks: exclusion of from political life, 2, 3, 7, 14, 129–30, 150; in agriculture, 4, 87; in fusion forces, 4–6; in General Assembly, 5, 32, 55, 125, 130, 139, 144–45, 147, 149, 152, 156–57, 159–60; disfranchisement of, 6–7, 8, 26, 51; spending on schools for, 7, 8, 63, 80; as percentage of population regionally and statewide, 17, 80, 130, 131, 145, 151, 158; affirmative action for, 21, 24, 43, 184; and traditionalists, 21, 135, 137, 141–46, 148, 155, 164, 167, 174, 175–76, 182–83, 214; and modernizers, 23–24, 134–35, 137, 138–39, 141, 146, 148, 153–54, 155, 157–58, 160; as Republicans/Republican voters, 25, 50, 135, 214; and economic populism, 27–28, 43, 62, 153, 156–59, 160, 218; and Helms, 30, 141, 142, 143–44, 151, 161, 164, 167, 169, 174, 175–76, 182–83, 191; as Democrats/Democratic voters, 32, 49, 130, 135–36, 148–49, 152, 159, 178, 179–80, 187, 189, 201, 206, 208, 217, 218; electoral gains of, 32, 125, 130, 139, 144–45, 149, 152, 153, 179, 199, 207–8; and Hunt, 33, 155, 157, 171, 175, 176, 178–79, 185; and Martin, 37, 196; 1950s out-migration of, 78; lack of economic opportunities for, 80, 129, 150, 156; and unions, 118, 122, 123; voter registration among, 130, 143, 144, 146, 169, 170, 185, 189, 192, 207, 208, 232; and redistricting, 130–31, 147, 148–50, 152, 153–55, 160, 208; tensions between Hispanics and, 132; white Democrats' representation of, 135–36, 146, 152–53; political participation by in Greensboro, 138–40; class differences among, 140; and "single-shooting," 144, 148, 150; obstacles to election victories by, 144, 146–48, 150–52; and Jordan, 196. *See also*

Dukakis, Michael, 198
Duke, Washington, 4
Duke family, 84
Duke Power Company, 103, 142, 225
Duke University, 28, 95, 120, 130
Duncan, Ann, 200
Duplin County, 73, 74, 86, 87, 90, 132
Durham, 2, 3, 13, 21, 28, 91, 95, 107, 116, 132, 210; tobacco industry in, 4, 84; growth and prosperity of, 4, 23, 89; citizen groups in, 39, 72, 126, 219; black political participation in, 148, 151
Durham Bulls, 98, 107
Durham County, 50, 88, 107, 151; Democrats and Democratic support in, 194, 196, 200

Easley, Mike, 180, 204
East, John, 176, 186, 192, 193, 194
Eastern Piedmont: tobacco cultivation in, 4, 89; blacks in, 14, 80; Democratic support in, 41, 54; region defined, 79; traditionalism in, 79–80; agriculture in, 80, 87, 89; relative economic disadvantages of, 84–85, 88, 89, 104, 105; educational levels in, 84–85, 90; economic development in, 103, 104; Helms/Republican support in, 192, 194
Eaton Corporation, 82
Economic conservatism, 36, 43
Economic development: and traditionalists, 20–21, 22, 97–104, 105; and issue of wages, 21, 34, 96–101; subsidies/tax incentives for, 21, 93, 94, 101–4, 106–9, 223–24, 225, 227–28; and modernizers, 23, 32–33, 63, 97–104, 105, 204, 222; and high-tech industry, 30; and low-wage industries, 30, 93, 98–99; and Hunt, 32–33, 34, 36, 38, 63, 99, 100, 101, 103, 109, 204, 225; and Democrats, 32–33, 104–5, 158, 204, 216; and trickle-down economics, 33, 43; and education, 34,

63–64, 94, 104; and Martin, 36, 38, 99, 101, 104–5, 115, 216–17; and highways, 38, 48, 72, 94, 104, 106; role of state government in, 48, 94, 104–5, 222; sports as, 58, 94, 106–9; and regional economic disparity, 65, 70; as "Buffalo Hunt," 93, 94, 103; and antiunionism, 94–96, 115, 117; in urban vs. rural areas, 96, 104–6, 109; and job training, 96, 196, 225; and Sanford, 96, 204; and Republicans, 104–5, 211, 216; and Jordan, 204
Economic Development Commission, 103
Economic liberalism, 36, 43–44
Economic populism: in Farmers' Alliance and fusion forces, 4–6; relative absence of in North Carolina politics, 8, 26, 157; vs. modernism and traditionalism, 20, 24; basic principles of, 20, 25, 26, 57; and business community, 20, 25, 26, 57, 106, 107, 108, 205, 225–26, 227–28; and taxation, 24, 26, 27–28, 43, 45, 62, 217, 224, 231, 232; and Democrats, 25–26, 41, 53, 202, 217, 218, 224, 234; in Congress, 25–26, 153, 157; unholy alliance of traditionalism and, 26–27, 45, 46, 62, 108, 156, 225–28; and modernizers, 27–28; in metro Piedmont, 53; in General Assembly, 62, 125–27, 135, 136, 156–57, 225–28; blacks and, 156–58, 159, 160, 184; and Wallace, 191; and Clinton, 204; and lottery proposals, 228
Edmisten, Rufus, 148, 196, 200, 202–3
Education, public, 4, 216, 232; and Democrats, 1, 7, 8, 12, 15, 65, 67–69, 158, 196, 204, 208, 230, 233, 234; and fusionists, 5, 8; and General Assembly, 8, 9, 11, 48, 49, 63–69, 133–34, 196, 208, 215, 230; and business community, 8, 34, 48, 63–64, 67, 69, 210, 224; and teachers' salaries, 9, 51, 55, 63, 67, 68–69, 157, 208, 215, 219; and

160; growing number/power of Republicans in, 189, 194–95, 197, 205; and health care, 224, 230; and citizen groups, 229–31. *See also* House of Representatives (N.C.); Senate (N.C.)

Georgia Pacific Corporation, 114
Gephardt, Dick, 25
Gibsonville, 13
Gingles, Ralph, 148, 149
Gingles v. Edmisten, 148–52, 154
Gingrich, Newt, 19, 25, 47, 205, 215
Glaxo, 21
Goldwater, Barry, 29, 190
Goode, Larry, 220
Goodman, Jim, 98, 107
Good Neighbor Councils, 142
Good Roads Association, 9
Gore, Al, 25, 204, 219
Government activism: as part of Democrats' progressive heritage, 1, 15, 18, 22, 49, 70, 134–35; Democratic commitment to, 1, 32, 216; business community as beneficiary of, 2, 8, 10, 18, 48, 95, 224; Helms/traditionalist opposition to, 20, 22, 30, 31; modernizer support for, 20, 24, 58, 222, 224; Hunt's commitment to, 32; Martin's acceptance of, 38, 39; taxation/spending to support, 43, 58–59; and economic development, 48, 49, 94, 222; support for in metro Piedmont, 79; and race relations, 134–35
Graham, Frank, 16–17, 150, 165–66, 179, 183
Great Depression, 10–11, 14, 52, 60
Green, Jimmy, 54, 150, 157, 158
Greensboro, 2, 9, 14, 40, 72, 83, 84, 90, 102, 124, 133, 148; and sports as economic development, 58, 108; prosperity relative to Triangle and Charlotte, 89, 101; race relations in, 129, 134, 136–40, 144–45, 147; Republicans and Republican support in, 147, 193, 196, 199

Greensboro Dialogue Task Force Committee, 138–39
Greensboro News and Record, 102, 220
Greensboro Sit-in, 136–37
Grissom, Eddie, 170
Grissom, James, 170
Gubernatorial succession, 34, 54
Guilford County, 40, 58, 89, 90, 101–2, 108–9, 139, 147; Republicans and Republican support in, 192, 194, 196
Guilford Mills, 57
Guillory, Ferrel, 169
Guinier, Lani, 149
Gulley, Wib, 67–68, 221
Gunter, Daniel, 117

Hackney, Joe, 53, 60
Hamlet, 84–85, 119–20
Hanes, Phillip, 9
Hanes, Robert, 95
Hanes Corporation, 101
Hardison, Harold, 200–202, 203–4
Harriet-Henderson Yarns, 15, 95, 120
Harvin, Lucius, III, 168, 170
Hastings, Jim, 215
Hawke, Jack, 213, 214
Haworth, Howard, 104
Hayes, Robin, 62, 214; as traditionalist, 43, 50–51, 67, 200, 207, 229, 235; in 1996 gubernatorial election, 50–51, 200, 212, 215, 226–27
Hazardous chemicals. *See* Right-to-know legislation
Health care, 7, 15, 42, 80, 153, 205, 230, 233, 234
Heinemann, Fred, 49–50, 112, 199
Helms, Dorothy Coble, 165
Helms, Jesse, 50, 66, 161, 193; and Smith-Graham senatorial contest, 16, 165, 179; as traditionalist, 20, 28–29, 30, 31, 35, 58, 97, 161, 163, 164, 167, 168–69, 173–74, 175, 181, 212; as Democrat, 20, 30; as TV editorialist, 28, 30, 31, 161, 166–67, 174, 175–76, 190, 192; anticommunism of, 28, 31,

Phosphates: ban on detergents containing, 39, 53
Piedmont, 78–79. *See also* Eastern Piedmont; Metro Piedmont; Western Piedmont
Piedmont Triad. *See* Triad
Pillowtex Corporation, 113
Pinehurst, 75, 78
Plutocracy, progressive: North Carolina as, 2, 48, 57, 219
Poll tax, 6, 7, 8, 26, 150
Pollution. *See* Environmentalism
Pope, Art, 231
Population: growth and distribution of, 77–80, 209
Populism. *See* Citizen groups; Economic populism; "Fusion"
Pork barrel spending, 55–56, 231
Poultry processing industry, 84–85, 119–20, 132
Powell, Colin, 160
Prayer: in public schools, 167, 176, 178, 186, 212
Preyer, Richardson, 142
Price, David, 50, 153, 211
Progressivism, 1–18
Property tax: state, 4, 10, 12, 60; local, 10, 11, 58, 235
Public School Forum, 64–65, 68

Quayle, Dan, 166

Race relations: North Carolina's reputation for moderation in, 1, 2, 3, 17, 129–30, 137, 141, 146; and business community, 3, 123, 137, 138–39, 142, 217; and Democrats, 5–8, 17–18, 134–36, 141–42, 148, 189, 205–6, 216, 217; and 1950 senatorial election, 16–18, 150, 165–66, 179, 183; and modernizers, 27, 134, 136, 137, 138–39, 141, 146, 148, 149, 153–54, 160, 193; and General Assembly, 27, 133–34, 144, 150; and Helms, 30, 31, 129, 135, 141, 142, 143–44, 151, 162,

164, 166, 173, 174, 175–76, 182–83, 186, 191, 212; and traditionalists, 30, 79–80, 135–36, 137, 141–46, 148, 175, 183; and Hunt, 32–33, 135–36, 145–46, 155, 169; and Martin, 37, 135; and federal courts, 133–34, 134, 148, 149, 152, 154–55; and Republicans, 134–35, 144, 147–48, 189, 211–12; and Sanford, 141–42; and Holshouser, 193. *See also* Blacks; Desegregation; King holiday; Racism; Segregation; Whites; White supremacy
Racism: and Democrats, 4, 6, 17, 150; electoral messages appealing to, 31, 140, 150–51, 182–83, 186, 187, 198. *See also* Ku Klux Klan; Race relations; White supremacy
Railroads, 5, 25
Rainbow Coalition, 41
Raleigh, 9, 13, 28, 78, 95, 108, 210–11; growth and prosperity of, 23, 88, 89, 208; transportation in, 71, 72; Democrats and Democratic support in, 148, 193–94; Republicans and Republican support in, 199, 235
Raleigh Times, 165
Ramsey, Liston, 48, 54, 71, 195, 197
Rand, Tony, 39, 41, 53, 195, 198, 202, 204
Randolph County, 54, 203
Reagan, Ronald, 70, 121, 163, 170, 185, 190, 210, 216; popularity and coattails of, 36, 38, 52, 162, 171, 193, 195, 196; and Congressional Club, 162, 163, 214; and Helms, 174, 175, 176
Real estate industry, 34, 85, 98–99
Red Shirts, 5, 6, 14
Reed, Ralph, 229
Religion, 3, 30, 31, 90–91. *See also* Baptist Church; Fundamentalist Protestantism; Roman Catholics
Religious right, 37, 49, 50, 56, 185, 197, 205, 210, 224, 229–30. *See also* Christian Coalition

Republicans/Republican Party: in
fusion forces, 4–6; and blacks and
race relations, 5, 25, 134–35, 140,
144, 147–48, 189, 211–12; and business community, 5, 29, 30, 56–58,
205, 208, 210, 217, 219, 228; and traditionalism, 19, 30, 161, 197–98, 205,
212–15; end Democrats' control of
General Assembly, 26, 42, 45, 47–48,
49, 54, 171, 178, 199, 205, 207, 213,
215; mainstream vs. Helms/religious-
right wing of, 29, 35, 163, 207, 210–
16, 235; 1972 electoral gains as watershed for, 29, 52, 189, 207; and modernism, 29–30, 35, 199, 207; and low-
wage industries, 30; Helms's role in,
31, 35, 162, 188; and environmentalism, 39–40, 74–75; and taxation,
45–46, 156, 208, 210, 217, 222, 224,
225, 226–27, 232, 235; and voter reg-
istration/mobilization, 50, 52, 173,
185, 190, 205, 215; and abortion, 50,
210, 212, 215, 229; regional distribution of strength of, 52, 54; and education, 66–67, 69, 210, 211, 215; and
economic development, 104–5, 211,
216; and labor relations, 111, 112,
118, 125; benefit from legislative
redistricting, 148, 149, 152; shift of
white voters from Democrats to, 168,
170, 189–90, 192–94, 195–96, 197,
210, 217, 218; challenge/future of,
181, 200, 205, 210–16, 234–35, 236;
gains of in local elections, 193, 195,
200, 205; and in-migrants, 193–94,
197, 236; 1980s electoral gains of,
194–97, 210–11; 1990s electoral gains
and losses of, 197–200; and highways,
210, 211; and campaign finance
reform, 220–21
Research Triangle area. *See* Triangle
Research Triangle Park, 21, 78, 91, 95,
194, 235
Retirees: in-migration of, 54, 70, 75, 78,
197, 210, 235

Reynolds, Dennis, 214
Reynolds, R. J., 4
Right-to-know legislation, 39, 126
Right-to-life groups, 37, 40
Right-to-work law, 51, 95
Riley, Richard, 44
R. J. Reynolds Industries, 84, 119
R. J. Reynolds/Nabisco, 101, 223
Roanoke Rapids, 114, 124
Robb, Chuck, 153
Robertson, Pat, 19, 213
Robeson County, 125, 130
Rockingham, 14
Roe, Emmett, 119
Roman Catholics, 90–91, 122
Roosevelt, Franklin D., 27, 52, 212, 234
Rose's Stores, 168, 170
Rough Riders, 5
Rouse, Frank, 176, 183
Roxboro, 88, 99–100
Roy, Gary, 168
Runoff primary: black opposition to,
150, 151, 217
Rural Economic Development Center,
105
Russell, Carolyn, 178
Russell, Daniel, 5, 6, 8
Russell, Richard, 166

Sales tax: introduction of, 11–12;
opposition to, 11–12, 45–46, 52, 58,
59–60, 108; rate of, 12, 13, 45, 58,
59–60, 225, 231; as regressive tax, 12,
24, 44, 46, 59, 224; vs. other taxes as
source of revenue, 24, 58, 59, 217,
224; and modernizers, 24, 36, 43–45,
46, 58–59, 224–25; and traditionalists, 24, 45; and economic populists,
26, 45, 231; reliance on, 44, 45, 224,
235. *See also* Food tax; Gasoline tax
Sanford, Terry, 158, 193, 229; and taxation, 12, 44, 61, 225; and education,
12, 44, 204; early career of, 15; as
modernizer, 20, 44, 61, 127, 141–42,
199, 204, 217, 225; and Kennedy, 33,

146, 169, 170, 185, 189, 192, 207,
208, 232; Democratic, 135, 170, 173,
190–91, 203, 205; Republican, 170,
173, 190, 205, 208; and unaffiliated
voters, 173, 190–91, 205, 208
Voting Rights Act (1965, 1982), 32, 130,
143, 146, 149, 150, 152

Wachovia Bank, 34, 58, 95, 108, 228
Wages: as issue in economic develop-
ment, 21, 34, 96–101; industrial, 33,
34, 82, 83, 84, 85, 88, 93, 115–16; in
tertiary sector, 85
Wake County, 148; Republicans and
Republican support in, 50, 192, 193–
94, 196; growth and prosperity of, 78,
88
Wake Forest College, 165
Wallace, George, 141, 165, 191, 192,
198, 211
Warren County, 88
Warrenton, 88
Washington Post, 169, 171
Watauga County, 78
Watergate, 34, 52, 202
Water/sewer lines, 12, 24, 34, 70, 106,
109, 159
Watkins, Billy, 54
Watson, Cindy, 75
Watt, Mel, 130–31, 153, 155, 182
Weld, William, 29, 162
Wellstone, Paul, 25, 184
Western Piedmont, 13, 108, 186, 208–9;
manufacturing in, 3, 81, 82, 88, 91,
100, 105; agriculture in, 4, 80, 87;
Republicans and Republican support
in, 52, 54, 185, 192, 193, 196, 232,
233; traditionalism in, 53, 79–80, 100,
185, 233; region defined, 79; blacks
in, 80; relative economic advantages
of, 88, 105–6; educational levels in,
90, 105
Whites: as textile workers, 3; in agriculture, 4; disfranchisement of poorer
segment of, 6, 7–8, 26, 51; political

disaffection of poorer segments of,
8, 164, 232; deference to authority
among, 21, 22; representation of
blacks by, 135–36, 146, 152–53; attitudes of toward black political candidates, 138–40, 144–45, 147–48,
150–53, 158–59, 184, 208; racial and
social traditionalism among, 141, 175,
181–82; Helms's support among,
167–70, 171, 174, 175, 178, 184–85,
197; Helms/Republican appeals to
racial and social traditionalism of,
175–76, 181–83, 184, 185, 187; in
1984 and 1990 senatorial elections,
184–87; as swing vote, 189; dealignment of from Democratic Party,
189–91, 192, 195–96, 197, 208, 217.
See also Desegregation; Race relations;
Segregation; White supremacy
White supremacy, 5, 7, 8, 51, 130
Whiting, Albert, 116
Whittle, Richard, 171
Wilder, Douglas, 24, 130
Wildlife Commission, 220
Williamson, Odell, 220
Wilmington, 6, 78, 85, 90, 129, 145, 199,
209
Wilmington Race Riot, 6
Wilmington Record, 6
Wilmington Ten, 129, 145–46, 149
Wilson County, 32, 220
Wingate University, 164
Winner, Leslie, 149
Winston-Salem, 2, 58, 89, 101–2, 108,
132, 134, 147, 148; tobacco industry
in, 4, 84, 101; Republicans and
Republican support in, 147, 152, 193
Winston-Salem Journal, 102, 220
Women: traditionalists and the role
and rights of, 21, 22, 30; affirmative
action for, 21, 43, 184; in low-wage
employment, 21, 85; modernizers and
the role and rights of, 23–24, 27; and
Helms, 30; and Hunt, 33, 217; Demo-
crats and issues involving, 200, 201,